'The architectural profession and society must co enant between us so that we may deliver the out both. Flora Samuel's excellent book throws light on the actual and potential contribution of architects to the prospect of social well-being and, more to the point, identifies ways in which we must go about realising this potential.'

Benjamin Derbyshire, President, Royal Institute of British Architects and Chair of HTA Design

'Architects are needed more than ever to address the challenges in the built environment. In this timely book Flora Samuel presents valuable insights for the profession's future development, which she argues depends on how it organises its knowledge. It is a must-read for architectural professionals in the 21st century.'

Fredrik Nilsson, Professor of Architectural Theory, Chalmers University of Technology, and Head of Research in Practice, Älvstranden Utveckling, AB, Sweden

'I have been teaching and preaching about the problems architecture as a profession and architects as practitioners face for the last five years. If only I had had this book to assign all along! It lays out so clearly the issues behind the ironic but tragic fact that the public and the architectural profession hate what architecture has become. The fact that no one in this binary is happy with a profession that is seen as effete and socially indifferent requires an analysis that goes beyond handwringing and cross accusations. This book is it, as it systematically analyzes both the history and structure of this dilemma.'

Peggy Deamer, Professor of Architecture, Yale University and Architecture Lobby, USA

Why Architects Matter

Why Architects Matter examines the key role of research-led, ethical architects in promoting wellbeing, sustainability and innovation. It argues that the profession needs to be clear about what it knows and the value of what it knows if it is to work successfully with others. Without this clarity, the marginalization of architects from the production of the built environment will continue, preventing clients, businesses and society from getting the buildings that they need.

The book offers a strategy for the development of a twenty-first-century knowledge-led built environment, including tools to help evidence, develop and communicate that value to those outside the field. Knowing how to demonstrate the impact and value of their work will strengthen practitioners' ability to pitch for work and access new funding streams. This is particularly important at a time of global economic downturn, with ever greater competition for contracts and funds driving down fees and making it imperative to prove value at every level.

Why Architects Matter straddles the spheres of 'Practice Management and Law', 'History and Theory', 'Design', 'Housing', 'Sustainability', 'Health', 'Marketing' and 'Advice for Clients', bringing them into an accessible whole. The book will therefore be of interest to professional architects, architecture students and anyone with an interest in our built environment and the role of professionals within it.

Flora Samuel is Professor of Architecture in the Built Environment and the first RIBA Vice President for Research. She was also the first woman Head of the University of Sheffield School of Architecture in the UK. This book was written as a result of her concern about the amount of waste and suffering caused by the poor quality of much of our built environment. She has received extensive funding from the Arts and Humanities Research Council for her work on the value of architects and on the way in which they evidence that value. Being passionate about breaking down the barriers between academia and architectural practice, she has, since 2012, embroiled herself in the activities of the Royal Institute of British Architects as a twice-elected National Council member and Chair of its Research and Innovation Group. She also delivers research training in practice and is a supervisor of practitioner PhDs. Flora Samuel is known for her unorthodox writings on Le Corbusier, about whom she has published extensively. A mother of three daughters, she is based in Wales.

Why Architects Matter

Evidencing and Communicating the Value of Architects

FLORA SAMUEL

Routledge
Taylor & Francis Group
LONDON AND NEW YORK

First published 2018
by Routledge
2 Park Square, Milton Park, Abingdon, Oxon OX14 4RN

and by Routledge
711 Third Avenue, New York, NY 10017

Routledge is an imprint of the Taylor & Francis Group, an informa business

British Library Cataloguing-in-Publication Data
A catalogue record for this book is available from the British Library

Library of Congress Cataloging-in-Publication Data
Names: Samuel, Flora, author.
Title: Why architects matter : evidencing and communicating the value of architects / Flora Samuel.
Description: New York : Routledge, 2018. | Includes bibliographical references and index.
Identifiers: LCCN 2017043980 | ISBN 9781138783928 (hb : alk. paper) | ISBN 9781138783935 (pb : alk. paper) | ISBN 9781315768373 (ebook)
Subjects: LCSH: Architectural practice–Social aspects. | Architects–Training of.
Classification: LCC NA1995 .S33 2018 | DDC 720.92–dc23
LC record available at https://lccn.loc.gov/2017043980

ISBN: 978-1-138-78392-8 (hbk)
ISBN: 978-1-138-78393-5 (pbk)
ISBN: 978-1-315-76837-3 (ebk)

Typeset in Univers LT Std
by Out of House Publishing

Printed in the United Kingdom
by Henry Ling Limited

What kind of house will you build for me, says the Lord, or what is the place of my rest? ACTS 7:47

Contents

List of illustrations

Acknowledgements

As economic historian, Chris Powell at Cardiff University heroically supervised the latter stages of my PhD on Le Corbusier. Looking back I realize what an important influence this extraordinary, forward-thinking, kind and funny man was on me. This book is in many ways in memory of him. I hope he would approve.

As the book progressed, I sense-checked its contents with multitudes of people both within and without architecture, some of whom are mentioned here. Dyfed Griffiths, Simon Foxell, Robin Nicholson and Walter Menteth gave me very useful comments on parts of the text. I have been the beneficiary of many conversations but all errors are entirely my own.

It is such a pleasure to be helping Lorraine Farrelly develop her vision for the new School of Architecture at the University of Reading. I find the professionalism and enthusiasm of my colleagues Oliver Froome Lewis, Daniela Perrotti, Carolina Vasilikou, Izabela Wieczorek and Penelope Plaza very inspiring. The school was the brainchild of Stuart Green in the School of Construction Management and I have benefited hugely from careful introductions to the research world of construction while working with colleagues there, among them John Connaughton, Roger Flanagan, Chris Harty, Will Hughes, Libby Schweber, Martin Sexton, Dylan Tutt, Dragana Nikolic, Ian Ewart, members of our Urban Living Research Group and colleagues from Real Estate and Planning, particularly David Clapham, Geoff Meen, Claudia Murray, Richard Nunes, Kathy Pain, Ruth Pugh and Emma Street. The DEGW archives currently being unpacked with great skill by Hiral Patel are in the Special Collections at Reading under the expert care of Guy Baxter. Spending time with Frank Duffy, John Worthington and the DEGW diaspora, notably Alastair Blyth, Steve Smith, Despina Katsikakis, Nicola Gillen and Stephen Greenberg, has been extremely inspiring.

I am also grateful to colleagues at the University of Sheffield School of Architecture when I was Head there. I was exposed to so many new things at this extraordinary politically driven school and by the people there, most notably Irena Bauman, Jian Kang, Doina Petrescu, Fionn Stevenson, Sarah Wigglesworth, Bryan Lawson, Judy Torrington, Stephen Walker, Prue Chiles, Renata Tyszczuk, Julia Udall and Peter Blundell Jones, the latter much missed. Important interdisciplinary influences at Sheffield were Jackie Harrison (Journalism), Jackie Marsh (Education), Carys Swanwick (Landscape), Craig Watkins (Planning), Gill Valentine (Geography) and Mary Vincent (Geography).

I am particularly indebted to the members of the Research Practice Leads group, who have made me so hopeful about the future of the profession – among them Darryl Chen (Hawkins\Brown), Craig Robertson (AHMM), Gillian Horn (Penoyre and Prasad), Mark Lumley (Architype), Aditya Aachi (Cullinan Studio), Malca Mizrahi (then Scott Brownrigg), Julia Park (Levitt Bernstein), Joe Jack Williams (FCBS), Peter Fisher (Bennetts), Elizabeth Kavanagh (Stride Treglown), Marilys Ramos (PRP), Rory Bergin and Phoebe Eustance (HTA), David Ayre (ACG), David Green (Perkins + Will), Emma Flynn (AStudio), Tom Dollard (PTE), Lucy Plumridge (HLM) and Veronica Simpson (Blueprint).

The ARENA network initiated by Murray Fraser has helped me develop a European perspective on the matter in hand. The late Johan Verbeke has done so much to promote the case of research in architectural practice, despite not being an architect. He will be sorely missed. I have enjoyed working closely with Fredrik Nilsson, Johan de Walsche, Oya Atalay Franck, Roberto Caballo and João Menezes de Sequeira.

There are some remarkable people working in and around the RIBA. The help and support of Presidents Jane Duncan and Ben Derbyshire and members of Council, especially student members Lily Ingleby and Simeon Shbutanaev, who have been right behind me on promoting research in the institution has been great. On staff, Lucy Carmichael, Anne Dye, Neal Shasore and Alex Tait have been particularly close and important collaborators as have staff in the RIBA Library including Kent Rawlinson. I am grateful to Hayley Russell and John Paul Nunes for supporting the development of the *RIBA Student Destination Survey*, which is now in its sixth year. Liam Foster (Sheffield) has been a generous and rigorous source of social science advice for its development and I am very glad that Kelly MacKinnon (Northumbria) has taken over its leadership to give it new life. It couldn't have been done without the seven schools that have co-operated in its development: Birmingham City University, Cardiff, Kingston, Northumbria, Sheffield, Queens University Belfast and Robert Gordon University Glasgow.

Nathan Baker (ICE), Brian Green (Brickonomics), David Hawkes and David Barnes (CIOB), Jeff Matsu (RICS), Tom Kenny (RTPI), Neil Paterson (BRE), Veronika Schropfer (ACE), Peter Mould (UIA), Jutta Hinterleitner and Jasper Kraaijeveld (BNA) have provided important perspectives from other kinds of professional institutions. The policy dimension has become much clearer to me following conversations with my local MP Jo Stevens, the experience of parliamentary launches facilitated by David Birkbeck of Design for Homes, and being part of meetings with Lord Waldegrave, Nick Raynsford and members of the DCLG.

I have had the privilege of working with two really excellent research assistants, Laura Coucill and Rowena Hay. I am really grateful to the CVoA team, Carolyn Butterworth, Sophie Handler, Jo Lintonbon and Nishat Awan, and the many people who helped us with the consultation. The Home Improvements team, Fiona McLachlan (Edinburgh), Stephen Spier (Kingston), David Birkbeck (Design for Homes), Nick Rogers (Taylor Wimpey), Jonathan Rickard (Radian), Sam Brown, David Rudlin, Cany Ash, Robert Sakula, Stewart Dodd, Robin Nicholson, Alan Jones, Kate Pahl, Paul Iddon and Simon Bradbury, did an excellent job on the CVoA Advisory Group. Robin is a very inspiring person with seemingly inexhaustible energy to fight the cause of good architecture. His introduction to the talented and highly resourceful Edge Group has been really important to me. Paddy Conaghan, Richard Lorch, Helen Taylor, Simon Foxell, Jane Briginshawe and Elanor Warwick. Important client viewpoints have been offered by John Davies (Derwent),Tim Helliwell (Royal College of Pathologists) and Lanra Gbolade (L & Q).

In no particular order I am grateful to these people for their advice and thoughts: Koen Steemers (Cambridge), Julie Godefroy, Edward Ng (Chinese University Hong Kong), Andy von Bradsky (PRP), Richard Saxon (former Chair of BDP), Peggy Deamer (Yale), Rob Imrie (King's College), Peter Clegg (FCBS), Danna Walker (Built by Us), Richard Brindley (ACE), Sunand Prasad and Greg Penoyre (Penoyre and Prasad), Denise and Rab Bennetts (Bennetts Associates), Roger Hawkins (Hawkins\Brown), Piers Taylor (Invisible Studio), Niall McLaughlin (Niall McLaughlin Architects), Dinah Bornat (ZCD), Walter Menteth (Project Compass), David Rudlin (URBED), Dyfed Griffiths (Bath), Simon Sturgis (Sturgis Carbon Profiling), Lynne Sullivan (Sustainable by Design), Pierre Wassenar (Stride Treglown), Andy Jobling (Levitt Bernstein), Anne Thorne and Fran Bradshaw (Anne Thorne Architects), Jen Forakakis (HOOP), Caroline Buckingham, Melodie Leung (ZHA), Carl Turner (Carl Turner Architects), Patrick Lynch (Lynch Architects), Dale Sinclair (AECOM), Alan Jones, Jane and Ron Darke, Louis Hellman, Casey Rutland (ARUP), Hans Wamelink and Marina Bos de Vos (Delft), Chris Williamson (Weston Williamson), John Cole (QUB), Oliver Smith (5th Studio), Deborah Saunt (LSA), James Soane (Project Orange), Maria Henshall (Sheffield), Sam Diston (Sheffield), Nigel Ostime (Hawkins\Brown), Karen Shook (Times Education Supplement), Richard Hayward, Bob Allies and Paul Appleton (Allies & Morrison), Nick Ray (Cambridge), Jon Ackroyd and Oliver Lowrie (Ackroyd Associates), Andrew Wright (Andrew Wright Associates), Matthew Gaunt (ACG), Peter Newton (Barton Wilmore), Martin Gledhill and Alex Wright (Bath), Adam Sharr and Graham Farmer (Newcastle), Paul Jones and Peter Holgate (Northumbria). I am also grateful for the thoughts of the practices that have invited me on fact-finding CPD sessions: Farrells, Penoyre and Prasad, Cullinan Studio, Levitt Bernstein, AHMM, Barton Wilmore, HLM, Pollard Thomas and Edwards, Scott Brownrigg (Edinburgh).

Being part of the Hong Kong Research Excellence Framework opened my eyes to the remarkable research work that is going on in Asia. Representing 'Europe zone 1' on the scientific committee of the 2017 UIA convention in Seoul was a mind-expanding experience which I really appreciated. My thanks are due to my reviewing colleagues and the amazing organizational team. My gratitude also goes to staff and students at Harbin University in China, where we developed a very educational (for me, anyway) architectural studio on 'urban atmosphere', the Built Environment panel of the Hong Kong Research Excellence Framework, which gave me a global perspective on the issues in hand, and the highly committed staff at Santo Tomas School of Architecture in Philippines, who reminded me of the desperate problems they face on a day-to-day basis as a result of climate change and inequality. I look forward to developing our PhD programme together.

My thanks also go to Fran Ford at Routledge, who had faith in the book, and Trudy Varcianna, who has been very patient and helpful for several years. Being a radical change of subject for me, it has been like doing a second PhD, but my conviction that this book is needed has kept me going, together with Alex, my husband, and home.

Research for this book was supported by three grants from the Arts and Humanities Research Council: Home Improvements, The Cultural Value of Architecture in Homes and Neighbourhoods and Evidencing and Communicating the Value of Architecture.

Introduction

Architects are not very good at explaining why what they do matters.
Alan Penn (Farrell, 2014, p. 65)

This is a book about why architects matter, why the quality of the built environment makes a difference, why more people need to get involved in architecture and what we need from architects to help them do so. In the words of Michael Sorkin (2011, p. 1), 'Architecture is for everyone' – so why aren't they getting it?

Our skylines are dominated by what I call narchitecture – narcissistic architecture – self referential, confusing (purposely or through lack of care), excluding and damaging to wellbeing and the environment. I was inspired to write this book when I wrote to complain to my local council about the design of the library at the edge of my local park. The response I received from 'the architect' was that 'good design costs money', something which I fundamentally refute. In my experience architects are remarkably good at making something from almost nothing. However, affordability is a design problem which architects are ruled out of (Dulaney, 2012), often because of erroneous assumptions about expense and risk, the result being the unloved, short-lived and soulless buildings that act as the scenery for most of our lives. The resultant waste is unacceptable (Osmani et al., 2008).

We are dependent on the environment around us, animate and inanimate, to self-actuate (Huskinson, 2018). *Why Architects Matter* is built on the premise that the built environment can impact strongly on quality of life and that good – and I mean good with all its moral associations – clients and project teams can do a great deal to promote wellbeing through their activities. 'We need to articulate who the baddies are. What is right and what is wrong' (Imrie, 2017). One of my fundamental premises is that not all architects are the same. I want to make the case that architects who are professional, research-focused, innovative and ethical do exist but need much greater acknowledgement and support. While I hope this book will inspire architects to be more effective, it is really written for non-architects – policymakers, clients, potential clients and potential architects – to get insight into why this particular field of expertise is so important and what they can do to help.

Some academics have turned their attention to theorizing the problems of other countries, attracted perhaps by their alluring otherness as well the fees of overseas students and potential research funding. Although it is always worthwhile to highlight the problems of the developing world, the distinctly unglamorous look of British deprivation often remains ignored. There is much work to be done at the neo-liberal coal face of value to focus attention back where it should be, on the key role that the built environment plays in the lives of people and to remember that it is possible to do economics, and indeed design, 'as if people mattered' (Schumacher, 1993). There is a chance that we can produce a built environment for future generations that we can be proud of by encouraging an understanding of value in its fullest sense.

'Collaboration' is a word that is prominent at this time, but it is rarely associated with its partner 'trust' or the conditions to support that trust, as these are bound up with the messy touchy-feely world of human relations. *Why Architects Matter* is written as a polemic with the aim of fostering trust and the conditions needed for trust – evidence, clarity and rigour, as well as shared ways of working. The possibility of a construction industry in which contractual complexity is replaced by trust, a recognition of competence through ties of familiarity, clear evidence and/or the potential for internet-based forms of highly visible feedback – think Airbnb and Uber – all enable the client to manage the risk of trusting their team and to work together for infinitely better results. This book is born out of the perhaps idealistic hope that advances in knowledge sharing and data collection can support the development of a culture of trust and the development of shared vision to eradicate the waste and misery caused by litigation and poor quality design. While I am under no illusion that much can be done to change the damaging and unethical attitudes of the build-it-and-flog-it school of development – one that many of us lazily promote through our pension funds and investments – I do believe there is much to be done to help owner-occupier clients, buyers and tenants ask more of their architects and their landlords.

To be a profession is to profess custody of a particular body of knowledge. In making the case for architects I am making the case for what it is that they know and what they do with that knowledge. I argue that architects are socio-spatial problem-solvers, integrators of complex bodies of information and masters in space-craft. Despite the fact that architectural practices are well known from outside to be 'knowledge-based organisations' (Winch and Schneider, 1993, p. 1), '"knowledge" is not a word with which most architects instinctively feel very comfortable as a way of describing the essence of their professional discipline' (Duffy, 1998, p. xiii), but it is my thesis that the knowledge and skills of architects need to be reframed and developed strategically for a twenty-first-century context of accelerated change. Discussions of knowledge seem to imply that it is a static resource to be exploited like money in the bank, which of course it isn't – hence recent emphasis on processes of 'organizational learning' and the structures needed to help this happen (Easterby-Smith and Lyles, 2011). However, both 'knowledge management' and 'organizational learning' are alien to most architects, so the subtle differences between them are slightly immaterial in this context. I want to highlight what it is that architects know in the hope of improving organizational learning. While my focus is on architects, conclusions may be drawn from this book with applicability to a range of learning and 'knowledge-based' organizations.

My difficult ambition has been to write a book that sits on a table between the shelves marked 'Practice Management and Law', 'History and Theory', 'Design', 'Housing', 'Sustainability', 'Health', 'Marketing' and 'Advice for Clients' in a typical architectural bookshop, bringing these aspects of the profession into an accessible whole. It has been conceived, in particular, to cross the uneasy cultural divide between architects and other built environment professionals. This book veers purposely between the extremes of creative expression and nitty-gritty aspects of contract law, because they are in reality linked. This is, however, largely uncharted research terrain. I am particularly concerned with making the business side of professional training more engaging by setting it within its cultural context, in this way encouraging critical engagement with this neglected area of practice. I take inspiration from Howard Davis, who gives a 'cross-cultural' take on building as a 'unified social process', but my emphasis is on the contribution of the architect to that process within the UK (Davis, 2006). Another key book in this area is Robert Gutman's excellent *Architectural Practice: A Critical View* (1988), which addresses a good deal of the territory covered here, albeit from a US angle and written some thirty years ago, but with minimal attention to the knowledge economy of the field and no attention to diversity. Steven Groak's unsurpassed *The Idea of Building* (1992), written from the perspective of a civil engineer, is a really important source. *Why Architects Matter* is also in some ways a response to Jeremy Till's *Architecture Depends* (Till, 2009). I will argue that architects are neither autonomous nor dependent (Imrie and Street, 2014). The book has been developed in conversation with Simon Foxell, whose *Professionalism for the Built Environment* is forthcoming. I should also mention the books *Architecture Matters* (Betsky, 2017) and *Why Architecture Matters* (Goldberger, 2011), which are both written from a US perspective. This book is about *architects*, not *architecture*, a subtle but important distinction to be discussed in Chapter 6, 'So what is an architect?'

My territory is what Ernest Boyer calls the 'scholarship of integration' and 'application', making connections across disciplines, 'placing specialities in larger context', often educating non-specialists too' (Boyer, 1997, p. 18). An additional aim is to offer researchers outside architecture a way into the field and to encourage them to help us investigate the links between the built environment and wellbeing. Such diversity is challenging at a methodological level, requiring what Abbott calls the 'usual disclaimer a synthetic writer makes to area specialists' (Abbott, 1988, p. xii). Further, it is hard to set the limits of a poorly defined entity, architects, in a constantly changing context with a paucity of evidence and hence 'to keep the coverage even', an academically desirable quality. One solution, adopted by Gutman (1988, p. 2), is to use a slightly different methodological framework for each chapter depending on the matter at hand, the whole stitched together with a consistent thread that winds through the narrative – architectural knowledge and its value.

Supporting the development of research in practice in order to generate the knowledge necessary to be more effective and more inclusive is a primary concern. Publishers of books aimed at industry generally suggest that the authors use extremely simple language and few or no footnotes, filling their books with bullet points and pull quotes for hard-pressed people to digest at speed. With this publication I have tried to offer a difficult middle ground between such industry-oriented writing and more highly theorized academic forms of communication. Parts I and II are built on more solid research than Part III, which is more speculative, with the aim of galvanizing an industry readership into action. I have peppered the text with references to other work partly, of course, to give acknowledgment to others, but partly also to show the extent of further reading that is possible, particularly within refereed journals, the highest quality information source, now more freely available over the internet. The intention is that these footnotes help provide solid back-up for arguments to be used by architects, clients and others in report presentations, funding applications and debate. I acknowledge more than a passing interest in 'evidence-based marketing', the use of data to promote the cause of the field. The references form the backbone of the online platform *Valuing Architects* developed in parallel with this book to help professionals communicate their offer and, unlike this book, designed for consumption at speed. Thinking fast and slow are radically different procedures, as Daniel Kahneman has shown (Kahneman, 2012).

To say that *Why Architects Matter* focuses on Western culture alone would be to stereotype what is Western and what is not (Bonnett, 2004). I take inspiration here from the work of anthropologist Aihwa Ong's work at Biopolis, a genomic research centre in Singapore, in which she argues that scientific outcomes are the result of complex mediations between 'global technologies' and situated forces framed by what she calls a 'global assemblage', a viewpoint that avoids overly simplistic contrasts between East and West, North and South. I argue that there are global lessons to be derived from UK practice set within the melting pot of knowledge which is the Royal Institute of British Architects (RIBA), an organization with members, chapters and schools across the world – some 17000 of its 40000 members are from outside the UK. At any point in time architects may be in demand on one side of the globe while floundering in recession on the other, with large global practices adjusting their services and presence accordingly. Its base, London, is arguably 'the world's global design hub' (Miller et al., 2013), being deemed a relatively stable world centre of finance and the epicentre of the former British Empire, in which a large proportion of the globe was oriented to UK ways of working and the English language system. In 2015 approximately 42.4% of the total gross value added of the UK architecture sector came from London, a figure that has been steadily rising over the last few years (GLA Economics, 2017, p. 8). Being an architect outside London is very different from being an architect in London, where architects' fees are but a small element of the overall real estate value of a project and the expectation of quality is much higher, but where the cost of living makes the lives of architects, young and old, almost untenable.

Ong is also inspirational in the way in which she draws on Donna Haraway's ideas of situated knowledge to make her own personal stake in her research very clear. 'No book about design is politically value free, whatever its apparent claim to objectivity' (Potter, 2002, p. 7). What then is the situated nature of my authorship? Well, a born and bred Londoner, I was a practitioner for eight years and have been an educator outside London for over twenty more, Head of the University of Sheffield School of Architecture for four of them. My interest in business and leadership was spawned when, like most academic leaders, I was catapulted into this role for which I had remarkably little training. I am now based in the newly created, industry-focused School of Architecture within the School of Built Environment at the University of Reading, conceived to deliver a truly research-based industry education, discussed in detail in Chapter 10. This book is based on knowledge gained through thirty years of active engagement in industry and education in an increasingly cross-disciplinary and global context.

The positions I have held have not traditionally been held by women (Samuel, 2016). One of the things that makes this book on the construction industry unusual is that it includes a consideration of the way in which women and indeed other minorities have been excluded from the way the built environment is made. Drawing on feminist approaches to writing, I dust my account with moments from my own highly subjective experience as a counterbalance to the academic argument. I hope it gives the book a different flavour, making it more widely accessible than some others in this territory. As a mother of three daughters I am fully aware of the difficulties faced by the next generation and I want to write a book that they can read.

Being the daughter of two architects, trained at the Architectural Association in London after World War II, I admit freely that my love-hate relationship with architecture is part of my 'family romance'. Hence, I think, my particular long-term interest in the Franco Swiss Modernist Le Corbusier, who explored in an extremely self-conscious way what it meant to be an architect, perhaps because he never went to architecture school. He understood that a difficult balance between the needs of 'the individual and the binomial' was actually at the core of what it is to be an architect, the paradoxical synthesis of poet and engineer, the scientific and the ineffable. This, in essence, was what I was investigating in the course of writing five books on his practice – research which will emerge from time to time in this book.

While in some ways I have been preparing to write this book ever since my youth, most of the writing took place during the years 2012–2017, a period of enormous flux, not least in the construction industry and related institutions, beginning with deep recession following on from the global financial crisis of 2008. I have had to repeatedly revise the text in the light of new developments, the UK's 2016 vote to exit the European Union (EU) being one; the 2017 Grenfell Tower disaster, the entirely unnecessary and tragic loss of life caused by a fire in a housing block in West London, being another. This book is a snapshot at a certain moment in time. Many of the conversations that informed its development happened as a result of my temporary and active engagement in the RIBA, as an elected and re-elected National member of Council and as Chair of its Research and Innovation group. As a trustee of the RIBA and a chartered architect I am bound by rules of professional conduct in reporting my observations. I have, however, been fortunate to be part of the RIBA during its current process of realignment towards research, as evidenced by its most recent strategy document developed under the auspices of the visionary RIBA President Jane Duncan (2015–2017), as well as her successor Ben Derbyshire (RIBA, 2016).

There is 'a new role for academia to link up with practice in order to carry out an archaeology of the processes of architectural production, in a non-threatening but critical manner' (Till, 2007, p. 4). I thought that being an academic would impede discussions with practitioners, but the opposite has been the case – they have opened up to me with remarkable generosity. As a piece of Participatory Action Research (essentially researching by doing things with other people) it has been challenging to fit within the established boundaries of university ethics procedures, which correctly favour extreme transparency (Hart et al., 2013), as the book encompasses thinking and encounters right across my professional career (Jarzombek, 2016). The need to develop practical ethical guidelines for collaborative work such as that done by architects and other construction professionals is urgent.

Words such as 'practice', 'technology', 'theory' and even 'science' have radically different meanings in different contexts and at different times (Groak, 1992, p. 72). Practice can be interpreted very differently by different theorists (see for example Pantzar and Shove, 2010). *Why Architects Matter* is a plaintive call for the role that history plays in understanding where we are now (Cayer et al., 2016). The history of the architecture profession has been eloquently set out by Andrew Saint in his book *The Image of the Architect* (1983), in which he builds on the work of Howard Colvin, Barrington Kaye and Frank Jenkins. Most histories foreground issues of design and philosophy, one result being that we have a very poor understanding of how architects have operated as professionals over time and in relationship with others. Did they, for example, deliver on time and on budget? Such issues, of low import to academia, continue to be neglected in professional education. In this book I will not dwell on the normative readings of history that make up the canon of architecture; my account is unbalanced by what I perceive as a need to bring in other voices.

On a similar note it is necessary to distinguish between 'traditional art' – often an object in a gallery which 'demands the physically distanced, passive contemplation of the viewer, for whom meaning is anchored to the artist' (Hill, 1998, p. 3) – and some forms of contemporary art in which 'the subject is recognized as an active, engaged participant' (Joselit, 2013, p. 2), exemplified perhaps by the work of the art/architecture co-operative Assemble, winners of the 2016 Turner Prize for Art. Unless stated otherwise, references to art refer to the former, traditional, category.

Part I of *Why Architects Matter* sets out the problem that I am seeking to address – the nature of the profession and its increasing marginalization from the construction industry. I argue that the key attributes of a profession are knowledge, ethics and professional judgement. However, lack of clarity about what it is that architects know makes it very difficult for them to defend their territory. The discussion will lead to the knowledge base of architects, concluding with a reflection on architecture's poor fit with the prevailing culture of audit and value. Part II starts with a working definition of the term 'architect' and then sets out some of the very different ways in which the profession brings benefits both to clients and to society, through economies of social value, cultural value and knowledge. Part III offers a strategy for developing a resilient, rigorous, respected research-led profession. This book is built on the scenario of business roughly as usual – developments such as climate change might change everything.

The way in which architects use their knowledge is at the foundation of three Arts and Humanities Research Council-funded studies, the primary research for which underpins the discussion in this book: *Home Improvements* (Samuel et al., 2014b), *Cultural Value of Architects* (Samuel et al., 2014a) and *Evidencing and Communicating the Value of Architects*, which included a study of UK architect attitudes to post-occupancy evaluation (Hay et al., 2017) and the growth of the Research Practice Leads group – individuals leading on the research agenda in twenty-five highly innovative architectural practices. This group has provided an important means to gather information and test some of the ideas herein. It also builds on the *RIBA Student Destinations Survey*, a ten-year longitudinal study of architecture graduates involving seven schools which I instigated in 2011. While, as Gutman found in 1988, there is more data available on architectural practice than is generally acknowledged, its quality is 'very uneven' (Gutman, 1988, p. 2). I am therefore very grateful to those researchers, often from Organization and Management Studies (OMS) and Science and Technology Studies (STS), who have focused their attention on architecture and professional practice in the construction industry, for example Lu and Sexton's empirical studies of knowledge exchange in small professional practices and Imrie and Street's work on attitudes to regulation in design practice. Such projects have provided me with rocks of rigorous research in a swirling miasma of hearsay, focus groups and spin exemplified by 'corporate social science'. Disagreements between architecture and the social sciences over the nature of rigour and the need to be propositional will emerge as a recurring theme in this book. If I go too far in generating conclusions from a set of dislocated circumstances (Abbott, 1988, p. 10), or in suggesting new categorizations, it is in the pragmatic name of a call to action.

References

Abbott, A., 1988. *The System of Professions*. University of Chicago Press, Chicago.

Betsky, A., 2017. *Architecture Matters*, 1st edition. Thames and Hudson, New York, NY.

Bonnett, A., 2004. *The Idea of the West: Politics, Culture and History*. Palgrave Macmillan, Basingstoke.

Boyer, E., 1997. *Scholarship Reconsidered: Priorities of the Professoriate*. John Wiley & Sons, London.

Cayer, A., Deamer, P., Korsh, S., Petersen, E., Shvartzberg, M. (eds), 2016. 'Asymmetric Labors: The Economy of Architecture in Theory and Practice'. www.academia.edu/28002267/Asymmetric_Labors_The_Economy_of_Architecture_in_Theory_and_Practice

Davis, H., 2006. *The Culture of Building*. Oxford University Press, Oxford.

Duffy, F., 1998. *Architectural Knowledge: The Idea of a Profession*. Spon, London.

Dulaney Jr., R., 2012. 'The Low-income Single-family House and the Effectiveness of Architects in Affecting Affordability'. *Enquiry*, 9, pp. 24–34.

Easterby-Smith, M., Lyles, M.A., 2011. *Wiley: Handbook of Organizational Learning and Knowledge Management*. Wiley, London.

Farrell, T., 2014. The Farrell Review of Architecture and the Built Environment. http://farrellreview.co.uk/downloads/The%20Farrell%20Review.pdf?t=1396343104

GLA Economics, 2017. 'London's Architectural Sector' (Working paper 86). www.london.gov.uk/business-and-economy-publications/londons-architectural-sector

Goldberger, P., 2011. *Why Architecture Matters*. Yale University Press, New Haven, CT.

Groak, S., 1992. *The Idea of Building: Thought and Action in the Design and Production of Buildings*. Taylor & Francis, Oxford.

Gutman, R., 1988. *Architectural Practice: A Critical View*. Princeton Architectural Press, New York.

Hart, A., Davies, C., Aumann, K., Wenger, E., Aranda, K., Heaver, B., Wolff, D., 2013. 'Mobilising Knowledge in Community–University Partnerships: What Does a Community of Practice Approach Contribute?' *Contemporary Social Science*, 8, 3, pp. 1–14.

Hay, R., Bradbury, S., Dixon, D., Martindale, K., Samuel, F., Tait, A., 2017. *Building Knowledge: Pathways to POE*. RIBA/University of Reading. www.architecture.com/knowledge-and-resources/resources-landing-page/post-occupancy-evaluation

Hill, J., 1998. *Occupying Architecture: Between the Architect and the User*. Routledge, London.

Huskinson, L., 2018. *Architecture and the Mimetic Self: A Psychoanalytic Study of How Buildings Make and Break Our Lives*. Routledge, Oxford.

Imrie, R., 2017. 'Autonomy and Architecture', Keynote speech, 28 April, Professional Practices in the Built Environment Conference, University of Reading, UK.

Imrie, R., Street, E., 2014. 'Autonomy and the socialisation of architects', *Journal of Architecture*, 19, 5, pp. 723–739.

Jarzombek, M., 2016. 'Work Time', in: Cayer, A., Deamer, P., Korsh, S., Petersen, E., Schvartzberg, M. (eds), *Assymetric Labours*, pp. 104–106. www.academia.edu/28002267/Asymmetric_Labors_The_Economy_of_Architecture_in_Theory_and_Practice

Joselit, D., 2013. *After Art*. Princeton University Press, Princeton, NJ.

Kahneman, D., 2012. *Thinking, Fast and Slow*. Penguin, London.

Miller, M., Brindley, R., Saxon, R., 2013. 'London: Global Design Hub, presentation to the City of London Corporation, 27 August 2013.

Osmani, M., Glass, J., Price, A.D.F., 2008. 'Architects' Perspectives on Construction Waste Reduction by Design'. *Waste Management*, 28, pp. 1147–1158. doi:10.1016/j.wasman.2007.05.011

Pantzar, M., Shove, E., 2010. 'Understanding Innovation in Practice: A Discussion of the Production and Re-production of Nordic Walking', *Technology Analysis and Strategic Management*, 22, 4, pp. 447–461.

Potter, N., 2002. *What is a Designer: Things, Places, Messages*. Hyphen, London.

RIBA, 2016. *Advancing Architecture: RIBA Strategy 2016–2020*. RIBA, London.

Saint, A., 1983. *The Image of the Architect*. Yale University Press, New Haven, CT.

Samuel, F., 2016. 'Symbolic Violence', in: Brown, J.B., Harriss, H., Morrow, R., Soane, J. (eds), *A Gendered Profession*. RIBA Publishing, London.

Samuel, F., Awan, N., Handler, S., Lintonbon, J., 2014a. 'Cultural Value of Architects in Homes and Neighbourhoods'. University of Sheffield/AHRC. www.shef.ac.uk/architecture/research/homeresearch/home_research_projects/cultural_value/index

Samuel, F., Coucill, L., Dye, A., 2014b. 'Home Improvements Knowledge Exchange in the Creative Economy Final Report'. University of Sheffield/AHRC. www.sheffield.ac.uk/polopoly_fs/1.359438!/file/FinalReport4.pdf

Schumacher, E.F., 1993. *Small Is Beautiful: A Study of Economics as if People Mattered*. Vintage, New York.

Sorkin, M., 2011. *All Over the Map: Writings on Buildings and Cities*. Verso, New York.

Till, J., 2009. *Architecture Depends*. MIT Press, Cambridge, MA.

Till, J., 2007. *What is Architectural Research?: Three Myths and One Model*, RIBA, London. www.architecture.com/Files/RIBAProfessionalServices/ResearchAndDevelopment/WhatisArchitecturalResearch.pdf

Winch, G., Schneider, E., 1993. 'Managing the Knowledge-based Organization: The Case of Architectural Practice'. *Journal of Management Studies*, 30, pp. 923–937. doi:10.1111/j.1467-6486.1993.tb00472.x

Part I

The undervaluing of architectural knowledge

Chapter 1

Public image, misinformation and the bogey of dispensability

While the architecture profession has been in 'crisis' since its very beginnings it seems clear that a new crossroads has been reached. A fundamental problem for architects is that what Kaye describes as the 'bogey of dispensability' (Kaye, 1960, p. 1968), the feeling that they aren't really necessary and that what they do do is of dubious worth.

> Reverence for beautiful buildings does not seem a high ambition on which to pin our hopes for happiness, at least when compared with the results we might associate with untying a scientific knot or falling in love, amassing a fortune or initiating a revolution. To care deeply about a field that achieves so little, and yet consumes so many of our resources, forces us to admit to a disturbing, even degrading lack of aspiration.
>
> (De Botton, 2006, p. 20)

It is perhaps this insecurity which causes architects to assert rather than evidence value, often in a manner which alienates others (Imrie and Street, 2011), contributing to the arrogant reputation of the profession. This chapter focuses on the professional identity of architects in Britain today – 'the relatively stable and enduring constellation of attributes, beliefs, values, motives, and experiences in terms of which people define themselves in a professional role' (Ibarra, 1999, p. 764).

Media representations of architects veer from adulation to contempt, the latter exemplified by this piece by Michele Hanson in *The Guardian* in support of the Japanese decision to shelve their planned Olympic stadium to be designed by Zaha Hadid Architects.

> But it's not just the monster egomaniac buildings that enrage me, the ones that heat up like a bakehouse, burn their surroundings, fall to bits, imperil window-cleaners, remain empty, cater only for millionaires, cock up our skylines, darken and oppress our streets. It's the rubbish built for the poor that is really sickening: cheap, dull, minimum-height ceilings, mean little square windows – no ornament at all, not even a sill – crappy materials and the crappiest possible design. Near me lives an elderly woman in sheltered accommodation, with the fire alarm placed above her cooker. She hasn't cooked

> a meal in months. But who cares? These places are for plebs. No architect would leave their dog in one overnight.
>
> (Hanson, 2015)

'Simple powerful messages about architecture are the ones that get remembered' (Brittain-Catlin, 2014, p. 20), so how have architects come to be so reviled?

1.1 The image of the profession

> Architect = An overworked and underpaid employee – of a pretentious registered practitioner of the arts (a prat). Many years in tertiary education have rendered the 'architect' bitter and in debt – and unable to relate to the remainder of society.
>
> (UrbanDictionary.com, 2015)

Architect-bashing is a national sport. They are an easy target as they have neither powerful patronage nor public sympathy and are, in general, poor at fighting back. It is for this reason that Prince Charles has been able to be a long-term and vociferous critic of the mainstream profession (Prince of Wales, 1989) with almost complete impunity. Architects are very often used as the butt of jokes. Recently I saw the product designer Sebastian Conran speaking jovially about what he called the 'three Fs of architecture' – 'finish, photograph and f. off', a response that elicited a hearty belly laugh from the large London audience, including some significant policy figures, but left us architects feeling distinctly uncomfortable (Conran, 2014).

In terms of career happiness a 2014 government poll had 'architects' ranked at 97th (Easton, 2014). Satisfaction with the choice of architecture as a career is deteriorating (ACE, 2012), as is student satisfaction with architectural education (RIBA, 2015a). Architects in the UK regularly work unpaid overtime (RIBA, 2015b) and their average income is little more than that of a train driver. The median gross hourly pay for architects in the UK has remained roughly static at around £17 from 2008 to 2016 (GLA Economics, 2017, p. 27). It is bizarre, given its poor prospects, that architecture remains an attractive choice of career for so many young people and their parents, despite the vast cost of five full-time years of study in a UK university. 'Through books, film, the Internet, and finally sheer willpower, the cultural idea and self-conception of the architect has enjoyed wild success, while architecture itself has failed both as a business model and as a tool for beneficial social change' (Ratti and Claudel, 2015, p. 22).

In 1934 Gotch made the wry observation that a '"rich architect" would strike most of us as a contradiction in terms' (Gotch, 1934, p. 1), yet rich-looking (male) architects abound in television and films. Architecture has traditionally been 'a gentleman's profession' (Saint, 1983, p. 160), but 'only just' (Summerson, 1973, p. 20). Architects have a status classification of 1.2 in the UK census, along with surveyors, airline pilots and doctors (AJ, 2001). At the same time architecture is well known to be the 'sexiest' profession for men; sexy here seemingly relating to the enduring 'romantic myth of the asocial, creative architect' (Jones, 2009, p. 2524), the dominating type characterized by Howard Roarke in Ayn Rand's famous novel and film *The Fountainhead* (1949) or the sensitive, but strong, architect using his drawing board to new ends in the film *Indecent Proposal* (1993) (ArchDaily, 2009).

Clothes play an important role in the construction of identity and the development of agency. For Georg Simmel social mobility takes place through adopting and impersonating the clothes of the elite (Simmel, 1957). A case in point might be the nineteenth-century fashion for bow ties among architects, worn to show they were artists and should not therefore be mistaken for the serving class (Shields, 1995) or indeed professionals. H.S. Goodhart-Rendel wrote in *The Professions* that: 'In those happy days artists behaved and dressed as a class apart, and professional men slept in their top hats' (1933). Nowadays fashion is more about the creation of identity than social mobility (Crane, 2001). Cordular Rau's book *Why Do Architects Wear Black?* (2001) explores the profession's obsession with this most negative of colours. The high priests and priestesses of architecture wear black, or its obverse extreme colour – Richard Rogers is famed for his red suits; ex-Mayor of Bristol and ex-President of the Royal Institute of British Architects (RIBA) George Ferguson is famed for his red trousers and so on. Is the shunning of the traditional grey business suit the twenty-first-century equivalent of the bow tie?

Architects are also known for being unintelligible. Porter's dictionary style book *Archispeak: An Illustrated Guide to Architectural Terms* (Porter, 2004) condones the use of 'archispeak' for 'helping students understand the nuances of this specialised language' and presumably learning to speak it themselves (Porter, 2004, preface). Craig Dykers of the Norwegian practice Snøhetta refers to the use of 'taciterms' in architecture 'uncommunicative but eager to be specific. It is easy to lop off loose bits of a concept to form a categorical some-such that sounds good to the ear while the meaning is lost' (Dykers, 2015). Such loose use of language may beguile students but generally fails to impress those beyond the profession. While archispeak might be important for the construction of group identity, it is also exclusionary (Richards, 2006).

Acceptance by peers seems to be more important to architects than public approval (Chaplin and Holding, 1998). It is possible that architects suffer from 'groupthink', which happens when 'members' strivings for unanimity override their motivation to realistically appraise alternative courses of action'. The result is a 'deterioration of mental efficiency, reality testing, and moral judgement that results from in-group pressures' (Janis, 1972, p. 9). Attoe argued that the multiple conflicting 'inner voices' working inside an architect can contribute to a sort of creative paralysis. 'Knowing that I shall fail, that decisions are ultimately unjustifiable, I avoid decisions' (Attoe, 1978, p. 132). It may be that architects end up hiding their 'true face' (Pels, 2000, p. 137) as they don't actually know what it is. The Farrell report talks about 'making the public better informed' (Farrell, 2014, p. 87), but is it actually architects who need to be better informed?

In 2012 94% of architects were white (Fulcher, 2012). The number of women registered with the ARB (the Architects Registration Board) has only just passed the 25% mark (Marrs, 2017), despite huge growth in the number of female students. The speed with which women have been accepted into the profession does not compare favourably with that of medicine and law (de Graft-Johnson et al., 2007, p. 162). Interestingly there are more women architects working in London than elsewhere (GLA Economics, 2017, p. 23). Those women who have managed to make it into the profession are generally in low-status roles. The gender pay gap across the UK was 9.9% in 2016 (GLA Economics, 2017, p. 28) and a shocking 40% across Europe in 2014 (ACE, 2014), a recent *Architects' Journal* survey suggesting a pay differential of some £50,000 at the top of the profession (Mark, 2017). Regardless of practice size, the percentage of women falls steadily by seniority, averaging 41% of architectural assistants but only 13% of Partners or Directors (RIBA, 2014, p. 1). Sociologists Fowler and Wilson have observed that there 'are few grounds for [the] belief that women are on the verge of "making it" in architecture' any time soon (Fowler and Wilson, 2004, p. 116). Many of the professions are experiencing a reduction of status in relation to their feminization (Bolton and Muzio, 2008), yet architecture seems to be experiencing a reduction in status even without being feminized. A lack of diversity in the profession continues to be a serious problem for its reception in the outside world (CABE, 2005; de Graft-Johnson et al., 2007, p. 179) and is a subject that will bubble to the surface repeatedly in this text. It is, however, important not to assume that things are the same across the globe, particularly on site.

1.2 Who needs an architect?

The architecture profession has developed in parallel with a growing interest in DIY and self-build. Indeed the DIY market in Britain expanded by 77% over the period 1990 to 2000 (Verdictonline, 2007), rendering architects seemingly more dispensable. The magazine *Popular Handicrafts* began to include articles on DIY in 1951, followed by the introduction of two new publications, *The Handyman* and *Do-It-Yourself*, in 1957 (Design Council, 1977; Powell, 1996). As people have grown more time-poor, DIY has started to decline (Powell, 2009), offering an opportunity for architects to step in to assist. However, the wide variety of material on the web, on the shelves of the newsagent WHSmith and in our libraries pertaining to the issue of home extensions does little to further the cause of the RIBA professional. Design is oddly absent from books such as the *Loft Conversion Projects Guide* (Construction Projects Association, 2010), suggesting that it is a non-issue. Paul Hymers, in his best-selling book *Home Conversion*, describes 'a good designer' solely as 'one who possesses the necessary skills of draughtsmanship and is familiar not only with the details of construction, but also with the problems and regulations relating to the work' (Hymers, 2003, p. 16). Time and time again the architect is depicted as a dispensable figure. The perception from the homeowners that I talked with is that the use of an architect worries builders, who do not want to work within a detailed contract, rendering them less likely to want a job, the result being higher tender figures – a further financial disincentive for the potential client, already daunted by the prospect of imagined architect's fees (Samuel, 2012). All this points to an emergent 'culture of amateurism', in which traditional professional roles are questioned (Leadbeater, 2003; Beegan and Atkinson, 2008).

Grand Designs is a popular UK television series which follows, with each programme, the progress of an individual self-build scheme. Its presenter, Kevin McCloud – not an architect but widely thought to be one – has done a great deal to put architects on the map, but not always in a positive light. *Grand Designs* was watched avidly by the group of homeowners that I interviewed about their house extensions, one of whom commented that on the rare occasions that the architect came into focus they were usually 'real prats'. She did, however, speak approvingly of the programme *Property Ladder*, 'which makes you feel you can do without them'. Another felt that the architects on *Grand Designs* were rather pushy, citing the example of one female architect who had been 'quite miffed' when things had not gone according to her plans (Samuel, 2012). While McCloud's aspiration has undoubtedly been to promote good design, the series failed to convince the homeowners I spoke to that architects are capable of bringing a project in on time and on budget. Ultimately the credit for a successful project rests firmly with the homeowners, not the team that brought it into being – and perhaps rightly so.

1.3 The reputational legacy of modernism

The legacy of post-war town planning still trails behind the architectural profession, the implication being that it followed sheep-like in the footsteps of Le Corbusier's megalomaniac vision to wipe out large swathes of existing cities and communities. It should, however, be remembered that his most contentious plans, the Ville Contemporaine and Plan Voisin for Paris, were conceived largely as a polemic to draw attention to the inadequate slum conditions persisting in France in his time. Le Corbusier's high-profile publicity stunts backfired when their headline characteristics – concrete, high rise and streets in the sky – were rolled out across the world by a novelty-hungry architectural profession in collusion with politicians uninterested in making them work in the long term. Negative perceptions were compounded by the Poulson Scandal of 1972, caused by an architect who had had remarkable success in bribing public officials to award him building contracts. It was at this point that high-rise estates came to be perceived as a social failure (Miller, 2009, p. 83). The Ronan Point disaster of 1968 – the collapse of an entire corner of a high-rise block following a gas explosion – left professionals with a negative view of prefabricated system building and the public with a negative view of professionals. It seems that 'the real quality problems associated with the high-rise experience of the 1960s owed more to inadequate research prior to widespread adoption of new construction techniques' as well as poor on-site supervision (Green, 2011, p. 8). The 2017 Grenfell Tower tragedy provides clear evidence of the failure of the construction industry to protect vulnerable people. 'It is clear that as an industry, we must atone for the dead by a root and branch re-appraisal of best practice to save lives in the future' (Kucharek, 2017, p. 36).

The blame for failed estates such as Broadwater Farm in London – known for a 1985 riot caused by the death of resident Cynthia Jarrett, during which PC Keith Blakelock was killed – is clearly shared. They were built too fast without the resources to provide the infrastructure and quality that was known, from past experiments, to be key to the success of mass housing. At Broadwater Farm cost-cutting exercises meant that the shops, pub, launderette and doctors' and dentists' surgeries that were planned for its success were not provided (Dillon and Fanning, 2011, p. 1), contributing to its social breakdown. Public perceptions of architects are still bound up with the social failure of twentieth-century experiments in housing and town planning, which, with true British stiff upper lip, the profession took on its shoulders without noticeable complaint or effective rebuttal. Where responsibility for the Grenfell Tower tragedy lies remains to be seen.

To the outside world, architects appear at once forward- and backward-looking, adding to the confusion about who they are. Some of the noisiest proponents of architecture, very often not architects themselves, are the historical lobbying groups such as the Georgian Group, the Victorian Society, and the Twentieth Century Society. Craggs and Geoghegan have made a study of the activities of the Twentieth Century Society and argue that 'amenity groups' and 'enthusiasts' play an increasingly important role in the making of our cities and that there is a need to engage critically with 'this challenge to conventional notions of expert, professional and lay-person' (Craggs et al., 2015, p. 374). Not long ago I attended a housing conference at which a right-wing councillor began by pronouncing on the ridiculousness of architects trying to save Allison and Peter Smithson's doomed Robin Hood Gardens Estate when nobody wanted to live there: 'I'd like to see those architects living there themselves – then they'd change their mind' – an observation that received hearty appreciation from the typically left-leaning academic audience. Robin Hood Gardens was earmarked for demolition apparently for reasons of tenant dissatisfaction. Whether it was the fault of the architects or because of the poor running of the estate is not clear. Either way I would suggest that the vociferous advocacy of this unpopular building by groups such as the Twentieth Century Society with the support of a high-profile group of architects has not been helpful to the profession's image.

1.4 Ethics

Architects then are generally the first to get the blame, as is currently the case with the proliferation of towers on the skyline of London (Prynn, 2015), when very often they are enacting the wishes of their funders. Nevertheless it cannot be denied that:

> The profession is looked upon as venal and selfish. Architects are perceived as people who are mainly interested in advancing, often on the basis of spurious arguments, the economic interests of building owners and developers; and therefore, indirectly, the wealth of professionals themselves. The public's trust in the fidelity of the profession is being undermined. The importance of this trust is the large part it plays in enforcing the client's respect

> for architects. This respect is based only circumstantially on confidence in technical skill. More important for the continuation of respect is the belief that architects will apply their skill not only for the benefit of the persons who pay their fees but also in response to the interests of persons, groups, and communities beyond the purview of the immediate client. For this reason, one can say that the public's and the user's conviction that the architect is indeed committed to the professional ideal is a fundamental source of the demand for the services of architectural firms. Architects who ignore this fact in their selling efforts imperil the future of their own practices and the practices of other architects.
>
> (Gutman, 1988, p. 21)

Public disappointment in architects is founded on the belief that architects have a collective ethical responsibility for public good. Since architecture is about making environments for people, with people, it will always have an ethical dimension. 'Professionals are expected to suppress individuality and personal creativity in the cause of shared "common sense", values that are assumed to be neutral and universal but in many cases primarily benefit a privileged minority'(Hill, 2003, p. 131).

Do UK architects have a responsibility for health and safety on building sites here and overseas? Ethical issues that the profession appears to condone include the poor working conditions in Qatar as it builds up to the 2022 World Cup and its involvement in industries that have a detrimental impact on the built environment such as air transport (Morrell, 2015, p. 49). '"If we didn't design it, someone else would"—only serves to highlight a worrying abdication of ethical responsibility by some of the world's leading design firms' (McNeill, 2006, p. 58). None of this helps the image of the architect.

1.5 Competitions

There are architectural competitions to select a design, competitions to select a designer and competitions to celebrate various kinds of achievement. Architects have learned through experience that the key to winning a competition of the first sort is to hastily create and sell an exciting solution to the jury, leaving more practical issues such as cost to be sorted out at a later date. The image that has been sold often becomes an impossible promise that cannot be translated into reality (Loe, 2000, p. 17). The result has been a series of highly visible competitions and controversies in which architects are once again the losers.

Apparently none of the finalists for the Scottish Parliament competition, launched in 1998, referred either to the brief or to the budget (Fraser, 2004, p. 63). The jury had relied on team 'assertions' that the project could be delivered within the £50 million budget (Fraser, 2004, p. 242). Despite this and despite the evident risk of working with the architects Enric Miralles/RMJM, the panel chose them as winners because of their 'presentation and concept' (Fraser, 2004, p. 63). It is instructive in this context to read the Holyrood Enquiry on the Scottish Assembly building, in which the setting-up of the legal framework between the architects was described as 'sloppy, unprofessional and fraught with danger' (Fraser, 2004,

p. 61). However, Lord Fraser observed that, while it was 'tempting to lay all the blame at the door of a deceased wayward Spanish architectural genius and his stylized way of working and the strained relationship between his widow and RMJM', he could not (Fraser, 2004, p. 240).

A wider issue, and one in which architects are complicit, is that clients expect an unrealistic amount of unpaid work to be done for competitions over an unrealistic time period – often driving architects to use unpaid interns and work the brutal unpaid overtime that pushes those with parental responsibilities, among others, out of the profession – with the most minute chances of success. In these unsustainable circumstances clients are bound to feel let down.

Historically among the major problems of competitions, which relate back to a general confusion about what constitutes good architecture, are the vague criteria for success (Lipstadt, 1989, p. 11; Rönn, 2009), a disgust with juries who have 'assumed to themselves the undefined and flattering attribute of taste' (Gotch, 1934, p. 103) and the frequent selection of a mediocre project as a compromise solution in the face of a judging impasse (Briggs et al., 1948, p. 489). Hannah Loftus made an astute observation on the online presentation of the 1715 entries for the Helsinki Guggenheim competition in 2014 that 'if you want a global icon stop pretending that it's about functionality for a given brief, and let's have the X factor vote' (Loftus, 2014, p. 21). When the project was shelved in December 2016, there was outrage on social media about the waste of architects' time entailed in this abortive venture and rightly so.

That prizes are being awarded for the wrong things has long been apparent to those architects keen to reward research-led practice (Manning, 1965). The RIBA runs a regular programme of awards, as do most other countries across the globe. The RIBA Gold Medal and the Pritzker Prize, two of the ultimate architectural accolades for architects, are awarded for lifetime achievement. A recommendation in the *Farrell Review of Architecture* was that awards need to focus more on everyday social value than on bespoke multimillion residential properties and the work of star architects (Farrell, 2014, p. 54). This is why the 2016 RIBAJ McEwen award for social architecture is such a welcome arrival on the scene, its first winners being ACG Architects, who with The Point, a new youth centre at Tadley, have managed to achieve a tricky balance between something designerly and something that its inhabitants enjoy (Figure 1.1). Perhaps the most prominent prize in the UK is the Stirling Prize, £20,000 'to the architects of the building which has been the most significant for the evolution of architecture in the past year', yet the way in which the building is significant is not specified. It is arguable that the Stirling Prize tells us more about the values of architectural culture than about architecture itself and that its opaque judging system devalues architecture in the eyes of the public. It is notable that the Stirling Prize-winning Peckham Library in London was singled out by residents of Peckham as being notable for eliciting 'negative emotions' (NEF, 2010, p. 23). The increased marginalization of the Stirling Prize from our television screens suggests that the public is not excited by the sight of architectural luvvies living it up (BD, 2011).

Ironically we have to turn to other organizations to find robust criteria for the valuation of architecture. English Heritage, for example, assesses buildings of

Figure 1.1
The Point Youth Centre in Tadley by ACG Architects (2016). Photo © Hufton and Crowe.

special architectural interest according to the importance of their 'design, decoration or craftsmanship', their display of 'technological innovation or virtuosity'. The Civic Trust prides itself on being 'the only 360 degree awards scheme in the world', examining entries to its awards through a variety of criteria, including 'positive community impact' and 'consultation with user groups' (Civic Trust, 2016). Until the profession presents some kind of united front on what constitutes good practice, the public will remain unimpressed. Unfortunately competitions are a very public way of showing our confusion in this area.

1.6 Starchitects

Public perceptions of the profession are, understandably, based largely on those architects who are most prominent, the so-called 'starchitects', a by-product of our industry:

> Here, reputation is built among key individuals in the commissioning process, such as development executives, chief executive officers, quantity surveyors, structural engineers, and so on, through the trade press, through word of mouth, through performance in design competitions, through excellence in particular sectors of construction (e.g. hospitals, office buildings, museums) through to the key 'bottom line' indicators of completing to budget and on time.
>
> (McNeill, 2005, p. 2004)

The final form of recognition is 'public recognition', expressed for example through a royal peerage and titles. To this end Lord Norman Foster has for several years been considered the architect who 'most inspires the work' of the *Architects' Journal*'s top 100 practices in the UK (Waite, 2016). Many architects identify with these elites whether they have any chance of reaching their elevated status or not (Spector, 2005).

There is a rich irony in the fact that the UK has produced more world famous 'starchitects' than any other country, yet the profession is so little valued over here. Starchitects, despite having large global practices, represent only a tiny proportion of architects and employ only a minute percentage of the profession. In London only 3.9% of architectural workplaces employ more than 50 people (GLA Economics, 2017, p. 12). It is unhelpful therefore to use them as exemplars for 'the 95 percent who will not begin to achieve that level of invention coupled with a necessarily ruthless approach to implementation' (Nicholson, 2000, p. xvi). This is especially the case if their activities are actually undermining the profession as a whole (Gutman, 1988; McNeill, 2005).

Fame sits awkwardly within a profession which frowns on self-publicity (Larson, 1993; McNeill, 2005) – in which 'a desire to be acknowledged without being seen to desire acknowledgement' (Chance and Schmiedeknecht, 1993, p. 5) is common. This might explain why Frank Gehry, architect of the Bilbao Guggenheim Museum, has referred to the word 'starchitect' as 'despicable' (Gehry, 2004). Another reason might be the emphasis that it gives to the single creative individual, other members of the team rarely receiving any credit (McNeill, 2006). When architects do try to acknowledge their teams, their words are often ironed out by the media, historians and other commentators, perhaps to save space or for the sake of a good story. The way in which building projects are credited has to change to show the full diversity of input from different members of the project team. This is a problem of architectural culture highlighted by the tendency, consolidated in schools of architecture, to reify individual architect masters by calling studio units after them – 'the Graves studio' and so on. While the canon of architecture often celebrates individual genius, architecture is always, in reality, a collective act (Larson, 1993, p. 5).

There is also a tendency to conflate all architects with starchitects, assuming that they are all capable of earning 'immense fees' (Risen, 2008, p. 3). While these highly successful architects may play up their role as creative form-makers, they are first and foremost excellent business people who are good at making money. Gehry states: 'I want to say something about how I run my world. Because it is very business like, and you will probably be very shocked to hear that. People think that we're flakey artists and that there is no bottom line, but I have a profitable office' (Gehry, 2004, p. 25). Starchitects have got where they are because they are good at winning competitions, they think globally, they are flexible about project delivery and are innovative when it comes to technology. They are also heavy with cultural capital, as will be discussed in Chapter 9. They are often hired by vast global contractors because of their particular ability to win competitions (Flanagan, 2017). Architects such as Gehry perhaps should be celebrated for their ability to 'recast the "hard" economic aspects of their role into "soft" aestheticized architectural frameworks' (Jones, 2009, p. 2532); then we might be able to change the widely held belief that architects are incompetent at business (RIBA, 2016).

Norman Foster recently stated: 'I have no power as an architect whatsoever' (Moore, 2015). While the power of starchitects to impact on policy may be relatively small, they have more power than the rest of the profession to influence the shape of the built environment. It is ironic, though, that people look to famous architects to change a system from which they have benefited and therefore have no interest in changing (Imrie and Street, 2011). Although these architects might be relatively powerless on the global stage, they have a great deal of influence on the younger generation:

> When I applied to study Architecture and Landscape at the University of Sheffield, I would consider my interpretation of the subject to have been distorted by the impressive physical qualities of iconic buildings by the likes of the greatest modern architects of today and that I only had a basic understanding of what an Architect was.
>
> (Year 1 student 2014/15)

Starchitects are of course carefully choreographed global super brands (Moore, 2002). It should, however, be noted that observations about their value are culturally specific. In China this kind of architecture can have associations with an anti-government stance, contributing to the 'cult status' of some architects over there (Ho, 2008, p. 278), perhaps a reason underpinning the Chinese President's desire for 'no more weird architecture' (Frearson, 2014). Rem Koolhaas's CCTV building in Beijing, known as 'Big Pants' by the locals, is an interesting case in point if his gnomic statements that 'it articulates the position and the situation of China' (Howarth, 2014) are taken at more than face value. Koolhaas has learned a great deal about using architecture as a Trojan Horse to bring in other ideas that were not necessarily part of the brief from his inspiration Le Corbusier, but is it really possible to be complicit and critical at the same time?

Conclusion

There is a mismatch between public perceptions of architects and what it is that they actually do, or believe that they are doing (Imrie and Street, 2011). When practices say one thing and do another, it is not surprising that the public is confused. 'As a result neither our working methods, nor our teachings, nor our values permit the profession to be effective' (Saint, 2007, p. 138). 'The resulting conflict confuses everyone, practitioners and clients, teachers and students alike. More importantly it prevents us from serving and sustaining the field as well as we could. Nor can the ordinary environment nourish us in return' (Habraken, 2005, p. x). This is why a key aim of this book is to achieve greater clarity on what architects actually do.

Although the profession has an enviable brand 'Architect', it has largely failed to come up with a service that meets the needs and aspirations of consumers

(Benedikt, 2007; Miles, 2010, p. 80). A recent survey by the RIBA showed that 'Two thirds of clients are "very" or "fairly" satisfied with the project, overall' (RIBA, 2016, p. 9). The real problem is those who choose not to employ an architect in the first place.

References

ACE, 2014. *The Architectural Profession in Europe*. Architects' Council of Europe, Brussels. www.ace-cae.eu/fileadmin/New_Upload/7._Publications/Sector_Study/2014/EN/2014_EN_FULL.pdf

AJ, 2001. 'Top Class: Architects Equal to Doctors in Census Categories'. http://m.architectsjournal.co.uk/180150.article (accessed 4.8.15).

ArchDaily, 2009. 'Fictional Architects in Movies'. *ArchDaily*. www.archdaily.com/33366/fictional-architects-in-movies/ (accessed 3.4.17).

Attoe, W., 1978. *Architecture and the Critical Imagination*. Wiley, Chichester.

BD, 2011. 'Stirling Prize'. *Building Design*, 14 October, p. 9.

Beegan, G., Atkinson, P., 2008. 'Professionalism, Amateurism and the Boundaries of Design'. *Journal of Design History*, 21, pp. 305–313.

Benedikt, M., 2007. 'Less for Less: On Architecture's Value(s) in the Marketplace', in: Saunders, W.S. (ed.), *Commodification and Spectacle in Architecture*. University of Minnesota Press, London, pp. 8–21.

Bolton, S., Muzio, D., 2008. 'The Paradoxical Processes of Feminization in the Professions: The Case of Established, Aspiring and Semi-professions'. *Work Employment and Society*, 22, pp. 281–299.

Briggs, M.S., Cross, K., Henniker, R.F., Rowland Pierce, S., 1948. 'The Work of the RIBA Part 1'. *RIBA Journal*, September, pp. 483–489.

Brittain-Catlin, T., 2014. *Bleak Houses: Disappointment and Failure in Architecture*. MIT Press, Cambridge, MA.

CABE, 2005. 'What Its Like to Live There: The View of Residents on the Design of New Housing'. http://webarchive.nationalarchives.gov.uk/20110118095356/http://www.cabe.org.uk/publications/what-its-like-to-live-there

Chance, J., Schmiedeknecht, T., 1993. Introduction, in: Chance, J., Larson, M.S. (eds), *Behind the Postmodern Facade: Architectural Change in Late Twentieth Century America*. University of California Press, Berkeley.

Chaplin, S., Holding, E., 1998. 'Consuming Architecture'. *Architectural Design Profile*, 131, pp. 7–9.

Civic Trust, 2016. 'Civic Trust Awards 2017'. www.civictrustawards.org.uk/about

Conran, S., 2014. 'Design and the Creative Economy'. AHRC Creative Economy Showcase. www.youtube.com/watch?v=gJuuukHAv4g

Construction Projects Association, 2010. *Loft Conversion Projects Guide*. RIBA, London.

Craggs, R., Geoghegan, H., Neate, H., 2015. 'Civic Geographies of Architectural Enthusiasm'. *ACME: An International Journal for Critical Geographies*, 14, pp. 367–376.

Crane, D., 2001. *Fashion and its Social Agendas: Class, Gender and Identity in Clothing*. University of Chicago Press, Chicago.

De Botton, A., 2006. *The Architecture of Happiness*. Hamish Hamilton, London.

de Graft-Johnson, A., Manley, S., Greed, C., 2007. 'The Gender Gap in Architectural Practice: Can We Afford it?', in: Dainty, A., Green, S., Bagilhole, B. (eds), *People and Culture in Construction*. Spon Research, London, pp. 159–183.

Design Council, 1977. *Leisure in the Twentieth Century*. Design Council, London.

Dillon, D., Fanning, B., 2011. *Lessons for the Big Society: Planning, Regeneration and the Politics of Community Participation*. Ashgate, Farnham.

Dykers, C., 2015. 'Listen 017'. *Blueprint*. www.exacteditions.com

Easton, M., 2014. 'Vicar or Publican – Which Jobs Make You Happy?' BBC. www.bbc.co.uk/news/magazine-26671221

Farrell, T., 2014. *The Farrell Review of Architecture and the Built Environment*. http://farrellreview.co.uk/downloads/The%20Farrell%20Review.pdf?t=1396343104

Flanagan, R., 2017. 'Global Construction Practice'. Presented at the Professional Practices in the Built Environment Conference, School of Architecture, University of Reading.

Fowler, B., Wilson, F., 2004. 'Women Architects and Their Discontents'. *Sociology*, 38, pp. 101–119.

Fraser, 2004. *The Holyrood Inquiry*. www.scottish.parliament.uk/SPICeResources/HolyroodInquiry.pdf (accessed 10.11.15).

Frearson, A., 2014. '"No more weird architecture" in China says Chinese president'. *Dezeen*. www.dezeen.com/2014/10/20/no-more-weird-architecture-in-china-says-chinese-president/ (accessed 3.4.17).

Fulcher, M., 2012. 'UK Architects are 94 per cent White'. www.architectsjournal.co.uk/news/daily-news/uk-architects-are-94-per-cent-white/8633432.article (accessed 4.8.15).

Gehry, F.O., 2004. 'Reflections on Design and Architectural Practice', in: Collopy, F. (ed.), *Managing as Design*. Stanford Business Books, Stanford University Press, Stanford, CA, pp. 19–36.

GLA Economics, 2017. 'London's Architectural Sector' (Working paper 86). www.london.gov.uk/business-and-economy-publications/londons-architectural-sector

Gotch, J.A. (ed.), 1934. *The Growth and Work of the Royal Institute of British Architects*. Simson and Co., London.

Green, S.D., 2011. *Making Sense of Construction Improvement: A Critical Review*. Wiley Blackwell, Chichester.

Gutman, R., 1988. *Architectural Practice: A Critical View*. Princeton Architectural Press, New York.

Habraken, N.J., 2005. *Palladio's Children*. Taylor & Francis, Oxford.

Hanson, M., 2015. 'Japan's heave-ho of Zaha Hadid's Olympic stadium is a win for the people'. *The Guardian*. www.theguardian.com/lifeandstyle/2015/jul/20/japan-zaha-hadid-olympic-stadium-architects-oppression (accessed 21.7.15).

Hill, J., 2003. *Actions of Architecture: Architects and Creative Users*. Routledge, London.

Ho, P.-P., 2008. 'Consuming Art in Middle Class China', in: van der Veer, P., Jaffrelot, C. (eds), *Patterns of Middle Class Consumption in India and China*. Sage, London, pp. 277–291.

Howarth, D., 2014. 'Rem Koolhaas: "Chinese Architecture Will Benefit" from CCTV Building'. *Dezeen*. www.dezeen.com/2014/11/26/rem-koolhaas-defends-cctv-building-beijing-china-architecture/ (accessed 21.1.16).

Hymers, P., 2003. *Home Conversion*. New Holland, London.

Ibarra, H., 1999. 'Provisional Selves: Experimenting with Image and Identity in Professional Adaptation'. *Administrative Science Quarterly*, 44, pp. 764–791.

Imrie, R., Street, E., 2011. *Architectural Design and Regulation*. Wiley Blackwell, Oxford.

Janis, I.L., 1972. *Victims of Groupthink*. Houghton-Mifflin, Boston, MA.

Jones, P., 2009. 'Putting Architecture in its Social Place: A Cultural and Political Economy of Architecture'. *Urban Studies*, 46, pp. 2519–2536.

Kaye, B., 1960. *The Development of the Architectural Profession in Britain: A Sociological Study*. Allen and Unwin, London.

Kucharek, J.-C., 2017. 'After Grenfell'. *RIBA Journal*, 124, pp. 35–38.

Larson, M.S., 1993. *Behind the Postmodern Facade: Architectural Change in Late Twentieth Century America*. University of California Press, Berkeley.

Leadbeater, C., 2003. 'Amateurs: A 21st Century Remake'. *RSA Journal*, June, 22–25.

Lipstadt, H. (ed.), 1989. *The Experimental Tradition: Essays on Competitions in Architecture*. Princeton Architectural Press, Princeton, NJ.

Loe, E., 2000. 'The Value of Architecture: Context and Current Thinking'. RIBA Future Studies. www.buildingfutures.org.uk/assets/downloads/pdffile_23.pdf

Loftus, H., 2014. 'And the Winner is …' *Architecture Today*, 253, p. 21.

Manning, P., 1965. 'Hard Facts on Research'. *Architects' Journal*, pp. 192–209.

Mark, L., 2017. 'Women in Architecture Survey Reveals Widening Gender Pay Gap'. *Architects' Journal*. www.architectsjournal.co.uk/news/women-in-architecture-survey-reveals-widening-gender-pay-gap/10017147.article (accessed 1.8.17).

Marrs, C., 2017. 'ARB Report: For First Time More Than a Quarter of Profession are Women'. *Architects' Journal*. www.architectsjournal.co.uk/news/arb-report-for-first-time-more-than-a-quarter-of-profession-are-women/10022181.article (accessed 2.8.17).

McNeill, D., 2006. 'Globalization and the Ethics of Architectural Design'. *City*, 10, pp. 49–58.

McNeill, D., 2005. 'In Search of the Global Architect: The Case of Norman Foster (and Partners)'. *International Journal of Urban and Regional Research*, 29, 3, pp. 501–515.

Miles, S., 2010. *Spaces for Consumption: Pleasure and Placelessness in the Modern Industrial City*. Sage, London.

Miller, D., 2009. *Stuff*. Polity, Cambridge.

Moore, R., 2015. 'Norman Foster: "I Have no Power as an Architect, None Whatsover"'. *The Guardian*. www.theguardian.com/artanddesign/2015/nov/22/norman-foster-i-have-no-power-as-an-architect-sustainability

Moore, R., 2002. 'Norman's Conquest'. *Prospect*, March, pp. 52–56. www.prospectmagazine.co.uk/magazine/norman-foster-profile

Morrell, P., 2015. *Collaboration for Change*. Edge, London. www.edgedebate.com/?page_id=2829

NEF, 2012. *Good Foundations: Towards a Low Carbon, High Well-being Built Environment*. http://b.3cdn.net/nefoundation/8b32051850bcf41dee_7bm62zt1o.pdf

Nicholson, R., 2000. 'Foreword', in: Nicol, D., Pilling, S. (eds), *Changing Architectural Education*. Spon, Oxford, p. xvi.

Pels, P., 2000. 'The Trickster's Dilemma: Ethics and the Technologies of the Anthropological Self', in: Strathern, M. (ed.), *Audit Cultures*. Routledge, London, pp. 136–172.

Porter, T., 2004. *Archispeak: An Illustrated Guide to Architectural Terms*. Spon, London.

Powell, C., 1996. *The British Building Industry since 1800*. Routledge, Oxford.

Powell, H., 2009. 'Time, Television and the Decline of DIY', *Home Cultures*, 6, 1, pp. 89–107.

Prince of Wales, H., 1989. *Vision of Britain: A Personal View of Architecture*. Doubleday, London.

Prynn, J., 2015. '"Starchitects" turn City Road into Skyscraper Highway'. *Evening Standard*. www.standard.co.uk/news/london/starchitects-turn-city-road-into-skyscraper-highway-8870844.html (accessed 22.7.15).

Ratti, C., Claudel, M. (eds), 2015. *Open Source Architecture*. Thames and Hudson, London.

Rau, C., 2001. *Why Do Architects Wear Black?*. Birkhauser, Basel.

RIBA, 2016. 'What Clients Think of Architects'. www.architecture.com/Files/RIBAProfessionalServices/ClientServices/RibaWorkingWithArchitectsOnlineReport2016.pdf (accessed 9.12.16).

RIBA, 2015a. *RIBA Student Destinations Survey 2015*. London. REPORTRIBAStudentDestinationsSurvey2015pdf.pdf

RIBA, 2015b. 'Education Statistics 2013–14'. www.architecture.com/Files/RIBAProfessionalServices/Education/Validation/EducationStatistics2012-13.pdf

RIBA, 2014. *RIBA Business Benchmarking Report 2013/14*. RIBA, London.

Richards, K., 2006. *Language and Professional Identity: Aspects of Professional Collaboration*. Palgrave Macmillan, Basingstoke.

Risen, C., 2008. 'The Conscience of a Constructor'. *Democracy*, 9, pp. 108–112.

Rönn, M., 2009. 'Judgment in the Architectural Competition'. *Nordic Journal of Architectural Research*, 21, pp. 52–67.

Saint, A., 2007. *Architect and Engineer: A Study in Sibling Rivalry*. Yale University Press, New Haven, CT.

Saint, A., 1983. *The Image of the Architect*. Yale University Press, New Haven, CT.

Samuel, F., 2012. 'Extension Stories', in: Sharr, A. (ed.), *Architecture and Culture*. Routledge, London, pp. 96–105.

Shields, R., 1995. 'A Tale of Three Louis: Ambiguity, Masculinity and Bowtie', in: Brydon, A., Niessen, S. (eds), *Consuming Fashion: Adorning the Transnational Body*. Berg, Oxford.

Simmel, G., 1957. 'Fashion', *American Journal of Sociologists*, 62, pp. 541–558.

Spector, T., 2005. 'Codes of Ethics and Coercion', in: Ray, N. (ed.), *Architecture and its Ethical Dilemmas*. Routledge, London, pp. 101–112.

Summerson, J., 1973. *The London Building World of the 1860s*. Thames and Hudson, London.

Till, J., 2009. *Architecture Depends*. MIT Press, Cambridge, MA.

UrbanDictionary.com, 2015. 'Architect'. www.urbandictionary.com/define.php?term=architect (accessed 3.4.17).

Verdictonline, 2007. www.verdictonline.co.uk/VerdictReports/EuroDIY01PRESS.HTM (accessed 7.9.07).

Waite, R., 2016. 'AJ100 Practices Vote Norman Foster "Most Influential" Architect'. *Architects' Journal*. www.architectsjournal.co.uk/news/aj100-practices-vote-norman-foster-most-influential-architect/10007343.article (accessed 20.8.17).

Chapter 2

The profession

Architects are members of a profession, but just what this means has been subject to considerable debate (Higgin, 1964; Till, 2009). The word 'profession' has etymological origins in the Latin word 'profiteri', which means to declare openly, in this case to declare possession of a special set of skills or training. Arguably all professions should have 'a skilled intellectual technique, a voluntary association and a code of conduct' (Kaye, 1960, p. 17). In the pages of *The Doctor's Dilemma,* George Bernard Shaw described the professions as 'conspiracies against the laity' (SPADA, 2009), reflecting here a deep ambivalence about their value (Abbott, 1988) and the opinion, still extant, that they exist only to control the market and are not to be trusted (Kaye, 1960; Sarfatti Larson, 1993 [1977]; Eraut, 1994).

The nature of the professions has been subject to very considerable social science and historical analysis, through a wide variety of methodological lenses (Abbott, 1988) since what is generally considered to be the first book on the subject, *The Professions*, by Carr-Saunders and Wilson (1933). The birth of the professions needs to be seen in the context of the disaggregation of universities into a range of academic disciplines, which have played an important role in bolstering up claims to expertise and also shooting them down. To this end Kay, Sarfatti Larson and Eraut use what Abbott calls the 'power' model to cast professions as 'market dominating institutions' operating in the private sector. In doing so they discount the existence of those professions that form part of the machinery of state such as the civil service and the army (Abbott, 1988, p. 6). 'The state offers legal protection, and a potential monopoly, to a profession in return for its safe management of an area of unsafe knowledge' (Hill, 2003, p. 132), yet we are now in a situation in the UK where legislative procedures seem to have displaced the professional institutions as custodians of standards (Hughes et al., 2015). This chapter provides an account of the development of the UK architecture profession, its relationship with other professions, and the difficulties it has had in adjusting to a private sector in which market forces rule. Its focus is on professional turf wars and their impact.

2.1 The origins of the architectural profession in the UK

The main driver for development of the professions was socio-technical change – new health requirements, new materials, new structural possibilities, new stylistic influences – caused by the advent of the industrial revolution (Wilton-Ely, 1977). These required new forms of representation as well as new collective, and sometimes global, ways of working, particularly when professions were servicing the commercial activities of Britain and its colonies. The architectural profession developed in a flurry of categorization characteristic of the Victorian era.

18th century		
1739	Solicitors	Law Society
1745	Surgeons	Company of Surgeons (1800 Royal College)
1791	Veterinary surgeons	Royal Veterinary College
19th century		
1818	Civil engineers	Institution of Civil Engineers
1834	Architects	Institute of British Architects
1841	Pharmacists	Pharmaceutical Society
1841	Chemists	Chemical Society
1847	Mechanical engineers	Institute of Mechanical Engineers
1848	Actuaries	Institute of Actuaries
1858	Accountants	Association of Accountants
1855	Dentists	Odontological Society
1868	Surveyors	Institute of Surveyors
1870	Teachers	National Association of Elementary Teachers (Kaye, 1960)
1914	Planners	Royal Town Planning Institute (rtpi.org.uk)
1922	Engineers	Institution of Structural Engineers (Powell, 1996)
1965	Architectural technicians	Society of Architectural and Associated Technicians (Powell, 1996)

The Institution of Civil Engineers, conceived to promote 'the arts and sciences of engineering' was ahead of the game not just temporally, but also in being canny enough to move to Great George St in London in 1839, just a stone's throw from parliament.

The Institute of Architects first came into being in 1834. Its original prospectus makes its purpose clear – the advancement of the knowledge of architects (Figure 2.1) (RIBA, 1834). It was not the first time that a group of architects had banded together for mutual support, but it was the most enduring association (Gotch, 1934). Right from the very beginning there was pressure to define the architect's role vis-à-vis others who might have a claim on the territory. Saint writes that at that time 'the only element in architecture to which some other professional group did not have a prior or better claim, was "art"', an assertion that was to make 'steady progress' over the years, particularly among the privately wealthy (Saint, 1983, p. 61). H.S. Goodhart-Rendel observed in his 1933 book, *The Professionals*:

> Norman Shaw, himself a practical man as well as a great artist, wrote an essay with a title 'That an Artist is not Necessarily Unpractical', and everybody agreed that he was not necessarily so with the inward reservation that more often than not he would be.
>
> (quoted in Kaye, 1960, p. 22)

Norman Shaw's book *Architecture as Profession or Art* (Norman Shaw and Jackson, 1892), emblematic of this discussion, was to cause a rift between the two parts of the nascent profession that remains alive to this day (Dodds, 2015).

In 1837 the Institute was transformed into the Royal Institute of British Architects in 1837 with the blessing of a Royal Charter:

> for promoting and facilitating the acquirement of the knowledge of the various arts and sciences connected therewith; it being an Art esteemed and encouraged in all enlightened nations, as tending greatly to promote the domestic convenience of citizens, and the public improvement and embellishment of Towns and Cities and have subscribed and paid considerable sums of money for those purposes and have formed a collection of Books and Works of Art and have established a Correspondence with Learned and Scientific men in Foreign Countries, for the purpose of inquiry and information upon the subject of the said art.
>
> (RIBA, 2009)

In the UK the Privy Council has charge of Royal Charters, which exist in the 'public interest' (Morrell, 2015, p. 45). Just who the public is, is of course debatable (Froud, 2015). T.L. Donaldson (1795–1885), the first secretary of the Royal Institute of British Architects (RIBA) – described by Prince Albert 'as the father of the Institute and of the profession' (Mace, 1986, p. xv) – observed that the architect members were to be 'men of taste, men of science and men of honour' (Walker, 1997, p. 9), a sentiment that reveals some of the complacencies of that time. The RIBA library was, according to Donaldson, put in place to 'direct the taste and warm the imagination of the Architect' (Gotch, 1934). The institution was to seal its status as a Learned Society, in doing so severing direct links with the craft trades (Powell, 1996), with the first publication of its *Transactions* in 1836. This was merged into the *RIBA Journal*, which was an important means to keep members in the provinces and overseas abreast of developments (Gotch, 1934). By 1934 its circulation had reached 10000 (Gotch, 1934, p. 156). In 1960, Barrington Kaye wrote a detailed account of the history of the RIBA (Kaye, 1960) but the last fifty years of the institute remains to be documented.

A legislative framework put in place in the name of public health arrived on the scene in the latter part of the nineteenth century, contributing to a fall in urban death rates while adding considerable complication to the building processes,

(a)

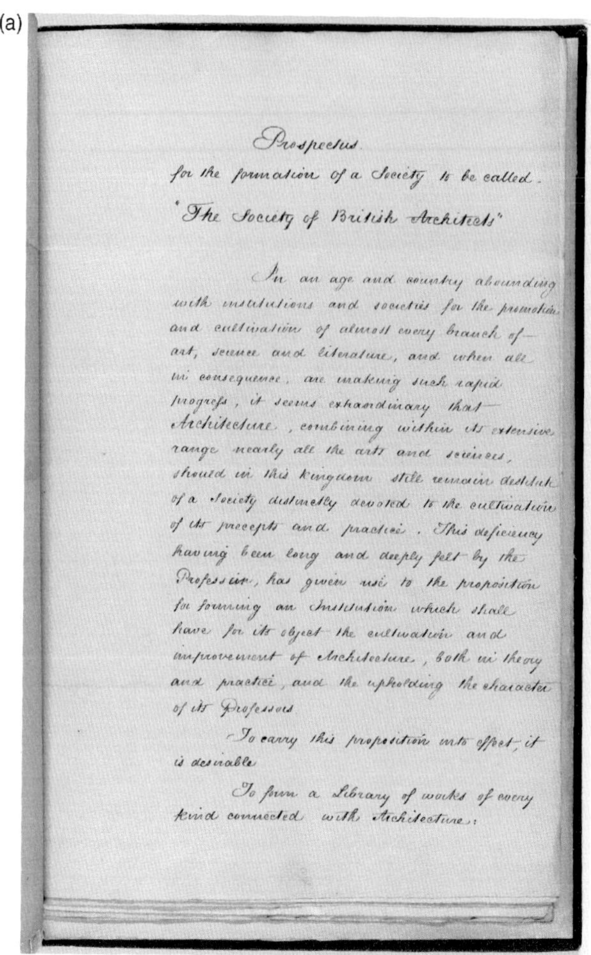

Prospectus

for the formation of a Society to be called

"The Society of British Architects"

In an age and country abounding with institutions and societies for the promotion and cultivation of almost every branch of art, science and literature, and when all in consequence, are making such rapid progress, it seems extraordinary that Architecture, combining within its extensive range nearly all the arts and sciences, should in this Kingdom still remain destitute of a Society distinctly devoted to the cultivation of its precepts and practice. This deficiency having been long and deeply felt by the Profession, has given rise to the proposition for forming an Institution which shall have for its object the cultivation and improvement of Architecture, both in theory and practice, and the upholding the character of its Professors.

To carry this proposition into effect, it is desirable

To form a Library of works of every kind connected with Architecture;

Figure 2.1 **'Prospectus for the formation of a society to be called "The Society of British Architects"' dated 15 February 1834. Reproduced with the permission of RIBA Collections.**

for example through the introduction of environmental services (Powell, 1996). That it was not well received by the profession is illustrated by Guy Dawber, then President of the Architectural Association, who voiced the following complaint on behalf of 'the poorest peasant':

> his antique smock has been discarded for the cheap tweed suit, his wooden clogs for newly made boots. His cottage too is changed, built now in depressing rows after the ugly model laid down by the Local Government Board, the open hearth has given way to the stove, the red tiled floor to the linoleum. The old fashioned lattice casement to sash windows and coloured glass – all things that doubtless conduce to his material advantage, but certainly to the great loss of picturesque effect
>
> (Dawber, 1904, p. 360)

(b)

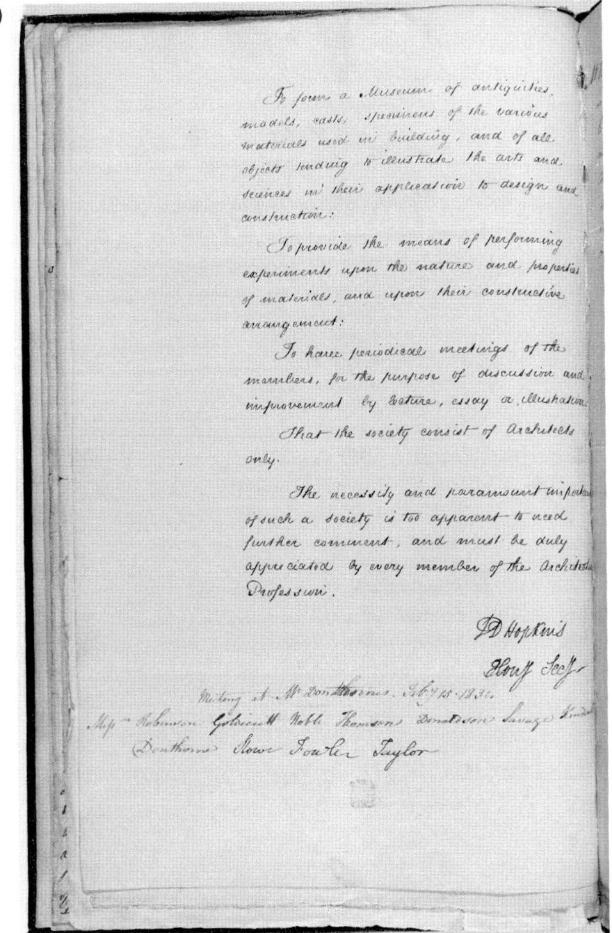

To form a Museum of antiquities, models, casts, specimens of the various materials used in building, and of all objects tending to illustrate the arts and sciences in their application to design and construction:

To provide the means of performing experiments upon the nature and properties of materials, and upon their constructive arrangement:

To have periodical meetings of the members, for the purpose of discussion and improvement by lecture, essay or illustration.

That the society consist of Architects only.

The necessity and paramount importance of such a society is too apparent to need further comment, and must be duly appreciated by every member of the Architectural Profession.

Hopkins
Hon. Secy

Meeting at Mr Donthorne's. Feby 15. 1831.
Messrs Robinson Goldicutt Noble Thomson Donaldson Savage Kendall
Donthorne Rowe Fowler Taylor

Figure 2.1 (***cont.***)

Complaints from architects realizing that their artistic freedom was about to be constrained resulted in 'a tightening of the defensive attitude' of the officers who had to enforce this legislation (Harper, 1977, p. 32), marking the beginning of a slightly unfortunate relationship between building regulation and architectural design in the UK in which regulation is treated as an unnecessary constraint (Imrie and Street, 2011).

Not all architects were so unethical as to resist positive social reforms. Social responsibility goes far back into the history of the profession, receiving clear expression in the philanthropic work of A.W. Pugin (Wilton-Ely, 1977), William Morris and others. This was also an area in which women had been instrumental, 'social welfare' and 'housing management' work having long been done on a voluntary basis by such women as Octavia Hill (Darling and Whitworth, 2007, p. 139), but this was made more difficult in the drive towards professionalization, prescription and legal redress. Women were not allowed to own and control property in the UK until the introduction of the Married Women's Property Act in 1882.

Almost as soon as the RIBA was created, the backlash began. A 'Memorial to the RIBA' was published in *The Times* in 1891 and signed by over seventy public figures including several artists. This list is itself instructive, as it shows how many of the architects who have gone down in history were *not* members of the RIBA, including Lethaby, Norman Shaw, Philip Webb and Gilbert Scott.

> No legislation can protect the public against bad design; nor could legislation help to prevent bad construction unless builders were required to pass the test of examination as well as Architects, in as much as Architects are not employed in the majority of cases.
>
> (Kaye, 1960, pp. 138–139)

Here Messrs Lethaby, Shaw, Webb and Scott made a powerful case for the better integration of the construction industry, rather than a separation into silos – an argument to which I will return.

The first RIBA Professional Practice Committee was set up in 1845 'to enquire as to the custom of architects in respect to professional charges and other matters connected with the practice of the profession, with such recommendations as they may think fit to ensure an uniformity in such proceedings', the result being the Scale of Professional Charges, the Form of Building Contract, the Declaration, the Bye-laws and the Code of Professional Practice (Gotch, 1934, p. 117). The professional association also had some important basic work to do such as standardizing the fee scale and agreeing on the ownership of drawings.

Right from the start the RIBA was conceived as a global institute. Donaldson was keenly interested in the development of international relations and developed a system of reciprocal hospitality for architects across the globe, which continued on into the twentieth century. More locally the development of the RIBA was accompanied by the development of the 'Allied Societies, regional branches both in the UK and overseas' (Gotch, 1934, p. 51). The next task was to develop an education system to ensure that the claims of the institute could be delivered (Gotch, 1934).

Three thousand 'architects' were registered in the 1851 census, many of whom would have been builders and members of other related trades, a number that rose to 8800 in 1940. Over the period the proportion who were members of the RIBA grew from 8% to 15%, still very much a minority (Powell, 1996, p. 76). The Registrations Acts of 1931 and 1938 meant that the title Architect was conferred only on those with the necessary qualifications, in this way giving it protected status. Today the title Architect is protected by the Architects Registration Board (ARB) with the more closely guarded title 'Chartered Architect' under the auspices of the RIBA. 'The RIBA and ARB are housed on adjacent sites in the centre of London, rather like the halves of a pantomime donkey bound together but pulling in different directions' (Hill, 2003, p. 133). The need for two organizations to guard the future of the profession is emblematic of the problems it faces in staking its unique claim.

The 1930s also saw official architects in local authority positions become more powerful and more numerous (Powell, 1996), a trajectory that continued into the 1940s and 1950s – by 1957 there were 135 local authority architects' departments (Powell, 1996, p. 171). During the early 1960s and 1970s around half the profession was employed in private practice (Powell, 1996, p. 171). However, the boundaries between the public and private sectors were not always clear as local authorities would also commission private practices when they offered particular specialisms. A radical shift from public funding to private funding, attributed to the free market policies of Margaret Thatcher's Conservative government, meant that the number of architects in private practice increased sharply (Lansley, 1997). There is hope that the tide might now finally be turning. Croydon Council in London has, for example, set up its own housing development company, Brick by Brick, and other local authorities are thinking more creatively about how best to use public funds to address the desperate shortage of affordable housing in the UK (Morphet and Clifford, 2017).

The RIBA's mandatory scale according to which architects' fees were based on a percentage of the final project cost applied until 1982 (see for example RIBA, 1971; Dobson, 2013), a disincentive for architects to save money for their clients or to demonstrate the value of what they did. Back in the 1860s architects earned a customary fee of 5% of building costs, based on the relative lack of complexity of early building work. As Powell notes, it must have been harder and harder to work within this tight margin (Powell, 1996). The customary fee went up to 6% in 1919 and then crept upwards (Gotch, 1934, p. 120) until the RIBA fee scale was introduced, reaching the giddy heights of 14% of the contract sum for domestic work. A *RIBA Journal* editorial in 1972 reports a series of attempts by public bodies to erode the fee scale.

> It is important for the whole profession – that is, both those in private practice and those in senior positions in client organisations – to continue to act with the solidarity which will establish the conditions of engagement in the minds of clients as the proper basis for the services which architects can provide.
>
> (RIBA, 1972, p. 1)

Indeed in 1974 the Architects' Revolutionary Council called for the abolition of the RIBA at a press conference, producing posters asking: 'If crime doesn't pay, where did Architects get all their money?' (Figure 2.2).

The fee scale continued in a suggested form until 2003, when it was abolished by the European Union (EU) Competitions Directive, on the basis that it encouraged collusion (Brindley, 2012) and unfair trading, despite the fact that architects were consistently found to be paid less than other comparable professions (UK Gov, 2001). A similar situation developed in the USA, leading to American Institute of Architects members being prevented from conferring on fees (Kubany and Linn, 1999). The Competitions Directive meant that UK architects were now allowed to market their services, something that had previously been prohibited.

The profession was now under pressure to demonstrate its added value. Its response was, in 2007, to set up the Chartered Practice route – intended to

Figure 2.2
Propaganda by Architects' Revolutionary Council.
Reproduced with the permission of the Architectural Association.

be a kitemark of excellence – and, in 2010, the RIBA Business Benchmarking survey, an important initiative which, through the provision of anonymized information, enables practices to measure themselves against what others are doing across the profession. Generally there is, however, a lack of information on fees at a regional level (GLA Economics, 2017) and they vary considerably (Grant Erskine Architects, 2017).

In the UK the graph showing suggested percentage fees was taken out of the *Client's Guide to Engaging an Architect* in 1999.

The problem was that the controls were taken away before the profession had enough solid knowledge of 'actual costs' or indeed was able to articulate its services in an effective way. After the dismantling of the fee scale architects undercut each other on price, reducing their ability to lead the team in the process and finding themselves managed by others (Saxon, 2006). A nadir was reached in the 2012 recession with the development of zero fees contracts. It is worth noting that, despite architects' reputation for being expensive, their 'charge-out rates for qualified staff are often a fifth of the equivalent lawyer (who qualifies faster) or half of an equivalent medic' (Pringle and Porter, 2015, p. 146).

Public loss of faith in the professions is paralleled by a suspicion among politicians, certainly in the UK, that regulated professions get in the way of growth. 'Cynics might argue that, whereas previously the State sought to protect its citizens from the unqualified practitioners, it now seeks to protect them from the qualified' (Eraut, 1994, p. 5). 'Government and its officials nonetheless increasingly look to the corporate world as a source of trusted advice' (Morrell, 2015, p. 24) and not the professions. 'The attitude that sometimes seems to prevail in the industry is that members of "other" professions are greedy, self righteous, dim or prima donnas' (Hughes et al., 2015, p. 13).

According to the Farrell Review, architects' share of responsibility in the built environment has reduced considerably over the last century and to a far greater extent than any of the other built environment professions (Farrell, 2014). There is, however, a notable lack of robust statistical information on the proportion of building work designed by architects, so it is really very hard to gauge the performance of the profession over the long term. According to one 1939 *RIBA Journal*:

> in general terms, of the nation's total annual expenditure on new building (about £255,000,000) the architect is responsible for 50 per cent. If, however, speculative and municipal housing are excluded, the architect is responsible for at least 85% of all other building work.
>
> (RIBA, 1939, p. 898)

Kaye writes of the belief in the late 1950s that only 5% of houses were built by an architect (Kaye, 1960). K. MacInnes has asserted that only 6% of self-builders contract an architectural firm (MacInnes, 1994). The proportion has traditionally been greater in the field of non-residential work. More recent statistics suggest that the figure is nearer 10%. Other figures suggest that buildings designed by architects account for no more than 2% of global construction (Ratti and Claudel, 2015, p. 21).Whatever the statistics, it seems that architects, the most highly trained members of the building team, have always been marginal to the production of the built environment. Architects have an important role to play in facilitating the adoption of sustainability (Hall, 2013). Their marginalization has not been helpful to this cause.

2.2 The construction improvement agenda

'The built world is not in very good shape, and the responsibility for this situation cannot be laid at the hands of any one profession' (Davis, 2006, p. 4). Conservative official estimates suggest that the construction industry accounts for 6.3% of gross domestic product (GDP). Looked at in another way 'the UK built environment accounts for 90% of the nation's physical assets and 84% of the nation's entire net worth' (CIOB, 2014, p. 6). Construction also has a profound impact on our society and its sustainability. As an enabler of the economy it plays an important role in social mobility (CIOB, 2016). Given the economic and strategic importance of the construction industry it is interesting that 'its role in society is often ignored or taken for granted' (Dainty et al., 2006, p. 174).

The history of the construction improvement agenda is in many ways an account of the failure of the industry to manage knowledge and therefore risk.

Its knee-jerk reaction has been to develop increasingly 'inflexible contractual and professional conventions' (Green, 2011, p. 13), which actually seem to be holding back the innovative potential of the industry as a whole. Green documents an important lineage of reports aimed at the improvement of the construction industry in his book *Making Sense of Construction Improvement* (2011) so there is no need to duplicate it here. It is, however, worth mentioning the Emmerson report of 1962, in which its author, Sir Harold Emmerson, argued that construction efficiency could be achieved only through the collaboration of the building owner, the professions and the contractor, a message that repeats across the years. At around that time a report by the Tavistock Institute suggested that the construction industry had 'a vested interest in preserving chaos and uncertainty' in order to gain short-term 'partisan advantage' (Tavistock Institute, 1966, p. 61). Woudhuysen and Abley's book *Why Is Construction So Backward?* describes a nervousness around innovation and the implementation of technology because of fears of job losses (Wouldhuysen and Abley, 2004).

Between the mid-1970s and the late 1980s public sector financing of the building industry fell from almost 60% to around 25% (Powell, 1996 p. 193). Speculative building grew with the rise of generic office or retail space built as an investment. 'Permanence was increasingly a liability; flexibility and adaptability, improvisation and short-life were at a premium' (Powell, 1996, p. 197) – hence a growing discourse about 'responding to change' (Duffy, 1998, p. 102), particularly in the context of office environments. Responsibility for a building owned by multinational conglomerates with multiple subsidiaries, often abroad, can often be obscure (Powell, 1996). When buildings become a fungible commodity to be traded from one disinterested hand to another, immeasurable damage is the result, particularly in developing countries where real estate development can fuel inequality and accelerate environmental damage.

At a time when the idea of the 'expert client' had not yet come to the fore, the architect was seen as the primary source of advice (Green, 2011, p. 10). This was a situation that was to radically change as efficiency and monetary rewad became the dominant issues, as exemplified by the Egan Report of 1998. In Green's opinion 'the shift to the political right was in part precipitated by the onset of globalisation', a cocktail of market forces caused by technical advances in communication which put the UK construction industry in direct competition with overseas industry. The corollary of all this was that some clients became much more demanding. Stuart Lipton of Stanhope, the client for the Broadgate development next to Liverpool Street Station in London, is one example, evidenced by his ability to get the project built in record time (Green, 2011).

New emphasis on satisfying clients meant a growth in diversity in the way in which buildings were procured. A greater need for flexibility resulted in the development of 'hollowed-out' construction firms with few, if any, directly employed 'operatives' (note the production line language). Older companies that had traditionally invested more in their workforce had to cut back to keep up with the cost-cutting drive. One of the characteristics of the construction industry is its project-based culture, often involving the employment of subcontractors to execute specialist tasks. With the advent of the new millennium, the use of *nominated* subcontractors, firms known and respected by the project team, was discouraged in favour of subcontractors, usually chosen for being cheap. The result was an erosion of trust and learning, with groups coming together for short periods and disbanding thereafter.

The delivery of projects then became the responsibility of teams of subcontractors (specialist leaders of work packages such as cladding or electrics) contracted by a management team (Green, 2011) – in large schemes there might be as many as five layers of subcontracting, meaning that money was to be made in pressing claims for responsibility for defects. Such lengthy supply chains meant that the responsibility for staff training has been devolved (Dainty et al., 2007), as has the responsibility for research and development and indeed the human rights of workers (CIOB, 2015). While the professions have been fighting turf wars over leadership, others have been ignored (Tutt et al., 2012).

What is the architect's ethical responsibility to the supply chain (Welsh Gov, 2017)? In the UK the industry itself is bound by law to put into effect the provisions of the Construction, Design and Management Act 2015 and to comply with the health and safety regulations that condition the operation of construction sites and the construction of buildings. Failure to comply is a criminal offence. Nevertheless, remarkably little attention has been paid to the terrible conditions of workers on building sites both overseas and in the UK and the dangers of working on site, many avoidable by design (Sacks et al., 2015). Home Office figures suggest that as many as 13000 people in the UK are in 'modern slavery', many of these on building sites (CIOB, 2015, p. 6). Forms of slavery include 'Bonded labour, delayed wages, abysmal working and living conditions, withholding of passports and limitations of movement' (CIOB, 2015, p. 4). Overseas, many construction workers are migrants who are not in a position to complain of their ill treatment (CIOB, 2015). The construction industry has an ethical duty to work together to improve performance on key issues such as site safety (Sacks et al., 2015). Until the professions marshal their forces into unified action, such atrocities will continue and a construction industry that can fulfil the innovation potential of the twenty-first century will remain a chimera.

Groak describes building practices which have been tried and tested over the years and are well understood by craftworkers, builders and architects as 'robust technologies' (a load-bearing brick wall might be an example), the opposite being 'sensitive technologies' (an example might be an 'intelligent' façade), which require precision in 'design, manufacture, assembly or use'. Unfortunately 'many of our robust technologies are becoming fragile' (Groak, 1992, p. 46). They have been pushed and pared down to the point that they are barely fit for purpose, the recent and spectacular failure of brick walls in a series of schools in Scotland being a case in point (Cole, 2017). Groak speculates that these technologies have become fragile because of the 'failure of traditional feedback mechanisms to keep these technologies within their robust limits' (Groak, 1992, p. 46). At the same time there is a major skills gap for the delivery of sensitive technologies. The result is that, whether intended or not, more and more projects are experimental.

Within the field of housing, the demise of innovative public sector clients and the vilifying of their outputs led to conservatism within the housing industry, reflected in its neo-vernacular outputs laid out according to the local authority design guidelines of cul-de-sacs and enclosed courts so popular in the 1970s (Powell, 1996). The recession of the 1990s consolidated this trend. 'The paradox of demand for old-looking exteriors with modern internal performance and comfort was sharpened by comparing the design of the house with that of another big consumer good, the car standing on the drive' (Powell, 1996, p. 208). Green places the blame for 'the homogeneous monotony of Britain's high streets' directly at the feet of enterprise culture (Green, 2011, p. 51). Our current housing crisis, lack of housing choice and indeed the Grenfell Tower tragedy (Braidwood, 2017) must be seen as symptoms of a collective failing of the construction industry to work collaboratively for the greater good.

2.3 The struggle for leadership in the built environment

The reluctance of architects to engage with new codes and standards during the Victorian era provided an opportunity to other types of professionals such as surveyors. Having been left out of the RIBA at its very beginnings (Mace, 1986), surveyors formed their own institution while positioning themselves as a vital element in the tendering team, sometimes being appointed before the architect. Civil engineers became an integral part of building design as they were needed to specify the frames and foundations necessary for complex, ever larger buildings. Another key profession, service engineers, evolved out of the plumbing and electrical trades. Whenever architects were asked to make calculations, develop processes or manage people or money, they were happy to step aside to let others do it in their place (Saxon, 2006). In this way 'The easy and finite, and their attendant fees, have been gifted to others, and the difficult, subjective and low-paid retained' (Pringle and Porter, 2015, p. 147).

> It is all rather dispiriting. Weak on specialist skills, many architects have turned themselves into irrelevant visionaries. For that they are ridiculed by other members of the project team, even though such people are themselves unable to make a good building without a clear architectural vision for it.
>
> (Woudhuysen and Abley, 2004, p. 7)

Roles and responsibilities in the construction team are constantly changing and very unclear. To combat this and to facilitate a discussion of responsibilities within construction contracts Hughes et al. posit 'five generic groups' within the building procurement process: 'builders, designers, regulators, purchasers and users'. Note that 'designers' are not necessarily 'architects'. The way that they come together is different for each project. Within this model 'it is useful to think of design as a once whole discipline that has been successfully eroded by more specific disciplines' (Hughes et al., 2015, p. 1).

Procurement is key to all this. Standard forms of contract came into being in the early twentieth century to avoid disagreement between different parties on the construction team (Powell, 1996) and have been constantly revised ever since under the auspices of organizations such as the Joint Contracts Tribunal (JCT) in the UK. With a traditional, standard or tripartite contract the architect prepares the design and specification in consultation with the client in enough detail that it can be priced with some precision by a building contractor. The architect then has a 'quasi-judicial role' arbitrating between the client and the contractor on delays, variations, additional sums and reparations. Until the 1940s RIBA contracts included a clause stating that 'the architect's decision was final' on matters such as work not in accordance with the contract (Turner, 1948, p. 9). A problem was, however, that architects had a reputation for being high-handed and intransigent on building sites with ancient class divides being enshrined into working practices.

> It is quite mistaken that the attitude of the architect is unimportant so far as the workmen are concerned. They are very quick to size up a man, both as regards his ability and his deportment. It goes without saying that a gentleman will treat everyone with courtesy and without 'swank'; but if an architect comes on to a job and assumes an air of importance and at the same time cannot hide his ignorance, he is not likely to gain the respect of the workmen. Some of you may think it does not matter; but, after all, it is the workmen who convert your designs into actual building, and they will certainly turn out better work if they have friendly feelings towards the architect.
> (Turner, 1948, p. 163)

It is perhaps worth mentioning that working-class bound masculinity remains an issue on construction sites to this day (Thiel, 2013).

Construction researchers Dainty, Moore and Murray write in aggrieved tones about guidance given in the *Architect's Handbook of Practice Management*, which advised architects not to discuss technical matters directly with subcontractors (Cox and Hamilton, 1998). Their complaint is that this 'rule book' has resulted 'in a legacy of disputes that continues to thwart improved interaction'; if only architects were prepared to work out issues at an informal and interpersonal level, then much effort would be saved (Dainty et al., 2006, p. 36). The idea that the architect designs everything so prevalent in the profession's discourse, leaves little room for the craftsperson's creativity or initiative (Saxon, 2006) and denies the collaborative nature of the building process.

The majority of architectural energy is spent of front-end services, not on building (RIBA, 2014). They rarely have control over the whole process but are bought in at strategic moments to deliver particular services such as 'pretty drawings' to get through planning. This has led to a further bifurcation of the profession into 'design' practices and 'delivery' or 'executive' practices (Winch, 2008), the latter being excellent at delivering quality work on time and on budget, sometimes for another practice. Just because a practice is good at design does not mean it is poor at management or vice versa. However, it could be argued that the 'most valuable type' are equally good at both (Hughes et al., 2015, p. 23).

Design creates competitive advantage, but it has been 'sold too cheap' (Flanagan, 2017). The key role of architects as translators between the client and the contractor has been largely lost with construction project managers now promoting themselves as 'an enabler of communication' (Dainty et al., 2006, p. 228) and the profession abdicating responsibility in the sphere of money, its incompetence in this area being a widely held belief. As clients became more demanding during the 1980s, the uptake of 'design and build' contracts became more widespread. Indeed by 2012, 50% of private contracts and 40% of public contracts were procured this way (RIBA, 2014). Here the architect is novated by the employer to the contractor – with the agreement of the contractor and the architect. The contractor then holds overall responsibility for the quality of the outputs, which theoretically makes things more straightforward for the client and also results in lower fees for the architect. If the architect has had no say in who the contractor might be or vice versa, continuity of trust and learning across construction teams is jeopardized.

Increasingly architects are having to vie with a range of other professionals for the role of 'independent client adviser', particularly when government money is being used (Designing Buildings Wiki, 2017). It's important to note that this is a separate function from being the architect, and combining the two would normally be a conflict of interest. In practice few architects are equipped for this role, although a larger number are suited to the (also independent) role of design adviser. Often architects are not with the client at the start of the process when the major strategic and financial decisions are being made. When the architect is on the side of the contractor, it may be necessary for the client to employ an agent to look after his or her interests, often in the form of a quantity surveyor or project manager. If the contractor is solely concerned with making money, rather than with the quality of the build, the results can be poor, as the architect has no power to influence the final outcome (Wigglesworth, 2012). The resultant

> design errors are a symptom of dysfunctional organisational and managerial practices that prevail within the construction industry. They significantly contribute to cost and schedule growth, and rework. Furthermore, they jeopardise safety and are major contributors to accidents that occur during and post construction.
>
> (Love et al., 2011, p. 685)

They also contribute to the huge amount of waste that the industry generates (Osmani et al., 2008). We are now in a very odd situation when large contractors such as McAlpine have a team of 'design managers', some of them architects, whose business is to reduce cost while preventing design errors, some created by architects.

> The real risk lies in the change of the design team which can happen two or three times during the life of a project as a result of re-tendering. Changing architects mid-project instantly transforms its development into a haphazard relay race where the baton of design responsibility is hastily handed from

> one architect to another. This is dangerous for clients because the new team will have little or no understanding of a project's design development history, and will need to rely solely on the client to ascertain why a project is like it is. Each baton change means knowledge and ownership for the concept diminishes as it moves through different hands, increasing project risk which is never adequately recognised by clients in tender appraisals.
>
> (Middleton, 2016)

A high-profile example of the costs caused by design errors is Fitzroy Place in London, a project that resulted in £89 million of losses for the contractor McAlpine, attributed in part to 'risk management during tendering and the management of our design responsibilities and changes' (Withers and Gardiner, 2015). Design errors may be a corollary of the architect's loss of status within the procurement process, which leaves the rest of the industry scrambling to compensate for what is widely seen as the architect's incompetence and leads to an increasing intolerance of architects' outdated claim to professional exceptionalism in design leadership. While some argue that the architect should have overall responsibility for managing a project in order to bring out its vision, others argue that an outside viewpoint is needed to weigh up the different 'constraints' in a more impartial way (Hughes et al., 2015, p. 23). Changing designer mid stream is likely to be detrimental to design quality, unless the different teams have achieved a degree of symbiotic continuity.

There is a confusion about names, particularly when it comes to design (Hughes et al., 2015). For example, design in the context of design and build is the terrain of the 'design manager', not necessarily of an architect. Hughes makes the extremely important point, which I suspect many would endorse, that whether the architect should be seen as the leader of the construction team depends very much on whether architecture is considered to be an art or a science.

> Architecture as art cannot effectively be subjected to external management: indeed it can only occur if the architect is in complete control. Architecture as science can be subjected to external controls because output can be measured against some predetermined objective set by the architect.
>
> (Hughes et al., 2015, p. 4)

'Predetermined objectives' don't just have to be about quantitatively measured performance; they could be tangible measures of atmosphere, conviviality, peacefulness or inspiration – not, however, something that can readily be handed over to others to manage into existence – but are more a product of professional judgement developed through practice requiring input at every stage of a project. This doesn't, however, mean that architecture has to be an art – a point that I will return to repeatedly in this narrative.

The Construction Industry Council, formed in 1988, was one of a succession of initiatives to bring together the disparate parts of the profession, not an easy process (Nicholson, 2000), culminating recently in the Edge Commission report *Collaboration for Change* (Morrell, 2015). As respondents to the 2016 National

Building Specification (NBS) National Construction Contracts and Law survey recently made clear, 'established divisions between professionals prevent collaboration' (Malleson, 2016, p. 62). What is needed is a procurement framework that truly incentivizes collaboration (Woudhuysen and Abley, 2004).

Building Information Modelling (BIM) is forcing the collaborative agenda. BIM models can be embedded with formulae just like an Excel spreadsheet. As the designer adjusts the model, information about relative performance/cost/value is generated. In the past drawings had to be sent to consultants for updating or for the creation of overlay drawings such as services or structure. The management of information was fiddly and susceptible to human error. Using BIM, all this information is contained in one model and that model is on a file sharer, meaning theoretically that it is always up to date. This approach requires certain protocols to be in place to make sure that everyone is working in the same way, using the same terms and so on, and that everyone is clear about who ultimately is responsible for the curation of the model. BIM allows a building system to be tested in the virtual world, meaning that errors in the integration of different work packages – services, structure and so on – can be identified before they are built. BIM can be a force for good – less waste, less environmental damage, less conflict, greater trust and greater sharing of knowledge (Malleson, 2016). BIM presents architects with an opportunity to communicate and collect different types of value, including their own, but this needs strategic leadership and 'effective communication' (Dainty et al., 2006, p. 7). Architects are well suited to take on the overall curatorship of the BIM model and must do so if they are not to be edged out of the process. This is why it is so important that architects can say what it is that they do and why indeed it matters.

Communication is of the utmost importance. A range of organization and management studies reveals just how much care needs to be taken in personal interaction (Dainty et al., 2006) and the extent to which jargon can cause misunderstandings (Dadji, 1988) and interfere with progress at project meetings (Gorse and Emmitt, 2003). Communication even between architects can be a problem, if the Fraser Inquiry into the Scottish Parliament Building is anything to go by (Fraser, 2004). An increasing number of practices are becoming multidisciplinary to sidestep this issue. An example is Hoare Lea, a so-called 'single discipline' engineering firm, operating in 26 fields of specialization served by people with unique postgraduate qualifications and particular skills offers.

Going forward, Flanagan argues that integrated service delivery (as currently modelled by practices such as Skidmore Owings and Merrill (SOM)), will be key in the future. Digitization has an obvious impact, and not only on BIM. The implications of digitization on EBusiness (transactions via the internet), document management, auto-ID (collection of information without manual data entry) and other industry working practices are set to be profound. At the same time there will be a convergence of companies and their information, leading to new systems and products such as off-site manufacturing. 'The interface between design and production is at the heart of the challenge' (Flanagan, 2017). If – and this is a big if – the industry can learn to work with environmental constraints of our planet, companies seem set to get bigger, far outgrowing the needs of their domestic markets, and may increasingly diversify into other industries.

2.4 The international scene

Other versions of architectural professionalism have of course been developing in parallel across the globe. US architects were quick to follow the RIBA by forming the American Institute of Architects in 1857. Significantly it was formed to promote the 'scientific and practical perfection of its members' and the profession in general (www.aia.org). Nowadays every country has its own professional association but there are few with the history and clout of the RIBA.

In 2013 the total European construction market was estimated at €1664 billion. Architecture is one of the largest 'internationally traded service sectors' (Winch, 2008). There are 565000 architects in Europe, 74% of whom are in one-person practices (ACE, 2014). The number of architects in Europe is growing while their share of the construction market is shrinking, meaning that it is increasingly for them to be given the opportunity to exercise their high-level design and research skills, usually honed over five years of university training, on the design of our built environment. As a whole the UK is a net exporter of architectural services, exporting £437 million more than it imported in 2015 (GLA Economics, 2017, p. 3), and there is potential for much growth in this area. The danger is that the opposite will happen, that others will start to make inroads into the European construction market with innovations and efficiencies that eclipse ours.

Radically different professional and legislative cultures across the construction industry make it difficult for all but the largest firms to gain traction in other countries (Lorenz and Marosszeky, 2007). Huge firms such as AECOM, Perkins + Will and Gensler have interdisciplinary offices all over the globe, helping them capitalize on growing markets. Smaller practices deliver projects outside their homeland often with the help of a local executive or delivery practice, whose name may be suppressed in publicity. Even the largest architecture practices are minute in comparison with the gargantuan global construction conglomerates that have recently come into being, for example the China Communications Construction Company Ltd (Flanagan, 2017). The constant game of merger and acquisition that is being played means that ultimate responsibility for a project can become quite difficult to pin down. We are in a situation where the largest practices seem set to be bought out and absorbed within large, hybrid built environment firms, in this way easing the advent of integrated project delivery, while the smallest practices will continue with their 'boutique' or local offer. Those in the middle will be under pressure to decide in which direction to jump, with their partners increasingly tempted to sell. This will have a significant impact on the organization of the built environment institutions, which will have to diversify – the Royal Institute of Chartered Surveyors (RICS) describes itself as 'the world's leading professional body for qualifications and standards in land, property, infrastructure and construction' (RICS, 2018) has been very successful at this – or become more specialized, perhaps offering 'Easyjet' additional services at a price.

Conclusion

So it seems that the architecture profession, in its current model, is not working very well in relation to colleagues in the built environment. In a prescient but seemingly ignored Strategic Study by the RIBA dated 1995, Frank Duffy, then its President, observed:

> We believe that the future prosperity of the construction industry, in this country and abroad, will depend not only on architects becoming more closely integrated with the skills, interests and concerns of our colleagues but equally on a much more precise and realistic calculation of our own specific contribution to shared success.
>
> (Duffy, 1995, p. 3)

This is particularly important as large built environment practices are increasingly developing into 'hybridised organisations' (Imrie and Street, 2011, p. 222), meaning that they encompass a wide variety of other professional skillsets enabling them to deliver a more integrated service. Within these organizations there will always be a place for specialized research-led architects. As Duffy has observed, 'The chance of any one profession monopolizing the built environment, or even the production of the built environment, is nil' (Duffy, 2008, p. 657).

References

Abbott, A., 1988. *The System of Professions: An Essay on the Division of Expert Labor.* The University of Chicago Press, Chicago.

ACE, 2014. *The Architectural Profession in Europe.* Architects' Council of Europe, Brussels.

Braidwood, E., 2017, 'Analysis: Grenfell Tragedy Highlights Architects' Marginalisation'. *Architects' Journal.* www.architectsjournal.co.uk/news/analysis-grenfell-tragedy-highlights-architects-marginalisation/10022066.article (accessed 1.8.17).

Brindley, R., 2012. 'Why Doesn't the RIBA Provide Fee Scales?', *Building Design.* www.bdonline.co.uk/why-doesn%E2%80%99t-the-riba-provide-fee-scales?/5041284.article

Carr-Saunders, A.M., Wilson, P.A., 1933. *The Professions.* Oxford University Press, Oxford.

CIOB, 2016. *Social Mobilty and Construction: Building Routes to Opportunity.* Chartered Institute of Building, London.

CIOB, 2015. *Modern Slavery: The Dark Side of Construction.* The Chartered Institute of Building, London.

CIOB, 2014. *The Real Face of Construction: A Socio-economic Analysis of the True Value of the Built Environment.* CIOB, London.

Cole, J., 2017. *Report of the Independent Inquiry into the Construction of Edinburgh Schools.* Edinburgh Council, Edinburgh.

Cox, S., Hamilton, A., 1998. *Architect's Handbook of Practice Management*, 6th edition. RIBA Publications, London.

Dadji, M., 1988. 'Are You Talking to M & E?'. *RIBA Journal Switch Supplement*, pp. 102–103.

Dainty, A., Green, S.D., Bagilhole, B. (eds), 2007. *People and Culture in Construction*. Spon Research, London.

Dainty, A., Moore, D., Murray, M., 2006. *Communication in Construction: Theory and Practice*. Taylor & Francis, Oxford.

Darling, E., Whitworth, L., 2007. *Women and the Making of Built Space in England, 1870–1950*. Ashgate Publishing, Farnham.

Davis, H., 2006. *The Culture of Building*. Oxford University Press, Oxford.

Dawber, G., 1904. 'Editorial'. *The Builder*, 87, p. 360.

Designing Buildings Wiki, 2017, 'Independent Client Adviser for Building Design and Construction'. www.designingbuildings.co.uk/wiki/Independent_client_adviser_for_building_design_and_construction (accessed 3. 1.17).

Dobson, A., 2013. *RIBA Fee Calculation, Negotiation and Management for Architects*. RIBA, London.

Dodds, M., 2015. 'Double Agency, The Art School, Critical Practice and Architecture', in: Harriss, H., Froud, D. (eds), *Radical Pedagogies*. RIBA Publishing, Newcastle-upon-Tyne, p. 22.

Duffy, F., 2008. 'Forum Linking Theory Back to Practice'. *Building Research and Information*, 36, 6, pp. 655–658.

Duffy, F., 1998. *Architectural Knowledge: The Idea of a Profession*. Spon, London.

Duffy, F., 1995. *Strategic Study of the Profession, Phases 3 & 4: The Way Forward*. RIBA, London.

Egan, J., 1998. *Rethinking Construction: The Report of the Construction Task Force to the Deputy Prime MinisterJohn Prescott on the Scope for Improving the Quality and Efficiencies of UK Construction*. DETR, London.

Emmerson, H.C., 1962. *Survey of Problems before the Construction Industries*. HMSO, London.

Eraut, M., 1994. *Developing Professional Knowledge and Competence*. Routledge, London; Washington, D.C.

Farrell, T., 2014. *The Farrell Review of Architecture and the Built Environment*. http://farrellreview.co.uk/downloads/The%20Farrell%20Review.pdf?t=1396343104

Flanagan, R., 2017. 'Global Construction Practice'. Presented at the Professional Practices in the Built Environment Conference, School of Architecture, University of Reading.

Fraser, P. 2004. 'The Holyrood Inquiry'. www.scottish.parliament.uk/SPICe Resources/HolyroodInquiry.pdf

Froud, D., 2015. 'You Will See Pictures of What is Bad and What is Good', in: Harriss, H., Froud, D. (eds), *Radical Pedagogies*. RIBA Enterprises, Newcastle-upon-Tyne, pp. 46–54.

GLA Economics, 2017. 'London's Architectural Sector' (Working paper 86). www.london.gov.uk/business-and-economy-publications/londons-architectural-sector

Gorse, C.A., Emmitt, S., 2003. 'Investigating Interpersonal Communication during Construction Progress Meetings: Challenges and Opportunities'. *Engineering Construction and Architectural Management*, 10, 4, pp. 234–244.

Gotch, J.A. (ed.), 1934. *The Growth and Work of the Royal Institute of British Architects*. Simson and Co., London.

Grant Erskine Architects, 2017. 'Architect's Fees'. www.designingbuildings.co.uk/wiki/Architect%27s_fees

Green, S.D., 2011. *Making Sense of Construction Improvement: A Critical Review*. Wiley Blackwell, Chichester and Ames, IA.

Groak, S., 1992. *The Idea of Building: Thought and Action in the Design and Production of Buildings*. Taylor & Francis, Oxford.

Hall, P., 2013. *Good Cities, Better Lives: How Europe Discovered the Lost Art of Urbanism*. Routledge, London.

Harper, R., 1977. 'The Conflict between English Building Regulations and Architectural Design 1890–1918'. *Journal of Architectural Research*, 6, pp. 24–25.

Higgin, G., 1964. 'The Architect as Professional'. *RIBA Journal*, 71, 1, pp. 139–145.

Hill, J., 2003. *Actions of Architecture: Architects and Creative Users*. Routledge, London.

Hughes, W., Champion, R., Murdoch, J., 2015. *Construction Contracts*. Routledge, London; New York.

Imrie, R., Street, E., 2011. *Architectural Design and Regulation*. Wiley Blackwell, Oxford.

Kaye, B., 1960. *The Development of the Architectural Profession in Britain: A Sociological Study*. Allen and Unwin, London.

Kubany, E.H., Linn, C., 1999. 'Why Architects Don't Charge Enough'. *Architectural Record*, 187, pp. 110–115.

Lansley, P.R., 1997. 'The Impact of BRE's Commercialisation on the Research Community'. *Building Research and Information*, 25, 5, pp. 301–312.

Latham, M., 1994. *Constructing the Team*. HMSO, London.

Lorenz, K., Marosszeky, M., 2007. 'Managing Cultural Difference in the Global Construction Industry: German and Austrian Engineers Working in Australia', in: Dainty, A. (ed.), *People and Culture in Construction*. Spon Research, London, pp. 184–203.

Love, P.E.D., Lopez, R., Edwards, D.J., 2011. 'Reviewing the Past to Learn in the Future: Making Sense of Design Errors and Failures in Construction'. *Structure and Infrastructure Engineering*, 9, 7, pp. 675–688.

Mace, A., 1986. *The Royal Institute of British Architects: A Guide to its Archive and History*. Mansell Publishing, London.

MacInnes, K., 1994. 'Here's One I Designed Earlier: How Architects Can Capitalise on the Growing Self Build Market'. *Architectural Design*, 64, pp. xvi–xvii.

Malleson, A., 2016. 'Now for the Fine Print …', *RIBA Journal*, 123, pp. 61–62.

Middleton, M., 2016. 'False Distinction between Design and Delivery Architects is Killing the Profession,' *Building Design*. www.bdonline.co.uk/comment/false-distinction-between-design-and-delivery-architects-is-killing-the-profession/5082085.article

Morphet, J., Clifford, B., 2017. *Local Authority Direct Provision of Housing*, RTPI London. http://b.3cdn.net/nefoundation/8b32051850bcf41dee_7bm62zt1o.pdf

Morrell, P., 2015. *Collaboration for Change*. Edge, London.

Nicholson, R., 2000. 'Foreword', in: Nicol, D., Pilling, S. (eds), *Changing Architectural Education*. Spon Press, Oxford, p. xvi.

Norman Shaw, R., Jackson, T.G., 1892. *Architecture: A Profession or an Art: Thirteen Short Essays on the Qualifications and Training of Architects*. John Murray, London.

Osmani, M., Glass, J., Price, A.D.F., 2008. 'Architects' Perspectives on Construction Waste Reduction by Design'. *Waste Management*, 28, 7, pp. 1147–1158. doi:10.1016/j.wasman.2007.05.011

Powell, C., 1996. *The British Building Industry since 1800*. Routledge, Oxford.

Pringle, J., Porter, H., 2015. 'Education to Reboot a Failed Profession', in: Harriss, H., Froud, D. (eds), *Radical Pedagogies*. RIBA Publishing, Newcastle-upon-Tyne, p. 146.

Ratti, C., Claudel, M. (eds), 2015. *Open Source Architecture*. Thames and Hudson, London.

RIBA, 2014. *RIBA Business Benchmarking Report 2013/14*. RIBA, London.

RIBA, 2009a. *Charter and Byelaws*. www.architecture.com/about/history-charter-and-byelaws

RIBA, 2009b. *Practice Bulletin*. RIBA, London.

RIBA, 1972. 'Establishing the fee scale'. *RIBA Journal*, 79, 1, p. 1.

RIBA, 1971. *RIBA Conditions of Engagement Mandatory Fee Scale*. RIBA, London.

RIBA, 1939. Editorial, *RIBA Journal*, XLVI, p. 898.

RIBA, 1834, 'Prospectus'. British Architectural Library, Shelfmark MS. X (06) (09).

RICS, 2018. Homepage. www.rics.org/uk

Sacks, R., Whyte, J., Swissa, D., Raviv, G., Zhou, W., Shapira, A., 2015. 'Safety by Design: Dialogues between Designers and Builders Using Virtual Reality'. *Construction Management and Economics*, 31, 1 pp. 55–72. doi:10.1080/01446193.2015.1029504

Saint, A., 1983. *The Image of the Architect*. Yale University Press, New Haven, CT.

Sarfatti Larson, M., 1993 [1977]. *The Rise of Professionalism: A Sociological Analysis*. University of California Press, Berkeley.

Saxon, R., 2006. 'The Future of the Architectural Profession: A Question of Values'. www.saxoncbe.com/profession-values.pdf

SPADA, 2009. 'British Professions Today: The State of the Sector'. www.ukipg.org.uk/executive_group_resources/spada-british-professions-today.pdf

Tavistock Institute, 1966. *Interdependence and Uncertainty (Digest of a Report from the Tavistock Institute to the Building Industry Communication Research Project)*. Tavistock Institution, London.

Thiel, D., 2013. 'Builders, Bodies and Bifurcations: How London Construction Workers "Learn to Labour"'. *Ethnography*, 14, 4, pp. 412–430. doi:10.1177/1466138112463656

Till, J., 2009. *Architecture Depends*. MIT Press, Cambridge, MA.

Turner, H.H., 1948. *Architectural Practice and Procedure*. Batsford, London.

Tutt, D., Pink, S., Dainty, A., Gibb, A., 2012. '"In the Air" and below the Horizon: Migrant Workers in UK Construction and the Practice-based Nature of Learning and Communicating OHS'. *Construction Management and Economics*, 31, 6, pp. 515–527.

UK Gov, 2001. *Competitions in Professions*. Office of Fair Trading.

Walker, L., 1997. *Drawing on Diversity: Women, Architecture and Practice*. RIBA Heinz Gallery, London.

Welsh Gov, 2017. 'Code of Practice: Ethical Employment in Supply Chains'. www.wales.gove.uk/code-of-practice

Wigglesworth, S., 2012. 'WLTM Caring Contractor: The Dating Game of Design and Build Contracts'. *ARQ Architectural Research Quarterly*, 16, 3, pp. 210–216.

Wilton-Ely, J., 1977. 'The Rise of the Professional Architect in England', in: Kostof, S. (ed.), *The Architect*. University of California Press, Berkeley, pp. 180–208.

Winch, G., 2008. 'Internationalisation Strategies in Business-to-business Services: The Case of Architectural Practice'. *Service Industries Journal*, 28, 1, pp. 1–13.

Withers, I., Gardiner, J., 2015. 'Sir Robert McAlpine Singles out Fitzroy Place after £89m Loss'. *Building*. www.building.co.uk/sir-robert-mcalpine-singles-out-fitzroy-place-after-%C2%A389m-loss/5075527.article

Woudhuysen, J., Abley, I., 2004. *Why Is Construction So Backward?* Wiley Academy, Chichester.

Chapter 3

Cracks in the professional foundations

The right body of knowledge

> *It still stings: you are a respected architect, you've recently spent a great deal of effort attempting to convince your valued client about something, and you believed you were right. Everything you have learned over your years of education and practice tells you that you were right. Why, then, does your client take the word of the less educated and less experienced program manager over yours? Why does your client, who has worked with you before, not seem to trust your professional opinions? For that matter, why has the client chosen to work with a program manager when he seems to do nothing that you are not qualified to do?*
>
> *(Kirk Hamilton and Watkins, 2009, p. 1)*

The focus of this chapter is what architects consider to be their knowledge base. Despite 'the construction of a pantheonic edifice of instruction, moral code, do's and don'ts' through which 'architecture as an academy is established' (Jacobs, 2015, p. 174), the knowledge base of architects remains remarkably unclear. 'Architecture was professionalized around the wrong body of knowledge' (van Schaik, 2008, p. 183), meaning that control of a body of knowledge, the defining characteristic of a profession, was never secured (Abbott, 1988). The profession has largely focused on nuances of aesthetics and form when it should, arguably, have been refining methodologies for investigating and improving the relationship between people and the built environment over time (Lansley, 2001; Schilling et al., 2012). The profession's confusion about whether it is an art or a science, or whether this is in fact an artificial divide (Latour, 1998) impacts upon the profession's production of knowledge and therefore its ability to innovate.

3.1 The canon: architectural history

The architect Cedric Price presciently observed back in 1964 that it was unlikely that the architectural profession would have any real impact on society 'until a total reappraisal of its particular expertise is self-imposed, or inflicted from outside' (Price, 1966, p. 483). It seems that time has come.

The intellectual basis of the profession is set out in its canon, extending back to Vitruvius's endlessly debated *De Architectura* (c. 30 BC) and even beyond. The canon forms the knowledge repository of our field, regularly aired in Architecture 101 modules across the globe and written into the criteria for validation for Royal Institute of British Architects (RIBA) architecture schools. It has a long record of being used to suggest that architects have access to unique and historical knowledge that goes back through the master builders and into the arcane practices of ancient Greece and even Egypt. Architectural fascination with geometry and its relationships with structure still flourishes in the profession, sometimes with hidden, or less hidden, quasi-mystical associations with nature, relying on faith for validation.

Until recently the canon was built on the work of very few very powerful historians, who wrote the story of architecture to suit their own agendas, a good example being Nikolaus Pevsner, who quietly excluded the emotional and the irrational from his account of the development of modernism, while at the same ruling it out as a concern of the profession more widely (Samuel and Linder-Gaillard, 2014). While few historians will ever enjoy the glory experienced by Pevsner – he achieved 'man of the year' status in the *Architectural Review* in the 1970s – the way in which historians and commentators have articulated what is important in narratives of the profession has inevitably impacted on its vision of itself and on the kind of knowledge it has to offer. Pevsner promoted a belief that there was one right and true way of doing things, a view which favoured the 'functional' in terms largely of process, technology and ergonomics, as well as those in power.

The downfall of the modernist project that came with the advent of postmodernism in the 1960s supposedly changed everything, but the recognition that each person has a unique viewpoint, and that each one is as valid as the next, has taken a long time to trickle into architecture. Architectural historians have been remarkably impervious to the tide of critical and feminist, political and postcolonial revisionist history that has engulfed the rest of the humanities. They have, however, been quick to edit spirituality and beauty out of their ruminations, except in all but the most anodyne terms. Architectural history as expressed through hegemonic discourse is very often presented as the truth when it is clearly only opinion (Samuel, 1998). The architectural canon is really an inward-looking account of breakthrough moments in design – what Sunand Prasad calls the 'relationship of the work to architectural culture' (interview in Odgers and Samuel, 2010, p. 50) – and is therefore of little use to those outside the field. Reframed, it could, however, be a remarkable resource for those interested in the balance between 'creativity, risk, and regulation' (Imrie and Street, 2011, p. 21).

A particular problem for architects is that 'traditional canons of thought and conduct which once underpinned High Culture have been officially demoted and relegated to marginal "options"' (Nowotny et al., 2001, p. 28). Adolf Loos' *Ornament and Crime* (Loos, 1998), an essential piece of the modernist canon, is deeply offensive on racial and gender grounds, though this is rarely mentioned. In order to present it as a totalizing universal truth it has been necessary to bracket out anything involving gender, ethnicity, sexuality or disability, as these necessarily entail multiple different experiences of the world (Baydar, 2004; Boys, 2014).

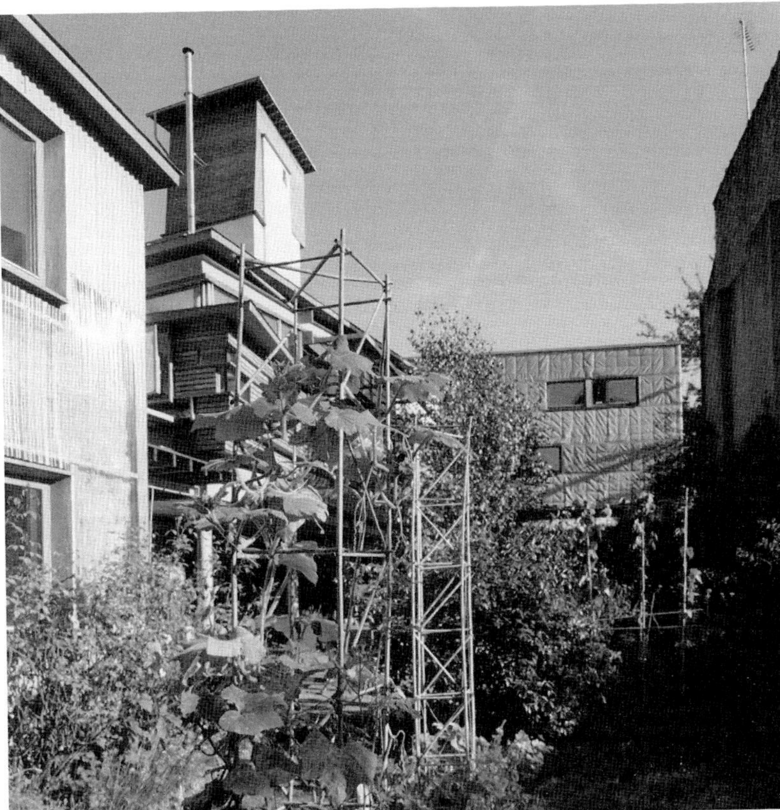

Figure 3.1 **Garden elevation, Stock Orchard St by Sarah Wigglesworth Architects. Photo © Paul Smoothy.**

This is what makes Sarah Wigglesworth's Stock Orchard Street, 'a polemical reconsideration of a few dearly held beliefs concerning the architectural canon' (Wigglesworth, 2006, p. 339), so interesting (Figure 3.1).

3.2 'Theory'

'History' and 'theory' are at the core of most architecture programmes. In my education it was a tacit understanding that 'theory' referred to the knowledge and ideas that underpin architectural design and/or ways of interpreting architectural design generally emanating from art and philosophy-based research.

Charles Jencks's well known 'Evolutionary Tree' diagram (Figure 3.2) represents an important attempt to map out across the twentieth century the huge range of experimental approaches or methodologies that architects have applied to architecture across a wide range of value systems, often derived from other fields. Lacking a strong research tradition of its own it has become overly reliant on those of others (Broadbent et al., 1970; Till, 2004), absorbed in a piecemeal way. It has also been swayed by fashion, tied up with a consumerist need for novelty.

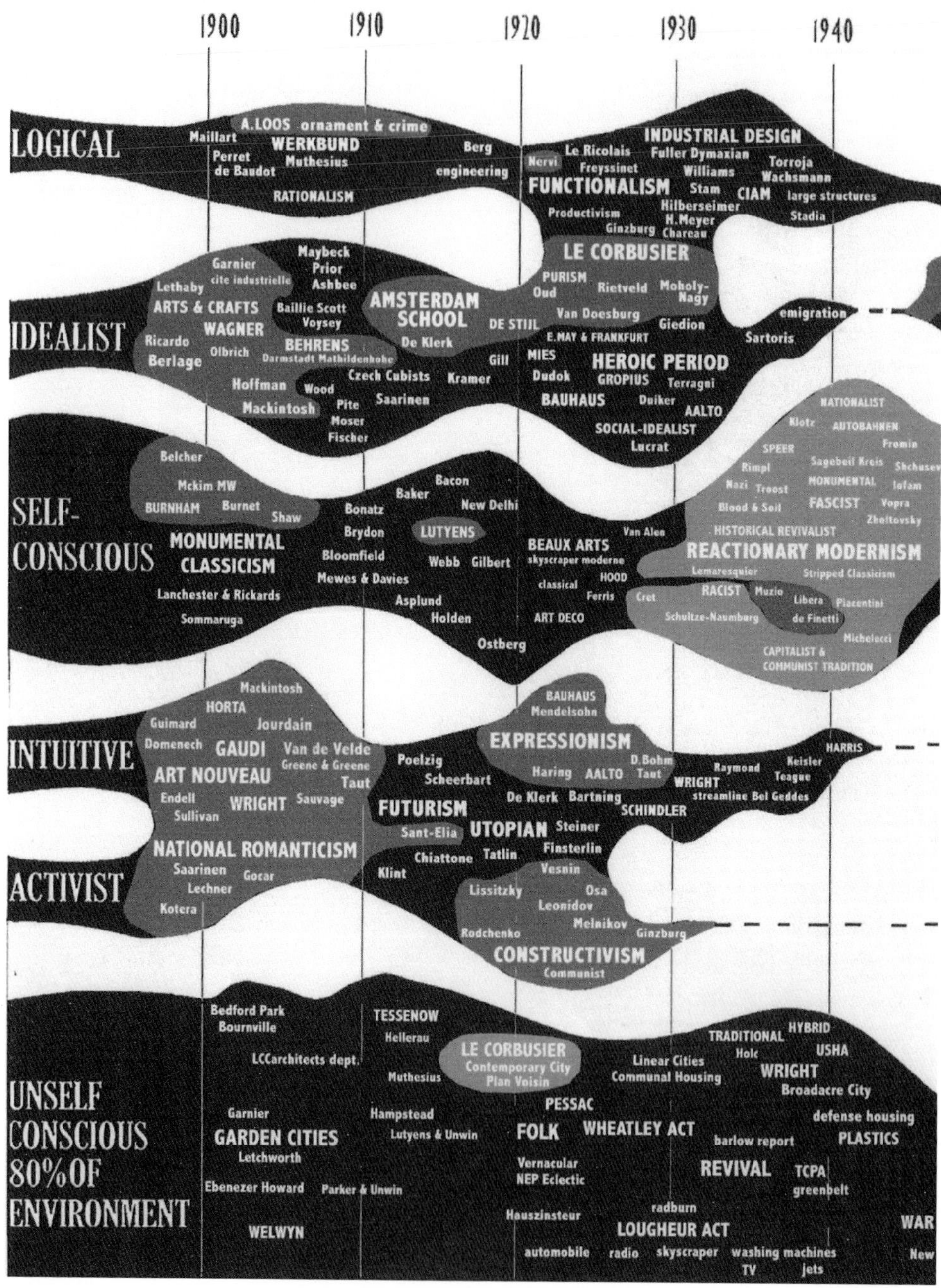

1900
1910
1920
1930
1940
LOGICAL
A.LOOS ornament & crime
Maillart
WERKBUND
Perret
de Baudot
Muthesius
Berg
engineering
RATIONALISM
INDUSTRIAL DESIGN
Le Ricolais
Fuller Dymaxian
Nervi
Freyssinet
Williams
Torroja
Wachsmann
FUNCTIONALISM
Stam
CIAM
large structures
Productivism
Hilberseimer
Stadia
H.Meyer
Ginzburg
Chareau
IDEALIST
Garnier
cite industrielle
Maybeck
Prior
Ashbee
Lethaby
ARTS & CRAFTS
Baillie Scott
Voysey
WAGNER
Ricardo
Olbrich
BEHRENS
Darmstadt Mathildenhohe
Berlage
Hoffman
Wood
Mackintosh
Pite
Moser
Fischer
AMSTERDAM SCHOOL
De Klerk
DE STIJL
Czech Cubists
Saarinen
Gill
Kramer
LE CORBUSIER
PURISM
Oud
Rietveld
Moholy-Nagy
Van Doesburg
Giedion
E.MAY & FRANKFURT
MIES
HEROIC PERIOD
Dudok
GROPIUS
Terragni
BAUHAUS
Duiker
AALTO
SOCIAL-IDEALIST
Lucrat
emigration
Sartoris
SELF-CONSCIOUS
Belcher
Mckim MW
BURNHAM
Burnet
Shaw
MONUMENTAL CLASSICISM
Lanchester & Rickards
Sommaruga
Bacon
Baker
New Delhi
Bonatz
Brydon
LUTYENS
Bloomfield
Webb
Gilbert
Mewes & Davies
Asplund
Holden
Ostberg
BEAUX ARTS
skyscraper moderne
Van Alen
classical
HOOD
Ferris
Cret
ART DECO
NATIONALIST
Klotz
AUTOBAHNEN
SPEER
Fromin
Rimpl
Sagebeil Kreis
Shchusev
Nazi
Troost
MONUMENTAL
Iofan
Blood & Soil
FASCIST
Vopra
Zholtovsky
HISTORICAL REVIVALIST
REACTIONARY MODERNISM
Lemaresquier
Stripped Classicism
RACIST
Muzio
Libera
Piacentini
Schultze-Naumburg
de Finetti
Michelucci
CAPITALIST & COMMUNIST TRADITION
INTUITIVE
Mackintosh
HORTA
Guimard
Jourdain
Domenech
GAUDI
Van de Velde
Greene & Greene
ART NOUVEAU
Taut
Endell
WRIGHT
Sauvage
Sullivan
NATIONAL ROMANTICISM
Saarinen
Lechner
Gocar
Kotera
ACTIVIST
Poelzig
Scheerbart
FUTURISM
Sant-Elia
Chiattone
Klint
BAUHAUS
Mendelsohn
EXPRESSIONISM
Haring
AALTO
D.Bohm
Taut
De Klerk
Bartning
UTOPIAN
Steiner
Tatlin
Finsterlin
Vesnin
Lissitzky
Osa
Leonidov
Melnikov
Rodchenko
Ginzburg
CONSTRUCTIVISM
Communist
Raymond
Keisler
Teague
HARRIS
WRIGHT
streamline Bel Geddes
SCHINDLER
UNSELF CONSCIOUS 80%OF ENVIRONMENT
Bedford Park
Bournville
LCCarchitects dept.
Garnier
GARDEN CITIES
Letchworth
Ebenezer Howard
Parker & Unwin
WELWYN
TESSENOW
Hellerau
Muthesius
Hampstead
Lutyens & Unwin
LE CORBUSIER
Contemporary City
Plan Voisin
PESSAC
FOLK
WHEATLEY ACT
Vernacular
NEP Eclectic
Hauszinsteur
Linear Cities
Communal Housing
TRADITIONAL
HYBRID
USHA
WRIGHT
Broadacre City
defense housing
barlow report
PLASTICS
REVIVAL
TCPA
greenbelt
radburn
LOUGHEUR ACT
automobile
radio
skyscraper
washing machines
TV
jets
WAR
New

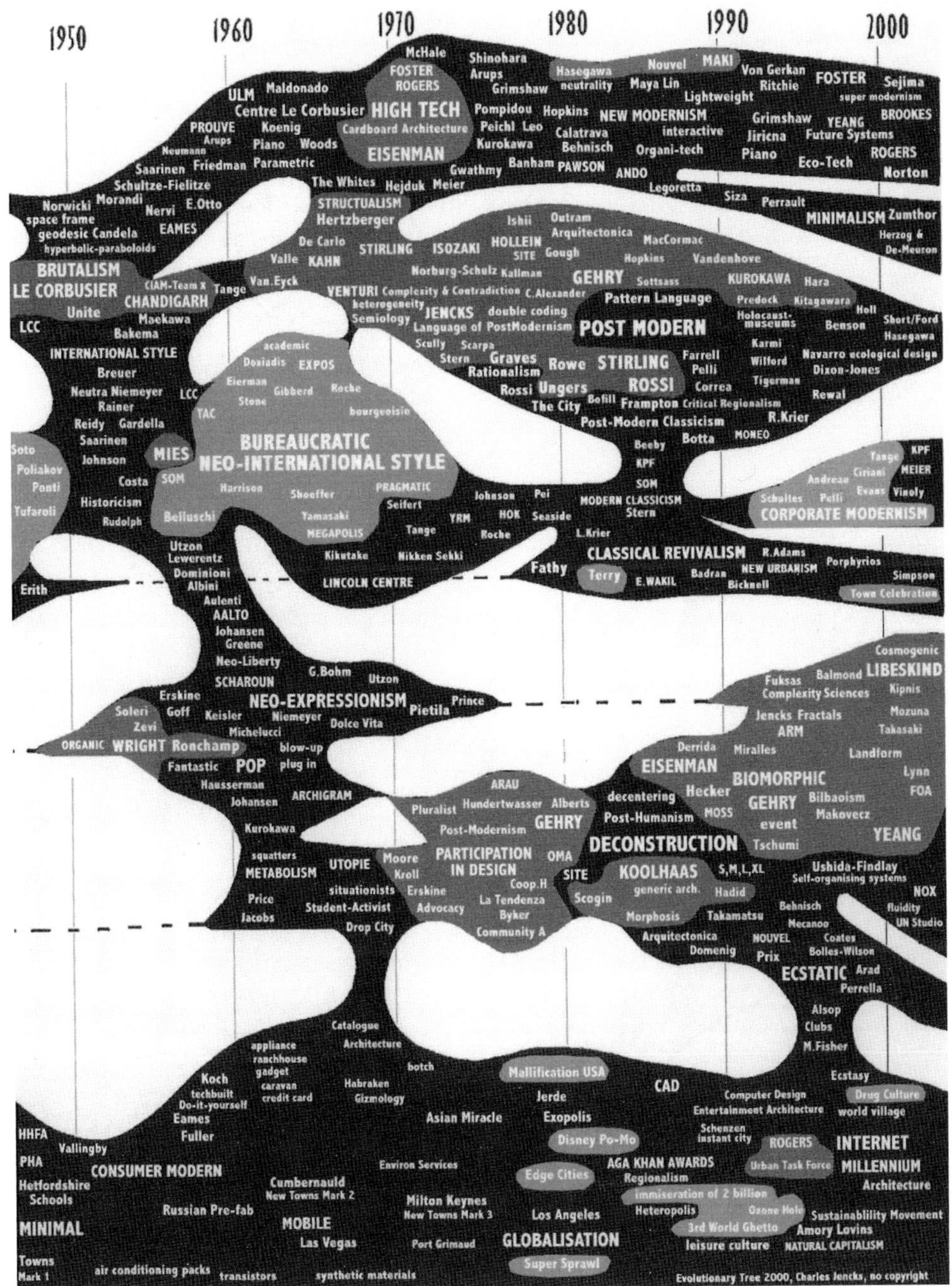

Figure 3.2

Evolutionary Tree of Modern Architecture (1970) by Charles Jencks. Reproduced with the permission of Charles Jencks.

At its best 'the struggle for theory' (Broadbent et al., 1980, p. xii) gets to the very core of what it is to be human and how this impacts on our conception of architecture. At its worst it is unintelligible (Brittain-Catlin, 2014) and full of 'encrusting jargon' (Miller, 2009, p. 3) sometimes used to 'make it critique proof' (Albrecht, 2002, p. 195). For this reason architects have come to believe that to do 'research' they have to 'stop practising and adopt arcane rituals and pseudo-objective writing styles' (van Schaik et al., 2010, p. 33). This situation has not been helped by the development of the rarefied theoretical discourse so prevalent in certain schools. See for example Roemer van Toorn's account of a Columbia University symposium in 'The State of Architecture at the Beginning of the 21st Century', a biting critique, if it is possible, of critical architecture (van Toorn, 2007, p. 1). The result is that, as Peggy Deamer notes, 'architectural history/ criticism/ theory is inherently conservative and intellectually risk-free' (Deamer, 2016) despite pretences otherwise (Miller, 2009, p. 80). The 'discourse of architecture is autonomous' as long as it focuses on the world of ideas (Larson, 1993; McNeill, 2005, p. 503). The problem for Till is exemplified through the career of Peter Eisenman:

> shifting from one linguistic critique to another in dizzying intellectual pirouettes which radically revise the forms of architecture, but leave its wider condition untouched. The fact that Eisenman concerns himself only with the formalist tendencies of his linguistic mentors (Chomsky in the seventies, Derrida in the eighties and Deleuze in the nineties) and not with their later political developments, is indicative of a wider problem of political myopia that the autonomy of architecture has led to.
>
> (Till, 1995, p. 1)

In such situations architecture disappears into the realm of the imagination without value judgement (Saint, 1983; Huxtable, 1997). Research problems are abstracted and focused using analytical barriers until they become 'soluble and interesting, rather than lifelike or relevant' (Broadbent et al., 1970, p. 3). This is why Williams ascribes the poor quality of our built environment to 'critical failure' (Williams, 2014) with a focus on the work of dead architects because they don't answer back (McNeill, 2005, p. 503). Better then to 'put theory to work' (Schweber, 2016, p. 840), to use it to make architectural research more reflective, more critical and ultimately more useful, to create what Duffy calls 'a powerful and concentrated intellectual searchlight (literally *search*light) which can be used to illuminate masses of empirically driven data which otherwise would remain obscure, entangled, scattered and meaningless' (Duffy, 2008, p. 656). The energy that goes into 'theory' needs to be reframed in the cross-disciplinary language of research methodology and brought to bear on what Habraken has named 'the ordinary built field' (Habraken, 2005, p. 28), at least in the short term, to help architects get out of their hole.

Christopher Frayling disaggregates 'Research in Art and Design' into three types: research *into* art and design – historical research, aesthetic research and so on; research *through* art and design – this could be materials research or action research; and the last, 'thorny' one, which is research *for* art – an example might be Picasso, whose process is embodied in the artefact, in other words 'the expressive tradition' (Frayling, 1993, p. 5). It is this last perhaps individualistic, tacit, spiritual and sometimes exclusionary category which has a disproportionate influence within the field of architecture, given its rarity.

'Destroying the mythology of the architect as visionary' (Hyde, 2011) is a necessary step, if only in the short term. In architecture culture a sense of the sacred tends to exist in a tacit form, cleansed of religious association in touchy-feely discussions of the body, memory, absence, geometry, atmosphere, tectonics and so on. The exclusion of religion from architectural discourse is political, based on assumptions of class, taste and background culminating in an ingrained inability to connect with theology or interfaith action – issues which of course underpin many of the conflicts in our world. Until the spiritual dimension of architecture is pulled out from under the carpet to receive a proper and just airing, I argue that emphasis should be given to more normative forms of research and knowledge generation that make up the bread and butter of what architects do. We really do need to know how to make architecture appropriate to its environment.

3.3 Evidence-based knowledge

In the early 1950s the sensual, spiritual, symbolic and seemingly irrational curves of Le Corbusier's chapel at Ronchamp caused a temporary wobble in the profession's sense of direction best exemplified by James Stirling's famous essay on the 'crisis' of rationalism in architecture (Stirling, 1956). Faced with such uncertainty, architects made a growing call for 'a scientific attitude towards design as a basis for a rich developing aesthetic', which could address fully the needs of people (Cox, 1949, p. 17).

> The closer the architect's contact with those for whom he designs the more he will come up against conflicting opinions, and the greater will be the demand upon his judgment to detect those which are valid. For sooner or later the architect himself must take sides if his buildings are to make a clear statement and not merely reflect a jumble of incompatible demands.
>
> (Cox, 1949, p. 18)

Evidence-based design emerged in the second half of the twentieth century as 'a process for the conscious, explicit, and judicious use of current best evidence from research and practice in making critical decisions, together with an informed client, about the design of each individual and unique project' (Kirk Hamilton and Watkins, 2009, p. 9). I use it here as an umbrella term for two particularly significant seams of empirical research-based activity, one in the UK and one in the USA.

Important protagonists of evidence-based and systems thinking (the clustering of data to inform decision-making) were Leslie Martin and Lionel March at Cambridge University and Richard Llewelyn Davies at University College

London, instigators of the 1958 Oxford Conference on Education, an attempt to place architecture within the academy of science-based research. Martin's principles were absorbed into a wide range of initiatives still thriving, for example the National Building Specification which defines and sets standards for construction. According to Adam Sharr this work also led to the inclusion of some aspects of post-occupancy evaluation within the first edition of the *RIBA Plan of Work* (RIBA, 1967). The idea of a feedback loop of evaluation and refinement is at the foundation of the UK's use of the Swedish CI/SfB system (AJ, 1972). Sharr ascribes such books as Adler's *AJ Metric Handbook of Planning and Design Data* (Adler, 1968) and *The Architect's Pocket Book* (Baden-Powell, 1997) to Martin's influence (Sharr, 2010). Such design guides were seen as 'generative rules' ripe with programming potential by early computing researchers (Sprunt, 1975, p. 15). At the same time systems thinkers worked steadily on the development of architectural computing and computer-aided design throughout the 1970s and 1980s (Samuel, 2014), laying the platform for parametric design through which data is seemingly translated into form by three-dimensional modelling software, Foreign Office Architects' Yokohama International Port Terminal (2002) being but one early example.

Even though their work was 'socially motivated and generous-spirited', Martin and Llewelyn Davis received considerable criticism from some influential figures (Sharr and Thornton, 2013, p. 198).

> A swathe of younger practitioners, among whom the Archigram group are now most famous, found it rigid and stifling. Phenomenologists criticized its inability to deal in sensory and emotional experiences, and its subjugation of the architect's individual creative judgement behind the operation of the prescribed systems. Critical theorists rallied against its elitism and essentialism, challenging its explicit hierarchies of professionals and inhabitants, and questioning both its tendency to treat individuals as 'users' and the singular authority that it accorded to functional 'truths'.
>
> (Sharr, 2010, p. 68)

A similar backlash took place in the USA, where Christopher Alexander's book *A Pattern Language* (Alexander et al., 1977), an odd combination of 'poetic perception and positivist prescription' (Ray, 2008, p. 22), was condemned by US theorists – along with works such as *Defensible Space* (Newman, 1978) and *Design with Nature* (McHarg, 1994) – who were, at the time, embracing deconstructivism, unintelligible to all but a few, partly in retaliation against the reductive suggestion that the built environment could be explained and its behaviour predicted (Dimendberg, 2013).

The knowledge generated by evidence-based approaches is often characterized as being overly simplistic and functionalist (Fraser, 2013), but an examination of its history and conversations with its advocates reveals that this was not the intention. For example, Hillier and Leaman, the brains behind Space Syntax (a platform which predicts pedestrian, and other, flows), wanted architecture to 'become a member of the community of truly modern sciences without sacrificing anything of its preoccupation with the human, the intuitive, and the free run of socio-spatial imagination' (Hillier and Leaman, 1976, p. 31). Unusual in having training in both psychology and architecture, Bryan Lawson wrote in *The Language of Space* of the futility of using measurement-based approaches to record our experience of the world because we 'do not ourselves experience the world around us as a series of discrete and independent dimensions' (Lawson, 1999, p. 246). He observed that it was, however, sometimes 'useful to atomize our reaction to the world in order to investigate what is otherwise an inaccessible mire of phenomenological existence', but this will 'inevitably introduce distortion and bias' (Lawson, 1999, p. 247).

Evidence-based design in the early 1970s relied on collaboration with social scientists, bringing into clear relief the tense relationship between the two fields (Broadbent, 1973; Reizenstein, 1975; Lipman, 1975) largely because of their radically different conceptions of research rigour and what constitutes good enough knowledge (Morris and Mogey, 1965; Canter, 1977). In the 1970s architects and planners were hungry for data on the interface between people and buildings (Gutman, 1972; Reizenstein, 1975), but only, it seems, if the results showed architects in a positive light (Broady, 1972). It was at this time that architects were accused of 'determinism', in other words of exaggerating their impact (Broady, 1968; Malpass, 1968; Lee, 1971; Lipman, 1975; Malpass, 1975; Mercer, 1975; Halpern, 1995; Richards, 2012) – a claim that caused great damage to the research culture of the profession, stunting its emergent knowledge base on the relationship between people and the environment (Darke, 1983; Macmillan, 2006). During this period architecture dropped the thread of environment–behaviour research, leaving it largely to environmental psychologists and others to unravel (Gifford, 1997). However, as Halpern has observed, 'there is no reason why links between the environment and behavior should be seen as deterministic or exclusive of other influences' (Halpern, 1995, p. 114). Environmental psychologists tend to take a deterministic view of the impact of the environment on people, while at the other end of the scale is the view, sometimes described as 'social constructionist', that the environment has no role at all. It is perhaps more fruitful to see the physical features of place and the actions of users as mutually dependent (Vischer, 2008).

Important, but often ignored, impetus for evidence-based design came from a growing band of feminists outraged at the way in which the built environment failed to address the problems of the disadvantaged, particularly women. Jane Darke's series of three articles in the 1984 edition of the refereed journal *Environment and Planning B*, based on her Sheffield University PhD with Bryan Lawson, reported her interviews with the architects of six public-sector (council) housing schemes in London designed during the mid- to late 1960s and completed in the early 1970s and constitutes a forensic critique of practitioner attitudes to knowledge. In the first she described the way in which architects conceived their clients as being 'generalized, imprecise and stereotyped'. 'The main problem was that architects made little if any attempt to evaluate the accuracy of

(a)

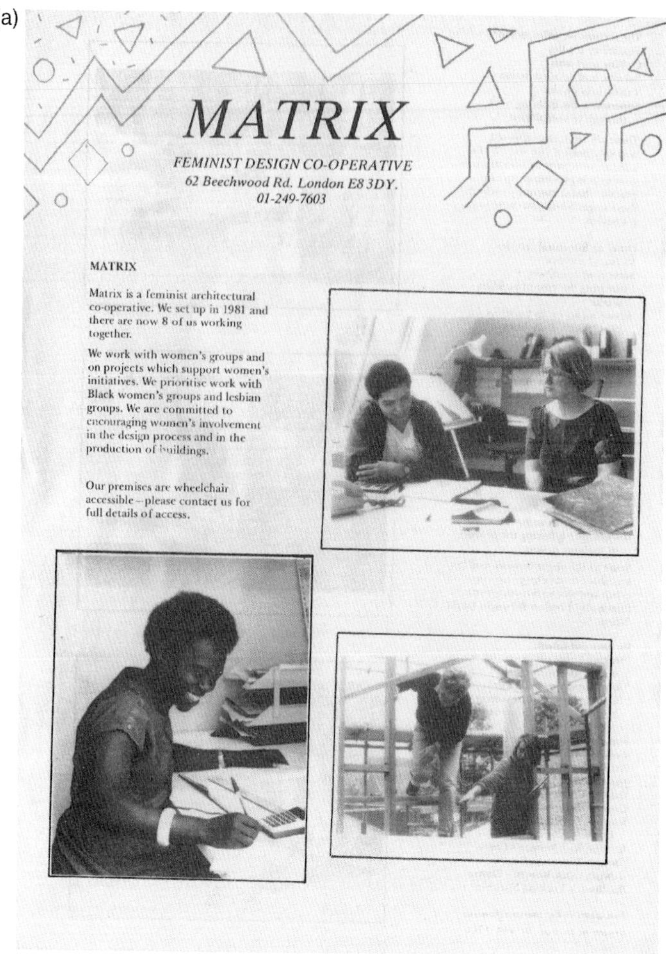

MATRIX

FEMINIST DESIGN CO-OPERATIVE
62 Beechwood Rd. London E8 3DY.
01-249-7603

MATRIX

Matrix is a feminist architectural co-operative. We set up in 1981 and there are now 8 of us working together.

We work with women's groups and on projects which support women's initiatives. We prioritise work with Black women's groups and lesbian groups. We are committed to encouraging women's involvement in the design process and in the production of buildings.

Our premises are wheelchair accessible – please contact us for full details of access.

Figure 3.3 **Matrix Feminist Design Co-operative leaflet. Reproduced with the permission of Anne Thorne.**

their images of the users'. The second paper examined the sources of architects' assumptions and revealed that they 'made only limited attempts to gain systematic information from the client, from social research findings, from observation and personal contact, or from feedback from completed schemes' (Darke, 1984a, p. 389). Instead they placed the greatest reliance on their own experience as a guide to the needs of others, a problem that surfaces repeatedly in the literature of that period (Reizenstein, 1975). Researchers in the 1960s became increasingly aware that architects were developing designs based on stereotyped conceptions of the council tenants they were to house (Morris and Mogey, 1965). Although they had little direct knowledge of council tenants, they never questioned the adequacy of their knowledge as a basis for design (Darke, 1984b). 'For all the lip service paid to the occupiers' desire to personalize their homes, actual scope for doing so was limited to conventional opportunities to choose furnishings' (Darke, 1984a, p. 393).

(b)

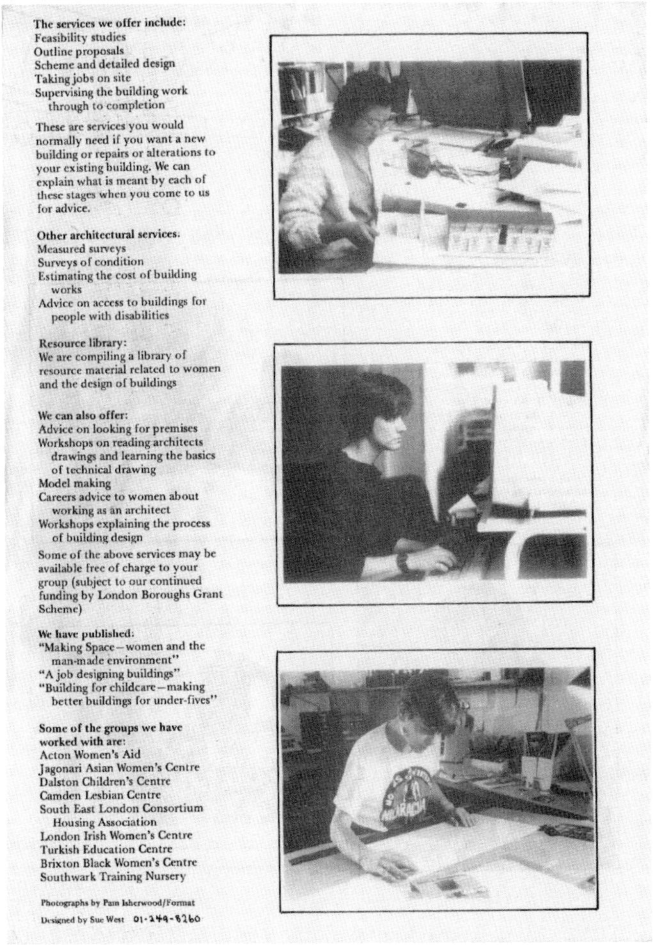

The services we offer include:
Feasibility studies
Outline proposals
Scheme and detailed design
Taking jobs on site
Supervising the building work through to completion

These are services you would normally need if you want a new building or repairs or alterations to your existing building. We can explain what is meant by each of these stages when you come to us for advice.

Other architectural services:
Measured surveys
Surveys of condition
Estimating the cost of building works
Advice on access to buildings for people with disabilities

Resource library:
We are compiling a library of resource material related to women and the design of buildings

We can also offer:
Advice on looking for premises
Workshops on reading architects drawings and learning the basics of technical drawing
Model making
Careers advice to women about working as an architect
Workshops explaining the process of building design
Some of the above services may be available free of charge to your group (subject to our continued funding by London Boroughs Grant Scheme)

We have published:
"Making Space—women and the man-made environment"
"A job designing buildings"
"Building for childcare—making better buildings for under-fives"

Some of the groups we have worked with are:
Acton Women's Aid
Jagonari Asian Women's Centre
Dalston Children's Centre
Camden Lesbian Centre
South East London Consortium Housing Association
London Irish Women's Centre
Turkish Education Centre
Brixton Black Women's Centre
Southwark Training Nursery

Photographs by Pam Isherwood/Format
Designed by Sue West 01-249-8260

Figure 3.3 (***cont.***)

Darke was part of a women's network that spread between Sheffield and London, including many of the founder members of the pioneering women's co-operative Matrix (Figure 3.3), perhaps the archetype of feminist practice, formed in 1980 – just at the moment when local authorities such as the London Borough of Haringey were shedding their design staff. With their book *Making Space: Women and the Man-made Environment*, they argued that the impact of design on women should be a subject of study and that women should be included in all stages of design (Matrix, 1984). This strand of evidence-based participatory practice persists today in the work of practices such as MUF, Anne Thorne Architects and Atelier d'Architecture Autogérée (Hoskyns and Petrescu, 2007, p. 21). Their preoccupation with giving a voice to the dispossessed has continued with Jos Boys' argument for an expanded notion of disability which addresses issues of powerlessness, otherness and mental health (Boys, 2014). What is common to all these practices is the knowledge that inclusive architecture cannot be

Figure 3.4 **Stonehenge Saucers. © Louis Hellman.**

made without research (Markus, 1967), and that it is vital to return to a project after completion to assess its efficacy and learn from mistakes (Figure 3.4).

3.4 Design research

> Research is a purposeful, systematic way to improve knowledge. Design can also contribute to a body of knowledge when designers commit themselves to share what they know, when they approach design problems as opportunities to learn what they do not know, and when they make design decisions that contribute to enquiry.
>
> (Zeisel, 1981, p. 231)

Zeisel was here talking about the strand of evidence-based design he called 'inquiry by design', closely linked to what is now known as 'design research'. This can be used to develop practical solutions to real world problems but is often used on theoretical explorations with no immediate applicability.

Design research is inherent in most architectural practice, but is in need of reframing and externalization to make it better utilized and understood. That it is an 'iterative process' should be 'proclaimed by architects without apology' as it allows for constant adjustment. This was something that the 'design methodologists' in the 1970s and 1980s tried to communicate but 'not very effectively' (Ray, 2008, p. 11):

> the hundreds of models and drawings produced in design form an artistically created primal matter that stimulates the haptic imagination, astonishes its

> creators instead of subserviently obeying them, and helps architects fix unfamiliar ideas, gain new knowledge about the building-to-come, and formulate new alternatives and 'options', new unforeseen scenarios of realization. To follow the evolution of drawings in an architectural studio is like witnessing the successive exertions of a juggler who keeps adding more and more balls to his skillful acrobatic show. Every new technique of drawing and modeling serves to absorb a new difficulty and add it to the accumulation of elements necessary to entertain the possibility of building anything.
>
> (Latour and Yaneva, 2008, p. 84)

The general confusion about what constitutes design research (Fraser, 2013) is underpinned by disciplinary border scuffles. Nigel Cross has made a helpful distinction between what he calls: 'scientific design' relating to the use of scientific evidence-based methods; 'design science', design as a systematically used research methodology; and 'a science of design', the scientific study of design (Cross, 2001, p. 4). In these terms this book is an argument for design science in the context of architecture, for the distinct nature of architectural problem-solving skills and for the value of research in the creation of knowledge. This involves a recognition that drawing, modelling and designing are all forms of thinking and that 'This should be no surprise, since we are used to the idea that speech, writing, mathematical reasoning, carving and hand-crafting are all ways of thinking, not records after the event' (Groak, 1992, p. 150). 'A building constitutes in many ways a set of hypotheses – assumptions and intentions about what will work' (Pavlides and Cranz, 2012, p. 300). Design research is not unique to architects. Indeed 'design thinking' is common currency in industrial design and marketing (Brown, 2009). There is a vast and ever growing array of design specialisms, with new ones continually being added to the mix (Preddy, 2011).

What is it that makes architectural design studio different from other types of design studio? Nicholas Ray argues that the architectural design process, based on a studio teaching model, is 'unique to architectural education and possibly our major contribution' (Ray, 2008, p. 19). Often described as a form of 'reflective practice', as outlined by the American philosopher Donald Schon (Schon, 1984), it involves the making of design decisions based on the synthesis and framing of large bodies of diverse knowledge and the communication of that synthesis to others in the form of drawings, models, reports and so on, creating new forms of knowledge along the way (Figure 3.5). Tom Holbrook writes of the work of his practice 5th Studio:

> we have developed our spatial thinking to achieve this bridge between strategy and detail: from the scale of furniture to infrastructure ... this approach is able to orientate and bring meaning to highly complex and conflicted sites through sustained and committed involvement.
>
> (Holbrook, 2017, p. 150)

The research methodology of architecture design studio is characterized by leaps in scale from the tiniest detail to the scale of cities and by the concomitant mix

Figure 3.5 **Design studio at Bath University. Photo author.**

of those that participate in it. This is what makes it different from other forms of design studio. 'Knowing through scaling' is an integral aspect of an architect's practice (Yaneva, 2005, p. 870). In her study of the practice Office of Metropolitan Architecture (OMA), 'materials, scoping instruments, and new knowledge "talk back" to the architects, and they are prepared to listen, thus triggering reinterpretations of interim results' (Yaneva, 2005, p. 870).

Considerable social science attention has been given to the way in which information crosses boundaries, sometimes with specific reference to the construction industry (Leigh Star and Griesemer, 1989; Ewenstein and Whyte, 2007a). Design studio, both in architecture and in other design disciplines, is a collective method of working in which multiple parties negotiate solutions through constant adjustment of 'artefacts of knowing' (Latour, 1986; Lynch and Woolgar, 1990; Ewenstein and Whyte, 2007a). Often visual, these can take the form of drawings, models and diagrams, but they can also be networks, processes and strategies.

'Artefacts of knowing' are closely related to the 'boundary objects' that have been extensively debated in Organization and Management Studies (OMS) and Science and Technology Studies (STS) as well as within the wider field of construction research (Ewenstein and Whyte, 2007a; Schweber and Harty, 2010). The representational capability of architects also plays an important role in the process as it can be 'an instrument of invention which is not an end product but an active component at phases of ideation, conceptualisation, experimentation and visualisation' (Reinhardt, 2008, p. 185). The locus of this process is the 'boundary object' through which meaning is negotiated.

Objects, models, maps, drawings and moving images are particularly effective if they translate knowledge from one community into another, but can be expensive and time-consuming to produce. They can simply act as a bridge between disciplines or can have more complex 'agency' depending on how they are viewed. They also have a temporal dimension and are repositories of knowledge to be exploited at a future time (Henderson, 1999; Ewenstein and Whyte, 2007a). If boundary objects are to work as tools of negotiation, they need to represent, learn about and transform knowledge (Carlile, 2002).

If architects are to be 'boundary spanners' using boundary objects across disciplinary divides (Carlile, 2002; Levina and Vaast, 2005), they need to be better at negotiating and externalizing the way in which they develop knowledge at the boundaries as well as articulating the impact of the boundary object on that negotiation. This merits considerably more exploration, as the collective design of space and systems negotiated through the use of media that become prosthetic tools for problem-solving is the key methodological contribution of architects. It is a process that requires the considerable use of embodied knowledge developed through repetitive practice as well as the synthetic professional judgement to decide what is good (Ewenstein and Whyte, 2007b).

3.5 Post-occupancy evaluation (POE)

It was not until the 1960s, in the context of rapid technological change, that a need for a more systematic approach to the measurement of building performance gained traction. The 1962 study on the state of architectural practice *The Architect and His Office*, commissioned by the RIBA, revealed a lack of learning from job to job and from practice to practice that is still prevalent today:

> There was a desire to know how their practice compared with others, and if there was some way in which their own methods of working might be improved. And yet most offices seemed to work in virtual isolation from one another. We found little interchange of information and experience on common or similar problems ... the isolation could be found even among working groups within the same office. The attitude that each problem of office organisation or of design must be tackled de novo is one which must be highly uneconomic for the profession and the building industry.
>
> (Derbyshire and Smith, 1962, p. 66)

The report's recommendations highlighted the need to capture common problems and solutions, and called for reflective research to be integrated into architectural processes. Subsequently, in 1964, the first *RIBA Plan of Work* was published and included *Stage M: Feedback*, which called for architects and their clients to inspect completed buildings two or three years after completion (Cooper, 2001).

In 1968 twenty architectural and engineering practices, together with the RIBA, *The Architects' Journal* and the then Ministry of Public Building and Works, co-sponsored the establishment of a Building Performance Research Unit in Strathclyde. This led to the formalization of design appraisal through the life of a building as set out in Markus et al.'s 1972 book *Building Performance*.

> Appraisal is a design activity. It is the continuous introspection of the designer whereby he monitors his own performance. Design is traditionally

> understood as taking place prior to the construction of a building, but it can also be seen as a continuous process lasting as long as the building itself, in which the design is present directly or variously through a successor, nominee, design tool or even computer program. In the former case appraisal has to be of design ideas: in the latter, of complete working buildings. Hence design is a central theme.
>
> (Markus, 1972, p. v)

At that time the field of building science was growing and developing in response to demand for energy-efficient buildings following the 1970s oil crisis and resulting problems associated with tight building envelopes and poor internal environmental quality on occupant health in the 1980s (Mallory-Hill et al., 2012). These areas of concern merged over subsequent decades into an urgent need to build environmentally sustainable buildings.

During the 1990s the PROBE case studies developed robust and systematic methodologies to measure the technical and energy performance of non-domestic buildings, as well as occupant perceptions of comfort and satisfaction (Bordass et al., 2001a, 2001b). The studies were particularly influential in highlighting the lack of engagement by designers, builders and procuring clients in POE and what later become known as the 'performance gap' between predicted and actual performance.

> Feedback need[s] to become routine: as a way of quality control in the more repetitive projects; as a necessary part of hypothesis testing in innovative ones; as a means of increasing awareness of chronic problems, changing requirements and emerging properties; and as a way of promoting fine-tuning and team learning.
>
> (Bordass and Leaman, 2005, p. 349)

At around the same time the practices DEGW and Ahrends Burton and Koralek (ABK) came together to develop the Building Use Studies (BUS) method under the leadership of Adrian Leaman (Duffy, 2008), begun in the 1980s and in use to this day (Arup, 2017). Despite this, post occupancy was 'quietly dropped' from the *RIBA Plan of Work* (Sharr and Thornton, 2013, p. 266), for reasons that remain unclear but may relate to the poor links between practice and research to be discussed in Chapter 4.

During the late 1990s and 2000s the Latham (1994) and Egan (1998) construction industry reviews – with their focus on collaborative working, performance measurement, client service and customer care – gave renewed impetus to POE (Cooper, 2001) and building performance evaluation (BPE). Broadly speaking, POE is the evaluation of a building in use, while BPE is the setting of targets and monitoring of performance at any point in the life of a building project. The Construction Industry Council and the Commission for Architecture and the Built Environment (CABE), established in 1999, sought to articulate and evidence the long-term benefits arising from investment in design. These included the cost savings made over the life cycle of a building (including energy, adaptation and disposal) and impacts on occupant productivity, health and attainment (in offices, hospitals and schools) (Chamberlain et al., 2015), as well as a set of less tangible outcomes like civic pride, social inclusion and wellbeing (in homes and neighbourhoods) (Macmillan, 2004, 2006; Samuel et al., 2014; Carmona and Natajaran, 2016). POE is not just about energy. The environment is a socio-technical problem and we know far too little about the way in which social and cultural factors impact on 'performance', not just in terms of energy but also in terms of important but intangible issues such as atmosphere and comfort. Design reduces the impact of climate control on the body in a range of significant and intangible ways (O'Hara and Holz, 2013). A discussion of heating, for example, is meaningless without a discussion of the 'cosiness' it imparts (Devine-Wright, 2014). Despite all this, it seems that only 3% of architectural practices undertake POE on a regular basis (Clark, 2015). Guesswork continues to be the preferred mode of operation.

Conclusion

This very brief account of what architects consider to be their knowledge shows just how little agreement there is on this issue. The result has been that the knowledge base of architects has 'developed only fitfully', meaning that 'architecture becomes increasingly irrelevant and, ultimately irresponsible' (Till, 2004, p. 1). The canon of architecture has focused on the ways in which buildings have changed in form and style over time, but it includes only a very limited and partial range of examples and is deeply excluding.

Theory, I have argued, has been overly inward-looking. It needs to be reframed as the study of 'research methodology' both to make the research content of architecture explicit and to facilitate exchange with other disciplines. While acknowledging that theories and methodologies are never perfect, these frameworks for thinking provide an important basis for action and need to be served up in a digestible, intelligible and provisional form which allows others to enter into the process. Nineteenth-century scientific research paradigms are no longer adequate to address the complexity of issues faced by the construction industry (Groak, 1992). Theory needs to be put to work on the very concrete problems we face, at least in the short term.

There is a profound need to reframe architectural knowledge around the relationship between people and place and the techniques necessary to explore such issues with others. That we know so very little about this is a sad indictment of the profession. The relationship between organizational culture, knowledge-generation and innovation has been subject to a large amount of academic attention, but not from within the field of architecture, with a few notable exceptions (Ewenstein and Whyte, 2007a).

The unique methodological contribution of architects resides within architecture design studio. I argue that this is different from other forms of design studio largely because of its subject matter, the vast range of issues it deals with, the spatial juxtapositions it tests, the diversity of people that are engaged in its negotiations and, most importantly, the scalar leaps that are characteristic of architectural design thinking. Far more research needs to go into doing architectural research better – in doing so, teasing out its distinctive value.

A nervousness about what constitutes architectural knowledge (Duffy, 1998) and what its value might be underpins the profession's attitude to fees. This nervousness does not, however, stop architects fighting for their intellectual property when necessary. The legal wrangle between Norman Foster and his former partner Ken Shuttleworth over the authorship of the design for the Swiss Re building in London is a case in point (Kaika, 2011). Architectural knowledge, to be disaggregated in detail in Chapter 6, is the profession's greatest asset. We neglect it at our peril.

References

Abbott, A., 1988. *The System of Professions: An Essay on the Division of Expert Labor.* University of Chicago Press, Chicago.

Adler, D., 1968. *AJ Metric Handbook of Planning and Design Data.* Architectural Press, London.

AJ, 1972. 'Guide to the AJ Information Library'. *Architects' Journal,* 41, pp. 833–848.

Albrecht, J., 2002. 'Against the Interpretation of Architecture'. *Journal of Architectural Education,* 55, pp. 194–196.

Alexander, C., Ishikawa, S., Silverstein, M., 1977. *A Pattern Language: Towns, Buildings, Construction.* Oxford University Press, New York.

Arup, 2017. 'Bus methodology'. www.busmethodology.org.uk/history/

Baden-Powell, C., 1997. *Architect's Pocket Book.* Architectural Press, London.

Baydar, G., 2004. 'The Cultural Burden of Architecture'. *Journal of Architectural Education,* 57, pp. 19–27.

Bordass, B., Leaman, A., 2005. 'Making Feedback and Post-occupancy Evaluation Routine 1: A Portfolio of Feedback Techniques'. *Building Research and Information,* 33, 4, pp. 347–352.

Bordass, B., Cohen, R., Standeven, M., Leaman, A., 2001a. Assessing Building Performance in Use 2: The Technical Performance of the Probe Buildings. *Building Research and Information,* 29, 2, pp. 103–113.

Bordass, B., Cohen, R., Standeven, M., Leaman, A., 2001b. 'Assessing Building Performance in Use: The PROBE Occupation Surveys and Their Implications. *Building Research and Information,* 29, 2, pp. 129–14.3

Boys, J., 2014. *Doing Disability Differently: An Alternative Handbook on Architecture, Dis/ability and Designing for Everyday Life.* Routledge, London.

Brittain-Catlin, T., 2014. *Bleak Houses: Disappointment and Failure in Architecture.* MIT Press, Cambridge, MA.

Broadbent, G., 1973. *Design in Architecture: Architecture and the Human Sciences.* Wiley, London.

Broadbent, G., Bunt, R., Llorens, T., 1980. *Meaning and Behaviour in the Built Environment.* Wiley, Chichester.

Broadbent, G., Hillier, B., Lipman, A., MacLeod, R., Musgrove, J., O'Sullivan, P., Wilson, B., 1970. 'Editorial'. *Architectural Research and Teaching,* 1, pp. 2–5.

Broady, M., 1972. 'Social Theory in Architectural Design', in: Gutman, R. (ed.), *People and Buildings*. Basic Books, New York, p. 179.

Broady, M., 1968. *Planning for People*. National Council for Social Service, London.

Brown, T., 2009. *Change by Design*. HarperCollins, London.

Carmona, M., Natajaran, L., 2016. *Design Governance: The CABE Experiment*. Routledge, London.

Canter, D., 1977. 'Priorities in Building Evaluation: Some Methodological Considerations'. *Journal of Architectural Research*, 6, pp. 38–40.

Carlile, P.R., 2002. 'A Pragmatic View of Knowledge and Boundaries: Boundary Objects in New Product Development'. *Organization Science*, 13, pp. 442–455.

Chamberlain, P., Wolstenholme, D., Dexter, M., Seals, E., 2015. 'The State of the Art of Design in Health: An Expert-led Review of the Extent of the Art of Design Theory and Practice in Health and Social Care'. www.researchgate.net/publication/281443863_The_State_of_the_Art_of_Design_in_Health_An_expert-led_review_of_the_extent_of_the_art_of_design_theory_and_practice_in_health_and_social_care

Clark, T., 2015. 'AJ Housing Survey: Post-occupancy Not on Architects' Radar'. www.architectsjournal.co.uk/news/daily-news/aj-housing-survey-post-occupancy-not-on-architects-radar/8678486.article (accessed 13.2.15).

Cooper, I., 2001. 'Post-occupancy Evaluation – Where Are You?', *Building Research and Information*, 29, 2, pp. 158–163.

Cox, O., 1949. 'Method in Design'. *Plan Architectural Association Students Journal*, 4, pp. 17–18.

Cross, N., 2001. 'Designerly Ways of Knowing: Design Discipline versus Design Science'. *Design Issues*, 17, pp. 49–55.

Darke, J., 1984a. 'Architects and User Requirements in Public-sector Housing: 1. Architects' Assumptions about the Users'. *Environment and Planning B: Planning and Design*, 11, pp. 398–404.

Darke, J., 1984b. 'Architects and User Requirements in Public-sector Housing: 2. The Sources for Architects' Assumptions'. *Environment and Planning B: Planning and Design*, 11, pp. 405–416.

Darke, J., 1983. 'The Design of Public Housing: Architects' Intentions and Users' Reactions'. Unpublished thesis, University of Sheffield.

Deamer, P., 2016. 'Architecture History/Criticism/Theory', in: Cayer, A., Deamer, P., Korsh, S., Petersen, E., Shvartzberg, M. (eds), *Asymmetric Labors: The Economy of Architecture in Theory and Practice*, pp. 33–35. www.academia.edu/28002267/Asymmetric_Labors_The_Economy_of_Architecture_in_Theory_and_Practice

Derbyshire, A., Smith, J., 1962. *The Architect and His Office*. RIBA, London.

Devine-Wright, P., 2014. 'Low Carbon Heating and Older Adults: Comfort, Cosiness and Glow'. *Building Research and Information*, 42, pp. 288–299.

Dimendberg, E., 2013. *Diller and Scofidio: Architecture after Images*. University of Chicago Press, Chicago.

Duffy, F., 2008. 'Forum: Linking Theory Back to Practice'. *Building Research and Information*, 36, pp. 655–658.

Duffy, F., 1998. *Architectural Knowledge: The Idea of a Profession.* Spon, London.

Egan, J., 2004. *The Egan Review: Skills for Sustainable Communities.* RIBA, London.

Ewenstein, B., Whyte, J., 2007a. 'Visual Representations as "Artefacts of Knowing"'. *Building Research and Information*, 35, pp. 81–89.

Ewenstein, B., Whyte, J., 2007b. 'Beyond Words: Aesthetic Knowledge in Organizations', *Organization Studies*, 28, pp. 689–708.

Fraser, M. (ed.), 2013. *Design Research in Architecture: An Overview.* Routledge, London.

Frayling, C., 1993. 'Research in Art and Design'. *Royal College of Art Research Papers*, 1, 1. http://researchonline.rca.ac.uk/384/

Gifford, R., 1997. *Environmental Psychology: Principles and Practice.* Allyn & Bacon, Boston, MA.

Groak, S., 1992. *The Idea of Building: Thought and Action in the Design and Production of Buildings.* Taylor & Francis, Oxford.

Gutman, R. (ed.), 1972. *People and Buildings.* Basic Books, New York.

Habraken, N.J., 2005. *Palladio's Children.* Taylor & Francis, Oxford.

Halpern, D., 1995. *Mental Health and the Built Environment: More than Bricks and Mortar?* Taylor & Francis, London; Bristol, PA.

Henderson, K., 1999. 'On Line and On Paper: Visual Representations'. *Visual Culture and Computer Graphics in Design Engineering.* MIT Press, Cambridge, MA.

Hillier, B., Leaman, A., 1976. 'Architecture as a Discipline'. *Journal of Architectural Research*, 5, pp. 28–32.

Holbrook, T., 2017. *Expanding Disciplinarity in Architectural Practice.* Routledge, Oxford.

Hoskyns, T., Petrescu, D., 2007. 'Taking Place and Altering It', in: Petrescu, D. (ed.), *Altering Practices.* Routledge, Oxford, pp. 15–38.

Huxtable, A.L., 1997. *The Unreal America: Architecture and Illusion.* The New Press, New York.

Hyde, R., 2011. 'Historian of the Present: Wouter Vanstiphout'. *Australian Design Review.* www.australiandesignreview.com/architecture/historian-of-the-present-wouter-vanstiphout/

Imrie, R., Street, E., 2011. *Architectural Design and Regulation.* Wiley Blackwell, Oxford.

Jacobs, S., 2015. 'Opening the Black Box/AA Night School', in: Harriss, H., Froud, D. (eds.), *Radical Pedagogies.* RIBA Publishing, Newcastle-upon-Tyne, p. 174.

Kaika, M., 2011. 'Autistic Architecture: The Fall of the Icon and the Rise of the Serial Object of Architecture'. *Environment and Planning D: Society and Space*, 29, 6, pp. 968–992.

Kirk Hamilton, D., Watkins, D., 2009. *Evidence Based Design for Multiple Building Types.* Wiley and Son, New York.

Lansley, P., 2001. 'Building Research and Quality of Life'. *Building Research and Information*, 29, 1, pp. 62–74.

Larson, M.S., 1993. *Behind the Postmodern Facade: Architectural Change in Late Twentieth Century America.* University of California Press, Berkeley.

Latham, M., 1994. *Constructing the Team*. HMSO, London.

Latour, B., 1998. 'How to be Iconophilic in Art, Science and Religion', in: Jones, C., Galison, P. (eds), *Picturing Science Producing Art*. Routledge, London, pp. 418–440.

Latour, B., 1986. 'Visualisation and Cognition: Thinking with Eyes and Hands'. *Knowledge and Society*, 6, 1, pp. 1–40.

Latour, B., Yaneva, A., 2008. 'Give Me a Gun and I Will Make All Buildings Move: An ANT's View of Architecture', in: Geiser, R. (ed.), *Explorations in Architecture: Teaching, Design, Research*. Birkhauser, Basel, pp. 80–89.

Lawson, B., 1999. *The Language of Space*. Architectural Press, London.

Lee, T., 1971. 'Psychology and Architectural Determinism'. *Architects' Journal*, 4 August, pp. 253–262.

Leigh Star, S., Griesemer, J.R., 1989. 'Institutional Ecology, "Translations" and Boundary Objects: Amateurs and Professionals in Berkeley's Museum of Vertebrate Zoology, 1907–39'. *Social Studies of Science*, 19, 3, pp. 387–420.

Levina, N., Vaast, E., 2005. 'The Emergence of Boundary Spanning Competence in Practice: Implications for Implementation and Use of Information Systems'. *Management Information Systems Quarterly*, 29, 2, pp. 335–363.

Lipman, A., 1975. *Aspects of the Professional Ideology of Architects: Social Engineering and Design Theory*. Welsh School of Architecture, Cardiff.

Loos, A., 1998. *Ornament and Crime. Selected Essays*. Ariadne Press, Riverside, CA.

Lynch, M., Woolgar, S., 1990. *Representation in Scientific Practice*. MIT Press, Cambridge, MA.

Macmillan, S., 2006. 'Added Value of Good Design'. *Building Research and Information*, 34, 3, pp. 257–271.

Macmillan, S., 2004. *Designing Better Buildings: Quality and Value in the Built Environment*. Spon, New York.

Mallory-Hill, S., Preiser, W.F.E., Watson, C., 2012. *Enhancing Building Performance*. Blackwell Publishing, Chichester.

Malpass, P., 1975. 'Professionalism and the Role of Architects in Local Authority Housing'. *RIBA Journal*, pp. 6–29.

Malpass, P., 1968. *People and Plans: Essays on Urban Problems and Solutions*. Basic Books, New York.

Markus, T.A., 1967. 'The Role of Building Performance Measurement and Appraisal in Design Method'. *Architects' Journal*, 20 December, pp. 1567–1573.

Markus, T.A., Whyman, P., Morgan, J., Whitton, D., Mayer, T., Canter, D., Fleming, J., 1972. *Building Performance*. Applied Science Publishers, Amsterdam.

Matrix, 1984. *Making Space: Women and the Man-made Environment*. Pluto, London.

McHarg, I.L., 1994. *Design with Nature*. J. Wiley, New York.

McNeill, D., 2005. 'In Search of the Global Architect: The Case of Norman Foster (and Partners)'. *International Journal of Urban and Regional Research*, 29, 3, pp. 501–515.

Mercer, C., 1975. *Living in Cities*. Penguin, Harmondsworth.

Miller, D., 2009. *Stuff*. Polity, Cambridge.

Morgan, G., 2006. *Images of Organization*. Sage, London.

Morris, R.N., Mogey, J., 1965. *The Sociology of Housing*. Routledge Kegan Paul, London.

Newman, O., 1978. *Defensible Space: Crime Prevention through Urban Design*. Collier Books, New York.

Nowotny, H., Scott, P., Gibbons, M., 2001. *Rethinking Science: Knowledge and the Public in an Age of Uncertainty*. Wiley, London.

Odgers, J., Samuel, F., 2010. 'Designing in Quality', in: Dutoit, A., Odgers, J., Sharr, A. (eds), *Quality Out of Control*. Routledge, London, pp. 41–54.

O'Hara, C.E., Holz, K., 2013. 'The Price of Comfort: How Landscape and Architectural Design Can Reduce Human Dependence on Climate Control'. *Journal of Green Building*, 8, 3, pp. 65–77.

Pavlides, E., Cranz, G., 2012. 'Use of Ethnographic Techniques in Architectural Education to Gain Deeper Insights into How Insiders Understand and Use Their Environments', in: Mallory-Hill, S., Preiser, W.F.E., Watson, C. (eds), *Enhancing Building Performance*. John Wiley & Sons, London.

Preddy, S., 2011. *How to Run a Successful Design Business*. Routledge, London.

Price, C., 1966. 'Life Conditioning'. *Architectural Design*, 36, pp. 483–494.

Ray, N., 2008. 'Studio Teaching for a Social Purpose'. *Open House International*, 33, 2, pp. 18–25.

Reinhardt, D., 2008. 'Representation as Research Design Model and Media Rotation'. *Journal of Architecture*, 13, 2, pp. 185–201.

Reizenstein, J.E., 1975. 'Linking Social Research and Design'. *Journal of Architectural Research*, 4, pp. 26–38.

RIBA, 1967. *Plan of Work*, 1st edition. RIBA, London.

Richards, S., 2012. *Architect Knows Best*. Ashgate, Farnham.

Saint, A., 1983. *The Image of the Architect*. Yale University Press, New Haven, CT.

Samuel, F., 2014. 'The Way We Were: The Changing Relationship of Research and Design'. RIBA Journal. www.ribaj.com/intelligence/the-way-we-were

Samuel, F., 1998. 'Lower Case History and the Development of Reflective Practice in Studio'. Architectural Education Exchange Conference, Cardiff. www.researchgate.net/publication/240638836_lower_case_history_and_the_development_of_reflective_practice_in_studio

Samuel, F., Linder-Gaillard, I., 2014. *Sacred Concrete: The Churches of Le Corbusier*. Birkhauser, Basel.

Schilling, A., Werr, A., Gand, S., Sardas, J.-C., 2012. 'Understanding Professionals' Reactions to Strategic Change: The Role of Threatened Professional Identities'. *The Service Industries Journal*, 32, 8, pp. 1229–1245.

Schon, D., 1984. *The Reflective Practitioner: How Professionals Think in Action*. Basic Books, New York.

Schweber, L., 2016. 'Putting Theory to Work: The Use of Theory in Construction Research'. *Construction Management and Economics*, 33, 10, pp. 840–860.

Schweber, L., Harty, C., 2010. 'Actors and Objects: A Socio-technical Networks Approach for Construction Management Research'. *Construction Management and Economics*, 28, 6, pp. 657–674.

Sharr, A., 2010. 'Leslie Martin and the Science of Architectural Form', in: Dutoit, A., Odgers, J., Sharr, A. (eds), *Quality Out of Control*. Routledge, London, pp. 67–78.

Sharr, A., Thornton, S., 2013. *Demolishing Whitehall*. Ashgate, Farnham.

Sprunt, R., 1975. 'Building Knowledge and Building Law'. *Journal of Architectural Research*, 4, pp. 10–16.

Stirling, J., 1956. 'Ronchamp: Le Corbusier's Chapel and the Crisis of Rationalism'. *Architectural Review*, pp. 155–161.

Till, J., 1995. 'Angels with Dirty Faces'. https://jeremytill.s3.amazonaws.com/uploads/post/attachment/43/1995_Angels_with_Dirty_Faces.pdf

van Schaik, L., 2008. *Spatial Intelligence: New Futures for Architecture*. Wiley, London.

van Schaik, L., London, G., George, B., 2010. *Procuring Innovative Architecture*. Routledge, Oxford.

van Toorn, R., 2007. 'No More Dreams? The Passion for Reality in Recent Dutch Architecture'. www.roemervantoorn.nl/Resources/Toorn,%20van_%20No%20More%20Dreams.pdf

Vischer, J.C., 2008. 'Towards a User-centred Theory of the Built Environment'. *Building Research and Information*, 36, 3, pp. 231–240.

Wigglesworth, S., 2006. 'Critical Practice'. *Journal of Architecture*, 10, 3, pp. 335–346.

Williams, R., 2014. 'Bleak Houses: Disappointment and Failure in Architecture, by Timothy Brittain-Catlin'. *Times Higher Education Supplement*. www.timeshighereducation.com/books/bleak-houses-disappointment-and-failure-in-architecture-by-timothy-brittain-catlin/2012078.article

Yaneva, A., 2009. *The Making of a Building: A Pragmatist Approach to Architecture*. Peter Lang, Oxford.

Zeisel, J., 1981. *Inquiry by Design: Tools for Environment – Behaviour Research*. Brooks/Cole Publishing Company, Monterey, CA.

Chapter 4

The research culture of architects

The key role of knowledge, and the research to generate that knowledge, in the promotion of a high-quality built environment has been 'undervalued by all sectors – profession, policy making, construction industry and even academia' (Campbell, 2012). So why is the architecture profession so confused about the nature of its knowledge? What is the research culture that has led to this state of affairs? I will begin with a brief description of the research scene in the UK generally before homing in on universities and their relationship with the institutions and architectural practice. The UK provides a particularly significant case study, not just because it has long considered itself a leader in architectural research (Musgrove et al., 1975), but also because UK universities have been compelled, since the advent of the Research Assessment Exercise (RAE), to be explicit about what their research is.

4.1 Research context of research

Research is a process of systematic and original investigation undertaken in order to gain knowledge and understanding and to de-risk innovation. It should ideally be disseminated to help the common cause. The ultimate aim of most research, as it has developed over the years through generations of scholars, is to anticipate the future and to gain advantage therein. Systematic research has been around for a very long time. I have no inclination to go back into the spaces of early Western modernism, which in philosophical terms was somewhere in the seventeenth century, or into the origins of 'scientific' methods, about which a great deal has been written (see for example Buchli, 2013). Suffice to say that this was a time when natural processes were artificially separated out from spiritual experience and became constructs formulated to help explain phenomena (Ray, 2008). Thomas Kuhn, famous for coining the term 'paradigm shift', argued that science accumulates knowledge within one overarching world view until the moment when a new discovery changes that paradigm, causing science to recalibrate itself and start a new normal (Kuhn, 1962). All knowledge is therefore provisional.

Science then is 'a systematic and rigorous approach encompassing a number of activities including research, measurement, comparison, evaluation, and feedback' (Mallory-Hill et al., 2012, p. 3). I prefer the European understanding of the word, which is not limited to technical issues as it seems to be in the UK (Snow,

1998). While the importance of scientific method and the replicability of results for the development of knowledge should not be downplayed, there has recently been greater acknowledgement of the creative element within science. Conversely the systematic nature of art practice has gained in recognition. Kyna Leski observes that the stages of creativity are essentially the same irrespective of whether the creativity is artistic, scientific, technical, business or whatever (Leski, 2015); all require rigorous testing. The boundaries between art and science are not really that clear cut (Latour, 1998). Although the research process may be systematic, it takes professional judgement to come up with the right question. This kind of 'creativity' is developed through the embodied experience of the repetitive actions of practice.

Architects are well known for describing their unique selling point as creativity but 'it is a weary effort to classify some people as "creative" and thus superior to others' (Groak, 1992, p. 62). Research is always creative, culturally and temporally specific, incomplete and highly contingent on the researcher's place in the world. This came into relief with the advent of postmodernism in the 1960s, shattering modernist conceptions of totalizing truth by recognizing the validity of a multiplicity of different viewpoints or subjectivities, most notably those of under-represented minorities, who each brought their own methods and viewpoint to the table. From then on reflexivity, acknowledging the limitations of one's own approach, has become a key element of high-quality research (Schweber, 2016) even in 'hard' science. It is also vital for sharing expert knowledge and risk with society (Beck, 1986; Nowotny et al., 2001).

Research is always highly political. Nowhere is this clearer than in the way in which it is funded, the allocation of research resource being an important tool for delivering government agendas and for impacting on policy. The US organization Battelle charts international shifts in research funding (Battelle, 2013) across the globe – the energy agenda is becoming increasingly important as military research is decreasing. Powerful companies and countries have the resources to fund research that works in their favour while hard-pressed universities and researchers tend to follow the money. Researchers and their teams have to continually think up new ideas so that they can apply for funding from a variety of national bodies – in the UK the research councils, charities and sometimes industry – or international bodies such as the European Research Council. Political imperatives mean that STEM (Science Technology Engineering Mathematics) subjects tend to be favoured over arts and humanities, at least in terms of funding pots. Research cultures vary considerably across the world, as does investment in research. In 2013 South Korea invested 4.15% of gross domestic product (GDP) in research, Sweden 3.3%, China 2.01% and the UK 1.63%. The results are there for all to see in the things in our homes.

4.2 The UK Research Excellence Framework

Research in UK universities and specialized research institutions has largely been funded through government, most notably through the University Grants Committee (Manning, 1965) and the Research Councils. Although research had been a priority during World Wars I and II, it quickly ceased to be a strategic priority

(Musgrove et al., 1975). How best to distribute limited funds in an increasingly audit-driven policy context became a pressing question, one that led to the development of the first Research Assessment Exercise, which took place in 1986. This was 'an explicit and formalized assessment process of the quality of research' (RAE, 2008), largely based on published outputs. The RAE rolled around again in 1989, 1992, 1996, 2001 and 2008, the periods between growing to accommodate the increasingly resource-hungry nature of the process. It was then recast as the Research Excellence Framework (REF) in 2014, which attempted to assess the very best work as judged through peer review and impact ratings.

The financial benefit to universities from an excellent performance in the REF, through 'quality-related (QR) funding' (HEFCE, 2017), has been depleting year on year. This impacts on status and recruitment through league tables for the lucrative overseas student market, the World University Rankings and national rankings such as the *Times Best University Guide*. It is also a significantly larger source than that allocated through the UK Research Councils (Keith, 2017). Large amounts of university energy are put into alignment with REF strategy, sometimes with a concomitant neglect of teaching – it is common practice to use student fees to subsidize research activity – something that the present government is trying to redress with the heavy-handed introduction of a Teaching Excellence Framework (TEF)(BIS, 2015). In the professions, research and teaching should not be disaggregated, as students need to be taught to work at the cutting edge of specialist knowledge.

The replacement of the university grants system, which offered a free education, with punitive fees is a major disincentive to undertake further study, particularly after five years of full-time architectural education. Now that the fee system has been extended to master's students, the number of 'home'-based UK master's-level students has plummeted, jeopardizing the flow of UK students up to PhD. Taking a master's degree, a traditional route for industry-based practitioners to develop expertise in a specialist area of knowledge, is now closed to all but the most affluent or lucky, with universities looking to the overseas market to up their postgraduate student intake. The result in the UK is an upskilling of countries other than our own. At the same time, many towns and cities in the UK have become worryingly reliant on a flow of overseas students to bolster spending in the local economy.

In the UK the majority of research funding comes via the Research Councils, each responsible for a different sphere of activity. One example is the Arts and Humanities Research Council, which funded the research for this book. The 2016 vote in favour of Britain leaving the European Union (EU) has resulted in a period of angst for UK academia in the face of uncertainties about access to European research funding – for example the €80 billion earmarked for the Horizon 2020 programme, an excellent resource for those who have learned how to access it. Coupled with shrinking resources, this event precipitated a review of specialist Research Council activity across the board and speculation as to where the UK contribution to the EU research pot would finally go. The result seems likely to be a relative growth in cross-council funding, a strategic push on interdisciplinarity and industry impact and the exploration of complex issues such as cities (Keith,

2017). This has created favourable conditions for the future of research in the built environment, but only for as long as the funds remain in place.

4.3 Construction research in the UK

It is widely felt that research in the built environment is not all it should be, as Green's book *Making Sense of Construction Improvement* makes clear (Green, 2011). In 1921 the Building Research Station (BRS) was set up, one of a series of government research organizations aimed at bringing the benefits of applied science to industry, and it was a significant moment for the formalizing of construction research. It began with experiments in traditional materials such as stone and thatch before moving on to geotechnical and structural engineering and then to the effect of bombs and explosions in WWII, with studies broadening out to encompass building physics, lighting and acoustics (including human factors) in the post-war years (Courtney, 1997, 2002). The height of the effort was in 1947, when the BRS employed over 300 people, but it slackened off thereafter (Figure 4.1).

The cheery post-World War II years are portrayed as a period when construction research 'enjoyed widespread and uncritical support' (Lansley, 1997, p. 320) and a pinnacle of research funding (Darke and Darke, 1979) as work was undertaken to develop methods to facilitate the speed and economy of the reconstruction. During this era there was a major push on codes of practice, standardization and non-traditional forms of construction, resulting in the creation of new directorates of Post-War Building, and Building Materials within the portfolio of the Minister of Works – a dedicated ministry being indicative of the support given to construction and infrastructure at that time.

Figure 4.1
The Building Research Station's first home, the Labs at East Acton. Reproduced with the permission of the BRE.

Research in the 1950s was focused on improving the functional relationship between space and activities, as well as the improved development of environment control. 'Each study was securely financed to its conclusion, and the pressures of the design/build process were taken off in the interests of careful testing of the proposed solutions' (Musgrove et al., 1975, p. 41). The experimental building system for the Hertfordshire Schools Programme was, for example, financed by the Ministry of Education (Keath, 1983).

In 1963 the National Joint Consultative Committee of Architects, Quantity Surveyors and Builders 'called a conference at Cambridge, representative of the whole building industry' (Tavistock Institute, 1966, p. 13). The outcome was a strategy, on an industry-wide scale, to develop The Building Industry Communications Research Project, the funds drawn almost equally from industry and government sources. Led by the Tavistock Institute, its primary intellectual aim was to develop theory in the context of practice (Duffy, 2008). The two-year project ran out of money along the way, but not before it had come to the conclusion that 'if the building industry is to reach the degree of efficiency it should attain … not only should there be greater co-operation between its various indispensable elements, but that co-operation must be based on knowledge and not merely on hunches' (Tavistock Institute, 1966, ix). Just how this 'long-term fundamental research' was to be paid for remains a key question.

The government became increasingly focused on technical and planning research in the 1970s, leaving the universities and the then polytechnic (now 'New University') schools of architecture to fill in the gaps (Musgrove et al., 1975). As there was little incentive for the schools to engage in research at that time, this was done in the rather haphazard and 'diffuse' way (Broadbent et al., 1970; Samuel, 2014) still common in countries where research is not actively promoted. Things were to become considerably worse as the monetarist policies of the Conservative government kicked in in the early 1980s. The translation of the BRS into the privatized Building Research Establishment, an important force in construction research to this day, has been chronicled in painful detail (Lansley, 1997).

Investment in research in construction relative to other industries has traditionally been low (Powell, 1996). External income for Architecture, Built Environment and Planning Research in UK universities amounted to £43.2 million in 2012/13, only 7.4% of this coming from industry (GLA Economics, 2017, p. 41). Groak marvels at how the industry can have invested so little in research and development (R & D) while still remaining as adaptable and innovative as it has. He suggests that hidden within the building process is a large network of 'informal or *de facto* R & D workers' who are not employed as researchers and would 'probably be surprised to be told that their work was in R & D' (Groak, 1992, p. 179). 'The sadness is that this informal R & D cohort do not mesh with the formally funded R & D programmes. In future each will increasingly need the other' (Groak, 1992, p.180).

The built environment is an interdisciplinary problem, yet, as Harvey has observed, 'Sociologists, economists, geographers, architects, city planners, and so on, all appear to plough lonely furrows and to live in their own confined conceptual worlds' (Harvey, 1973, p. 22). A special 2008 edition of the highly rated peer-reviewed journal *Building Research and Information* set out with clarity the need for 'models and processes of research that can assist with addressing the complexity and vast theoretical territory constituting the built environment' (Duffy, 2008, p. 655). Work is needed at multiple levels to enable the construction professions to develop a shared, reflexive, rigorous and efficient research culture, one that has the power to influence policy and research funders in positive ways while allowing for greater interdisciplinary connection.

4.4 Architecture research in UK universities

Is the study of the built environment a subject in its own right or is it simply the meeting ground for a number of disciplines? Should environmental studies be a loose faculty arrangement in the university, with architecture as one of a number of 'related disciplines' grouped around a problem area? Or is there some sense in which the study of the built environment can arise naturally from the activity of architecture (Hillier and Leaman, 1976)? The names of university departments across Britain and the situation of architecture within them sometimes reflect ideological differences about the character of research in the construction industry – my title is 'Professor of Architecture in the Built Environment', though people constantly change it to 'and the Built Environment', a subtle but significant distancing between the two. Titles also reflect the diversity of opinion about what constitutes 'architecture', a subject I will return to in Chapter 6.

There has been a long-term aspiration, largely unrealized for financial reasons, that every architecture school should have a 'Building Laboratory' which systematically explores more technical issues within the field – 'The ghost of the missing Building Laboratory, symbolising the range of architectural engagement that is not primarily aesthetic, hovers over the artistic basis of schools to this day' (Powers, 2015, p. 10). Many schools of architecture, for example that at the University of Sheffield, were built on and around strengths in technical research with clear overlaps into engineering and the sciences (Blundell-Jones, 2008) in collaboration with key practices such as the Building Design Partnership (BDP). Others, for example the University of Liverpool, were able to leverage funding from manufacturers to form bodies such as the Pilkington Research Unit, which began business in 1959 (Manning, 1965), and the Nuffield Foundation.

In 1965 the Royal Institute of British Architecture (RIBA) conducted a survey of current research in schools of architecture, the results of which 'could then be summarized on a single sheet of paper' (Broadbent et al., 1970, p. 3), an extremely disappointing result. The journal *Research and Teaching* was set up to correct this situation, to provide an outlet for university-located research and facilitate the 'application of research findings to design practice and teaching' (Broadbent et al., 1970, p. 3), but its existence was brief, a sorry reflection on 'the ability of researchers, practitioners and educators themselves to sustain a high level of constructive discourse, criticism and collaboration in improving the knowledge base of their work' (Musgrove et al., 1975). Fragmentary knowledge of diverse quality continues to pile up in 'a heap, not a structure' (Rapoport, 1982, p. 278), rendering it largely useless.

Architectural researchers have long been dogged by difficulties in convincing funders of the worth of their activities. This begins at the very start of the process when submitting a funding bid. Applicants have to choose their panel based on a list of expertise (for example OECD, 2007) in which architecture is nowhere to be seen. It is at this point that they are faced with the conundrum as to whether the bid should be assessed by an art, engineering or social science panel when in reality it should sit somewhere in between. Time and time again I have seen architecture-based bids being given a mediocre mark by reviewers with little or no understanding of what it is that architects do, when it is well known that excellent marks across the board are vital to ensure funding. Getting into a panel where architecture is understood and valued is crucial, as is the inclusion of architectural panellists (a rare breed).

Architecture schools generally submit their work to the Built Environment Panel of the REF, meaning that their work is scrutinized by a variety of experts from across the construction industry. The panel has always resisted the use of 'impact factors' such as the number of times a paper has been cited by other researchers or other indicators of esteem to establish the quality of work, relying instead on members of the panel reading hundreds if not thousands of submissions in an extremely short time. It would be impractical to use 'impact factors' in architecture as the discipline has never really played this game, perhaps because of the diversity of its outputs (meaning that data cannot readily be collected) or perhaps because of a potentially embarrassing seeming lack of impact. A window into the impact of architectural research is given by the SCImago Journal and Country Rank, which shows the impact of research across the globe. The highly esteemed *Journal of Architecture*, for example, has a Scientific Journal Ranking of 2.9 while the top world journal has a rating of 37.384, an extremely crude indicator of the relative insignificance of our knowledge (SCImago, 2007), which must in part be attributed to the opacity of architecture's methods and the indistinct nature of its knowledge base, as described in Chapter 3.

The REF in its earliest days paid attention principally to the 'outputs' of academics, with 'textbooks' or teaching materials largely excluded from consideration. This has been problematic for a number of reasons, not least that pedagogical and knowledge exchange activity, being complex, localized, people-oriented and messy, is risky to submit; it is difficult to give it the coveted gloss of 'global' significance and rigour so necessary to satisfy the most picky of peer reviewers. There was a general feeling that the safest kinds of submissions were highly academic, well-referenced and rigorous and, ideally, were published in peer-reviewed journals – an alien source of knowledge for most architects. A key moment for architectural education was the 2001 REF, in which the technically oriented Cardiff University was announced as the top architecture school in the Built Environment Unit of Assessment 33 (RAE, 2001), to the surprise of certain other schools and even some members of the press. A subsequent post-mortem revealed that more work needed to be done on mastering the submission of design research or built projects to the panel. This forced extensive debate on the nature of design research, as discussed in Chapter 3, and a general recognition that design needed to be aligned with normative research methodologies if it was to enter into dialogue with other disciplines (Till, 2007). From then on, much as in Art and Design disciplines, a project, exhibition, walk or event could be presented to the REF accompanied by a written statement on the nature of research encapsulated therein. The significance of this moment was that architects were at last starting to claim a territory of knowledge of their own.

The way in which research has developed in universities has contributed to a highly destructive cultural chasm between architectural academia and its profession (Musgrove, 1974; Duffy, 2008; Kirk Hamilton and Watkins, 2009; Samuel et al., 2013) and other stakeholders (Burney and Claflin, 2015). Indeed it forced architects in academia (myself included) to give up practice in order to gain the necessary PhDs and publications that would secure their advancement. This compounded an artificial and unhelpful division between research and teaching in many schools (van Schaik et al., 2010), with the subsequent impacts on education that will be discussed in Chapter 10. Doing a PhD for four years on top of a seven-year architectural training is a lot to ask for. While many are fully aware of the disgraceful situation in which architectural practices ask students and interns to work for free, what is less well publicized is the hardships suffered by architects hoping to enter academia (Cayer et al., 2016). The situation would be greatly improved if work in practice was considered to be research. At the same time, post-doctoral researchers returning to practice sometimes have to play down their research achievements and hide their skills in order to re-enter in an office environment (Murray, 2002).

Architecture schools are often marginalized within universities because the subject sits 'outside the dominant research based model developed from the sciences'. University architecture departments have been dominated by practitioners rather than traditional academics until very recently (McClean, 2009, p. 28), the result being that 'as a discipline [architecture] has suffered from low levels of respect from an institutional perspective' (McClean, 2009, p. 29). A considerable amount of my time is spent trying to convince sceptical non-architect academics that their architectural colleagues' efforts in research are worthy of reward through jobs and promotion. The result of this is that you don't generally find architects at the top of the academic tree as Pro Vice Chancellors or similar. Architectural knowledge is poorly understood or respected in an academic context. As an aside, this may be why so many schools of architecture have so little say concerning the activities of their university's estates department. It seems all wrong that universities should ignore the potential of high-quality architecture while happily accepting the fees of architectural students.

None of this is helped by radical divergences of opinion on what constitutes research globally, or even within London. The research culture of the Architectural Association (AA), which remains outside the Research Assessment process, and its near neighbour the Bartlett School at University College London are very different. The former is part of a star system of global research, often driven by tacit knowledge, the latter is an active participant in shaping the Research Assessment game and is therefore committed to dissemination by academic outputs. A tweet from UK-based architectural critic Oliver Wainwright prompted by the news that the then director of the AA was moving to become Dean of the School of Arts and Architecture at UCLA in the USA seems relevant here: 'interesting to see if the Architectural Association will now engage with the real world or drift further into meaningless obscurity' (15.12.2016). While countries such as Australia, Hong Kong and Sweden have taken a strong interest in UK Research Excellence, other countries, most notably the USA, operate quite differently. What is considered good research globally is heavily skewed by cultural capital and architectural preferences for research that is pleasing to the architect's eye. This then feeds back into ideas about what is good architecture.

4.5 Research in practice

Broadly speaking there are three different generic research activities that currently take place in practice: knowledge management, including post-occupancy evaluation (POE); design development; and research projects (Samuel et al., 2013). That the term 'research' has long been conflated with 'technical research' in the minds of many architects can be seen from a special edition of the *Architectural Review* edited by Peter Manning, then Research Editor of the *Architects' Journal* (Manning, 1965, p. 192). It is salutary to look through classic architectural management texts such as *The Architect in Practice*, which contains not one single reference to research or knowledge development (Chappell and Willis, 2005). Research has always been fundamental to the most innovative types of practice (as implied by Jencks's 'Evolutionary Tree', Figure 3.2), but it has rarely been articulated as such. It is therefore notably lacking from most historical accounts. An early example (1836) is a prizewinning essay by George Godwin on the history and uses of concrete in the *Transactions of the Institute of British Architects* (Godwin, 2017). Almost 100 years later another pioneer of concrete, Le Corbusier, described his practice as an 'atelier of patient research' and encouraged the Congrès Internationaux d'Architecture Moderne to present their work using the famous CIAM grid. Urban research was presented in a uniform tabular format for ease of comparison (Avermaete, 2008, p. 114). It is worth noting that the USA-based Graham Foundation funded some extremely influential research work from both UK and USA-based architects including Archigram's *Instant City* (1964), Reyner Banham's *Los Angeles: The Architecture of the Four Ecologies* (1971) and Robert Venturi's extraordinarily influential book *Complexity and Contradiction in Architecture* (1966) (Varnelis, 2007). Venturi, Scott Brown and Izenour's subsequent book *Learning from Las Vegas* was the product of a 'research studio' that they tutored jointly at Yale University in the autumn of 1968 (Stierli, 2008, p. 48). Rem Koolhaas's book *Delirious New York* (1978) is another example of 'polemical architectural "research"', leading to the development of a methodology utilized by his practice Office of Metropolitan Architecture (OMA) 'of transferring Manhattan's genetic code onto the field of their various projects' (Simpson, 2008, p. 12). The profession has always been methodologically minded, using 'concepts' and 'ideas' as the armature of design.

As mentioned in Chapter 2, a great many architects in the early twentieth century were 'salaried', working for government or councils across Britain, some of them in government-funded research institutions. At that time, because of their position within local authorities, architects were often 'concerned with the creation of a large number of good buildings rather than a few exceptional ones' and therefore had 'an unusually extensive involvement in designing the total built product' (Hillier and Leaman, 1972, p. 517). A mass production approach meant that time and effort could be put into research and development. The guarantee of large contracts then made it feasible to develop off-site building systems in factories, a high-investment procedure. As councils and government departments began to shed their architects from the 1980s, the profession had to reposition itself into private practice. At this point research and innovation became nice-to-haves rather than vital ingredients. That the profession was unable to reconstitute its innovation effort within the context of private practice has been ascribed to the 'inefficiency and folly' of architects (Powell, 1996, p. 173). It has also been argued that the standard agreed fee structure based on the contract sum, then prevailing, made economy, itself an incentive for innovation, unattractive (Bowley, 1966).

The construction industry suffers from 'weak linkage to the research communities when compared with medicine and other professions' (The Edge, 2016). There are a number of major hindrances to the development of work in practice including a hostility to the word 'research' with its overly academic associations (Dye, 2014), lack of research training in architecture schools, lack of investment in research (Lu and Sexton, 2009), lack of support from the academic community, as mentioned above, and a 'papyrophobic' reluctance to commit experiments to paper in a systematic manner (Groak, 1992, p. 170). However, practitioners themselves believe that the most relevant and innovative research is happening in practice (Samuel et al., 2013) and 'Research performed by practitioners has an important role to play in the development of the field' (Kirk Hamilton and Watkins, 2009, p. 39). Unfortunately it is difficult to verify this supposition or to access this research, as so few practitioners write up their experiments. If practitioners publish research, it tends to be in 'grey literature', documents which are produced by government departments, academic institutions, private companies and more. Yet, as a recent Australian study has shown, although the community spends in excess of $30 billion a year on projects which produce grey literature, a standardized mechanism for ordering it or finding it is lacking (McCallum, 2016), nor are these industry outputs searchable through library databases, the result being that their impact is minimal.

I was fortunate to be part of a focus group leading up to the RIBA report *Architects and Research-based Knowledge* (RIBA, 2014), in which it became apparent that the last place practitioners look for knowledge is academic refereed journals, their preferred sources being Google or their colleague at the next table. Academic knowledge rarely makes it into the industry press and, until the recent UK requirement for free open access, refereed journals were too costly for practices to access. Even if practitioners did access them, they often found the writing inaccessible and unfamiliar. Fortunately the curation and distribution of such knowledge in a user-friendly format is under way, led by the cross-construction industry think tank The Edge (2016).

4.6 RIBA and the institutions

One of the key purposes of the RIBA, as stated in its Charter, is 'information and enquiry'. In its beginnings the objective of being a learned society was taken very seriously by the RIBA, partly in an effort to outdo its nearest competitor, the Architectural Society (Mace, 1986), and the resultant growth of the library caused the Institute to move to a larger building in 1845. At that time the RIBA developed a custom of discussing 'learned papers on a great variety of artistic, archaeological historical, scientific and technical subjects' at its 'Ordinary General Meetings', which were then published in the *Transactions* (Mace, 1986, p. xvii).

At its foundation, Professor Robert Kerr, an active Fellow of the RIBA, suggested that the 'academical' work of the Institute, at that time unrelated, should be pulled together in four large 'standing committees for Art, Science, Practice and Literature' (Mace, 1986, p. xx). Art was concerned with design, archaeology and conservation; Science was concerned with construction and technical issues; Practice was concerned with business and procurement; and Literature included the library, the lectures and overseas relationships. The presence of 'academical' work within Practice was an important innovation subsequently lost. What appears to have been missing, or subsumed within 'Literature', was an overarching concern for the curatorship of architectural knowledge as a whole.

The body that represents research at the RIBA, which I will refer to as the 'Research Group', has morphed slowly over the years: from the Intelligence Unit (which included Hillier and Leaman), to the RIBA Research Steering Group in 1976 and to the RIBA Research and Development Committee (2004), and to the Research and Innovation Group in 2010, each name reflecting the buzzwords of that time (Hay et al., 2018). A point that has been made repeatedly by the group is the urgent need for a 'conceptual framework for research' in architecture to encourage 'continuous critical analysis or the assumptions on which research is based, rather than a conclusion to the debate' (Broadbent et al., 1970, p. 5). Another repetitive mantra has been the need to improve connections between practice and academic research (Duffy and Worthington, 1977, p. 9), increasingly driven apart by academic procedure. As RIBA President (1993–1995), Frank Duffy was also instrumental in driving 'architectural knowledge' up the agenda of the Institute (Duffy, 1998), but this good work was quickly dismantled by others. The President is in post for two years – a very short period to implement significant change even if they hit the ground running.

The structure and hierarchy of RIBA committees is indicative of the status of the knowledge within the Institution's remit. In the UK, architects are compulsorily members of the Architects Registration Board (ARB) and, by choice, a member of the RIBA. As an RIBA member, an architect will belong to one of its regions (and it is important to remember that London too is a region). Regional, national and international members can put themselves up for election to the RIBA Council. The Council delegates administrative power to the Board, which includes a set of elected Vice Presidents and is chaired by the President in close association with the Chief Executive, who runs the business aspects of the Charity. Each Vice President chairs one of seven committees, each of which builds on the work of several advisory groups. The Practice Committee is extreme in encompassing 13 advisory groups, one of which is Research and Innovation, which until recently had very little connection with the policy arm of the institution. The creation of a new Vice President for Research role in September 2017 at the instigation of the President Ben Derbyshire brings research to the top table of the RIBA and is an extremely important opportunity.

The RIBA has an excellent conduit for disseminating architectural research in international policy circles through the international networks of which it is a part. Among the Vice Presidents of the RIBA is the Vice President International, who works closely with staff members in the RIBA to connect to the Architects' Council of Europe (ACE) and the European Forum for Architectural Policies (EFAP). ACE is very active in the European research scene, much of its work focusing on technological aspects of sustainability. ACE and EFAP are in turn connected through membership of the global organization International Union of Architects (UIA), which has five chapters across the world (and a very large congress once every three years).

The institutions play an extremely important role in disseminating high-quality research to practice. They need to make research easy and impactful for practitioners and universities, an issue that came to the fore with the UK Edge report *Collaboration for Change* (Morrell, 2015). Organizations such as the RIBA are regularly asked to comment on policy issues but because of resources they are very selective about the issues that they can address.

Institutions need to make research-based speculations on what information will be needed and have solutions at the ready, produced as a result of an effective institutional knowledge policy.

> As a major procurer of buildings and services, Government should play a lead role in encouraging high design standards and sharing best practice with the private sector. Ministers should co-ordinate the work of research councils to promote longitudinal studies into the built environment, especially post-occupancy evaluation and learning, as well as investigating long-term trends.
> (Design Commission, 2017, p. 7)

The government needs the right information from the institutions to make this happen. It needs to know 'what works' (LSE, 2017), a question which the profession is singularly unprepared to answer at this time.

Conclusion

It is necessary to shed old preconceptions of what research is or might be if the profession is to trace its impact, learn from its mistakes and plan for its future. In this chapter I have examined some of the structural reasons that underpin architecture's dysfunctional research culture, manifested in a disconnect between practice and academia, and have shown how in the UK government policy has forced universities to be explicit about the nature, quality and impact of their work, a pressure for which both architectural academics and practitioners are poorly prepared. While architects remain unclear about what their knowledge might look like and where it might be going, their research culture remains inaccessible to others, the result being its continued atrophy with long-term impacts on the profession, the construction industry more widely, related academic fields and indeed the quality of our built environment.

Equally importantly, research makes practice much more intellectually stimulating and purposeful. My experience of being a practitioner in the 1980s, not helped by being at the bottom of the pile in a recession, was that architecture was a brain-numbing activity, its tediousness unalloyed by cycles of REM on my Walkman. This should not be the case.

References

Avermaete, T., 2008. 'A Web of Research on Socio-Plastics: Team 10 and the Critical Framing of Everyday Urban Environments', in: Geiser, R. (ed.), *Explorations*. Birkhauser, Basel, pp. 114–115.

Battelle, 2013. '2014 Global R & D Funding Forecast'. www.battelle.org/docs/default-source/misc/2014-rd-funding-forecast.pdf?sfvrsn=2

Beck, U., 1986. *Risk Society: Towards a New Modernity*. Sage, London.

BIS, 2015. *Fulfilling Our Potential: Teaching Excellence, Social Mobility and Student Choice*. Department for Business and Innovation, London.

Blundell-Jones, P., 2008. *University of Sheffield: School of Architecture 1908–2008*. University of Sheffield.

Bowley, M., 1966. *The British Building Industry: Four Studies in Response and Resistance to Change*. Cambridge University Press, Cambridge.

Broadbent, G., Hillier, B., Lipman, A., MacLeod, R., Musgrove, J., O'Sullivan, P., Wilson, B., 1970. 'Editorial'. *Architectural Research and Teaching*, 1, pp. 2–5.

Buchli, V., 2013. *An Anthropology of Architecture*. Berg, London; New York.

Burney, D., Claflin, A., 2015. 'Practical Considerations for Implementing Research on the Indoor Built Environment'. *Building Research and Information*, 44, 3, pp. 342–344.

Campbell, H., 2012. 'Research in Architecture Scoping Study 2012: Government Policy on Architecture 2009–2015'. Department of Arts, Heritage and the Gaelteacht, University College Dublin.

Cayer, A., Deamer, P., Korsh, S., Petersen, E., Shvartzberg, M. (eds), 2016. 'Asymmetric Labors: The Economy of Architecture in Theory and Practice'. www.academia.edu/28002267/Asymmetric_Labors_The_Economy_of_Architecture_in_Theory_and_Practice

Chappell, D., Willis, A., 2005. *The Architect in Practice*. Blackwell, Oxford.

Courtney, R., 2002. 'Implications of the Fairclough Review for UK Building Research'. *Building Research and Information*, 30, 5, pp. 322–327.

Courtney, R., 1997. 'Building Research Establishment: Past, Present and Future'. *Building Research and Information*, 25, 5, pp. 285–291.

Darke, J., Darke, R., 1979. *Who Needs Housing?* Macmillan, London.

Design Commission, 2017. *People and Places*. www.policyconnect.org.uk/apdig/research/design-commission-people-and-places-design-built-environment-and-behaviour

Duffy, F., 2008. 'Forum Linking Theory Back to Practice'. *Building Research and Information*, 36, 6, pp. 655–658.

Duffy, F., 1998. *Architectural Knowledge: The Idea of a Profession*. Spon, London.

Duffy, F., Worthington, J., 1977. 'Organizational Design'. *Journal of Architectural Research*, 6, 1, pp. 4–9.

Dye, A., 2014. *Architects and Research-based Knowledge*. RIBA, London.

Edge, The, 2016. 'Edge Report 2016'. www.edgedebate.com/wp-content/uploads/2017/01/edge-report-2016.pdf

GLA Economics, 2017. 'London's Architectural Sector' (Working paper 86). www.london.gov.uk/business-and-economy-publications/londons-architectural-sector

Godwin, G., 2017 [1836]. 'From the Transactions of the Institute of British Architects'. Reproduced in the *Journal of Architecture*, 22, 1, pp. 153–183.

Green, S.D., 2011. *Making Sense of Construction Improvement: A Critical Review*. Wiley Blackwell, Chichester.

Groak, S., 1992. *The Idea of Building: Thought and Action in the Design and Production of Buildings*. Taylor & Francis, Oxford.

Harvey, D., 1973. *Social Justice and the City*. Edward Arnold, London.

Hay, R., Shasore, N., Samuel, F., 2018. 'Research at the RIBA: An Institutional History 1958–1971'. *Architectural Research Quarterly*, forthcoming.

HEFCE, 2017. 'How We Fund Research'. www.hefce.ac.uk/rsrch/funding/mainstream

Hillier, B., Leaman, A., 1976. 'Architecture as a Discipline'. *Journal of Architectural Research*, 5, pp. 28–32.

Hillier, B., Leaman, A., 1972. 'New Approaches to Architectural Research'. *RIBA Journal*, 79, pp. 517–521.

Keath, M.P., 1983. 'The Development of School Construction Systems in Hertfordshire 1946–1964'. Unpublished PhD thesis, Thames Polytechnic, London. http://gala.gre.ac.uk/8740/1/Michael_P._K._Keath_1983.pdf

Keith, M., 2017. 'Urban Research and Policy Priorities', presentation at Urban Living Lab Symposium, 33 Finsbury Square London, 27 January.

Kirk Hamilton, D., Watkins, D., 2009. *Evidence-based Design for Multiple Building Types*. Wiley and Son, New York.

Kuhn, T., 1962. *The Structure of Scientific Revolutions*. University of Chicago Press, Chicago.

Lansley, P.R., 1997. 'The Impact of BRE's Commercialisation on the Research Community'. *Building Research and Information*, 25, 5, pp. 301–312.

Latour, B., 1998. 'From the World of Science to the World of Research?' *Science*, 280, pp. 208–209.

Leski, K., 2015. *The Storm of Creativity*. MIT Press, Cambridge, MA.

LSE, 2017. 'Two Year Extension of What Works Centre for Local Economic Growth'. www.lse.ac.uk/News/Latest-news-from-LSE/2017/07-July-2017/What-Works-Centre-for-Local-Economic-Growth-awarded-additional-funding (accessed 4.8.17).

Lu, S., Sexton, M., 2009. *Innovation in Small Professional Practices in the Built Environment*. Wiley Blackwell, Oxford.

Mace, A., 1986. *The Royal Institute of British Architects: A Guide to its Archive and History*. Mansell, London.

Mallory-Hill, S., Preiser, W.F.E., Watson, C. (eds), 2012. *Enhancing Building Performance*. Wiley, Hoboken, NJ.

Manning, P., 1965. 'Hard Facts on Research'. *Architects' Journal*, 20 January, pp. 192–209.

McCallum, T., 2016. 'How Australia Produces $30 Billion Worth of "Grey Literature" that We Can't Read'. The Conversation. http://theconversation.com/how-australia-produces-30-billion-worth-of-grey-literature-that-we-cant-read-56584 (accessed 27. 4.16).

McClean, D., 2009. 'Embedding Learner Independence in Architecture Education: Reconsidering Design Studio'. Unpublished PhD thesis, Robert Gordon University, Glasgow.

Morrell, P., 2015. *Collaboration for Change*. Edge, London.

Murray, G., 2002. 'Teaching, Research and Practice: Establishing a Productive Balance'. *ARQ Architectural Research Quarterly*, 6, 4, pp. 297–299.

Musgrove, J., 1974. 'Editorial'. *Journal of Architectural Research*, 4, 1, p. 3.

Musgrove, J., O'Sullivan, P., Territ, C., Hillier, B., Leaman, A., 1975. 'Architectural Research: Problems of Organization and Funding in the United Kingdom'. *Journal of Architectural Research*, 4, 2, pp. 41–46.

Nowotny, H., Scott, P., Gibbons, M., 2001. *Rethinking Science: Knowledge and the Public in an Age of Uncertainty*. Wiley, London.

OECD, 2007. 'Revised Field of Science and Technology (FOS) Classification in the Frascati Manual'. www.oecd.org/science/inno/38235147.pdf

Powell, C., 1996. *The British Building Industry since 1800: An Economic History*. Routledge, Oxford.

Powers, A., 2015. 'The Fiction of Architectural Education', in: *Radical Pedagogies*. RIBA Publishing, Newcastle-upon-Tyne, p. 4.

RAE, 2008. 'History of the RAE'. www.rae.ac.uk/aboutus/history.asp

RAE, 2001. 'RAE 2001: Results UOA 33'. www.rae.ac.uk/2001/results/byuoa/43.htm

Rapoport, A., 1982. *The Meaning of the Built Environment*. Sage, Beverly Hills, CA.

Ray, N., 2008. 'Studio Teaching for a Social Purpose'. *Open House International*, 33, pp. 18–25.

RIBA, 2014. *Architects and Research-based Knowledge*. www.architecture.com/-/media/gathercontent/architects-and-research-based-knowledge/additional-documents/architectsandresearchbasedknowledgeliteraturereviewpdf.pdf (accessed 27.4.16).

Samuel, F., 2014. 'The Way We Were: The Changing Relationship of Research and Design'. *RIBA Journal*. www.ribaj.com/intelligence/the-way-we-were

Samuel, F., Coucill, L., Tait, A., Dye, A., 2013. *RIBA Home Improvements: Report on Research in Housing Practice*. RIBA.

Schon, D., 1984. *The Reflective Practitioner: How Professionals Think in Action*. Basic Books, New York.

Schweber, L., 2016. 'Putting Theory to Work: The Use of Theory in Construction Research'. *Construction Management and Economics*, 33, 10, pp. 840–860.
SCImago, 2007. *SJR — SCImago Journal & Country Rank*. www.scimagojr.com
Simpson, D., 2008. 'Performative Modernities: Rem Koolaas's Delirious New York as Inductive Research', in: Geiser, R. (ed.), *Explorations*. Birkhauser, Basel, pp. 12–13.
Snow, C.P., 1998/1959. *The Two Cultures*. Canto Classics, Cambridge.
Stierli, M., 2008. 'Methodology: Historical Case Study', in: Geiser, R. (ed.), *Explorations*. Birkhauser, Basel, pp. 48–50.
Tavistock Institute, 1966. *Interdependence and Uncertainty (Digest of a Report from the Tavistock Institute to the Building Industry Communication Research Project)*. Tavistock Institution, London.
Till, J., 2007. *What is Architectural Research?* RIBA, London.
van Schaik, L., London, G., George, B., 2010. *Procuring Innovative Architecture*. Routledge, Oxford.
Varnelis, K., 2007. 'Is There Research in the Studio?' *Journal of Architectural Research*, 61, pp. 11–14.

Chapter 5

The value agenda

We are estranged from reality and inclined to treat as valueless everything that we have not made ourselves.

(Schumacher, 1993, p. 3)

Unfortunately the focus of architectural practice is generally on the cost of what it does in the short term rather than its long-term value, arguably its market niche (Wigglesworth, 2006; van Toorn, 2007). Architecture is essentially a holistic activity. Breaking it down into increments of value goes against its very grain unless done with great care. While the demonstration of value will never be an exact science it is one in which architects have to engage if they are to be heard. If a profession is to flourish, it needs to take control of the statistics through which it is presented to those in power, something that can be achieved only with a healthy and critical research culture. While it is very clear that the organic line between research findings and policy has dissolved, our only hope of policy impact lies in speaking the language of its makers (Crossick and Kaszynska, 2016).

There are of course many different types of value, as *The Value Handbook* produced for the Commission for Architecture and the Built Environment (CABE, 2016) makes clear. Examples are exchange value, use value, image value, environmental value and cultural value. This chapter begins with a discussion of the growth of audit culture, focusing on the UK, before examining the ways in which its tendrils have extended into architecture and the wider built environment. It provides the context for Part II, which focuses on how the value of architects might be evidenced.

Value is a contradictory word. On the one hand it is 'the capitalist category par excellence' (Phillips, 2015). On the other, like the architectural conception of transparency, it can be a tool for accountability, and inclusion, but also a medium of control (Groak, 1992). Value is often described as instrumental or intrinsic (Bunting, 2008). Instrumental value lends itself to expression through numbers while 'intrinsic aspects of experience are best evaluated qualitatively, or with a mixture of qualitative and quantitative methods' (Crossick and Kaszynska, 2016). Despite a general recognition that quantitative measures alone are inadequate as a source of information, 'social processes mean that they occupy a privileged position in Western culture' (Nowotny, 2015), the overall result being the advancement of the instrumental over the intrinsic, often played out as artificial debates over dualities such as art versus science, rational versus irrational and spirit versus body when life is never really so black and white.

5.1 Audit culture

Audit always begins with classification, and classifications are 'powerful technologies' that are both 'political and ethical' (Bowker and Leigh Star, 1999). Audit cultures are evidence of the spread of neo-liberal values:

> On the one hand, they accompany high hopes about a transformation of transnational relationships in the direction of good governance and an increasing transparency of the organization of the state and civil society; on the other, they generate the fear that this transformation of liberal morality cloaks a novel order of increasing global inequalities.
>
> (Pels, 2000, p. 136)

In an audit culture, organizational performance is measured against predetermined targets. The basis for government decision-making is the *Green Book* (UK Gov, 2013a), which focuses on cost–benefit analysis, nearly always in the short term. Put simply, 'the worthiness of an intervention' can be 'based on the generated benefits compared to the costs of implementation' (Fujiwara, 2014, p. 8). There is, however, a mismatch between the kind of research produced by academia and the kind of cost–benefit research needed by government (UK Gov, 2013b).

In the UK the government has been 'interested in developing a stronger evidence base to help make decisions about its funding' (Donovan 2013, p. 4). It has also tried to put in place measures that favour types of value other than money, for example the 'Procuring for Growth Balanced Scorecard' (UK Gov, 2016), which, anecdotally, seems to have had little impact. Without a stronger evidence base such initiatives are likely to be fairly meaningless anyway.

Evidence-based information has a powerful pull but, 'as many subjective forces counterbalance objectivity', care must be taken in its presentation to government (Simmons, 2015, p. 407). It is for this reason that the Design Council, which reports to policymakers on the activities of architects and others, purposely aligns its impact measures with that of government, in particular the Creative Industries Economic Estimates (Design Council, 2007).

The problematic nature of defining the value of the arts and culture was the subject of a wide review by the Arts and Humanities Research Council, which funded a range of projects in this area including the Cultural Value of Architecture and Homes and Neighbourhoods Project, the research for which underpins parts of this book. The overall project report written by Crossick and Kaszynska revealed a need for 'multi-criteria analyses and a range of approaches' to express the depth of value of the arts. It acknowledged that, although this type of research was unlikely to produce the kind of simple headline results that are useful for accountability, it had an important role as a tool for learning. At the same time the team observed that much of the evidence available on the value of arts and culture was of little use because it did not meet the 'necessary standards of rigour in specification and research design', a situation which they felt was particularly bad in the field of qualitative research. They questioned a seeming 'hierarchy of evidence', with 'experimental methods and randomized controlled trials' (in other words instrumental quantitative research) being highly favoured over other forms of research even if it was difficult to 'isolate variables' in 'complex situations'. 'The issue is the character of the knowledge and understanding that is being sought, because each approach will have its own benefits and drawbacks' (Crossick and Kaszynska, 2016, p. 8). Qualitative and quantitative research need to be applied discerningly.

A further issue seems to be the magnitude of some of the events that the government is trying to evaluate, for example the 'thousands of pages of data' that went into demonstrating the success of the 'legacy' of the London 2012 Olympics (DCMS, 2012). As we get further and further removed from the models, assumptions and variables at the core of such calculations, it becomes increasingly difficult to critically engage, and headline statistics feel like meaningless soundbites. An incremental case study approach with detailed qualitative as well as quantitative data feels far more convincing, but resists the modelling which policymakers like. Economists – of which there are many schools – are good at developing quantified impacts which slide comfortably into the *Green Book*. However, there is always the danger that researchers render their subjects one-dimensional through the overzealous use of overly simple models and variables that have little relationship with lived experience. The complexity of construction economics is set out in Myers's book of the same name (Myers, 2008). My experience as an academic reviewer has shown me that economists have difficulty in including issues such as design quality in their models, partly because the field of architecture is so opaque, but change appears to be in the air. In this context Ahlfeldt and Homan have made a valiant attempt to financially evaluate the value of an aesthetically pleasing architectural environment using conservation areas in the UK as the locus of study, concluding that 'design value is large' (Ahlfeldt and Holman, 2015, p. 33), while Colander et al. observe that economists are becoming much more used to open transdisciplinary working, questioning the assumptions that lie behind models and relinquishing the supremacy of the economic viewpoint over others (Colander et al., 2004, p. 496). It is time, therefore, to engage with economists in the creation of these models to offer more nuanced interpretations of 'cost' and value.

The advent of the Social Value Act 2012, which requires buildings that are procured with public money to be of demonstrable social value, was an initiative for which architects were notably unprepared (UK Gov, 2012; Battle, 2016). However, adoption of the Act has been inconsistent across local authorities. Small and medium-sized enterprises (SMEs), which are often the organizations left to actually deliver social value outcomes, tend to be unaware of the act and its wider aims (Burke and King, 2015, p. 395).

In the UK construction sector statistical consultants such as Brickonomics provide data to the industry across the board and research consultants are commissioned to write reports, but they need better and more evidence to work with (Green, 2016). There are very few economists with a specific interest in architecture – there are a few working on market predictions within the professional institutions (AIA, 2016); some are engaged with translating the wellbeing aspects of housing in financial terms (Watkins and McMaster, 2011; Fujiwara, 2014); some are engaged in large interdisciplinary firms (ARUP, 2016) and in the teaching and scholarship of planning (Adams and Watkins, 2014) – but more are needed. The impact of investment in construction is categorized according to: impact on economic activity; contribution to employment; and lastly 'benefits of investment' (LEK Consulting, 2009, p. 5).

The statistics for architecture do not make comfortable reading. Architecture is a relatively small sector (DCMS, 2016) in which the majority of people work in extremely small firms (ACE, 2014). It appears to offer very few concrete benefits to governments in search of votes. This contributes to its marginalization from both public debate and policy (Waite, 2014). It seems baffling that, at a time when the creative industries are taking over from financial services as the biggest generator of UK gross domestic product (GDP) (Cadman, 2016), the market share of architects appears to be decreasing. Is this related to a drop in the number of architects from a peak of 58,322 in 2013 to 43,702 in 2016 (Green, 2016)? Even allowing for the fact that these were recessionary years, is it right that the export value of architecture barely changed during the years 2009–13 (DCMS, 2016, p. 28)? Furthermore, how could it be that architecture accounted for only 4% of the 'Gross Value Added' of the creative industries overall in 2015 (GLA Economics, 2017, p. 16)? The profession needs to help the government answer such questions. An Australian study on the 'value add' of architecture concluded that 'architectural services are conservatively underreported by 15%, and that more than AUD 1 billion (15.43% of industry revenue) is not accounted for in the sector when the areas of technology development, business development, cultural contribution and education are considered' (Reinmuth et al., 2016). The problem is not just one of architecture's performance; it also relates to how that performance is measured.

Many architects are sceptical about the need for research to prove what they feel to be 'common sense' (Watson, 2016). The trouble is that their view of common sense can differ greatly from that of others (Darke, 1984). The value of quantitative research has recently been subject to extensive feminist debate (Spierings, 2012). I place temporary emphasis on quantitative evidence, often treated with suspicion in architecture, but, as Lisanne Gibson argues, there is a case for instrumental value discussions when organizations are internally divided and persist in paying lip service to the political imperative of being more inclusive (Gibson, 2008). I argue that the profession – notorious for its exclusivity in terms of gender, race and class – is a case in point and it is time for the field to see its own impact expressed in stark, rigorous, instrumental terms as a wake-up call.

5.2 Design value in the UK context

Such is the complexity of this issue that most discussions of value in architecture foundered in a quagmire of theory (Benedikt, 1997; Saunders, 2007). However, such debates have to be set temporarily to one side or saved for an architectural audience as policymakers and clients, the patrons of architects, don't generally share in such critical niceties.

The recent history of construction in the UK has been one in which quantitative performance indicators such as economic performance dominate through 'value management' (BSI, 2000), 'value engineering' (Kelly et al., 2010) and 'value analysis' (Designing Buildings Wiki, 2017), 'an approach by which supposed sub-systems in a design are further optimized against a constant performance requirement' (Groak, 1992, p. 93). The problem here is that the 'constant performance requirement' rarely takes into account the long-term impact of good design. Value engineering works hand in hand with management frameworks such as risk assessment, which anticipate and reduce problems. Little consideration is given to the long-term risks of buildings that are damaging to wellbeing and the environment, as these are not the problem of the project manager and are paid for out of somebody else's budget.

Although critical of what he sees as a peculiarly nineteenth-century tendency to reduce projects to their constituent elements, Groak (1992, p. 101) lists some of the ways in which a building might typically be evaluated financially:

- Land costs;
- Infrastructure costs;
- Initial building costs;
- Disruption costs (e.g. decanting employees during construction work);
- Fitting-out costs (including the expensive machines now installed in many buildings);
- Refitting or rehabilitation costs;
- Running and maintenance costs;
- Potential rent or sale value or other income from the building;
- Potential asset value;
- Opportunity costs (i.e. of alternative projects which could have been financed from the same resources);
- The cost of employing the people to work in the building over its useful life.

Here little or no consideration is given to third-party value (Loe, 2000, p. 19), intangible factors such as place or organizational branding benefits, or the impact of the building on a city or on the environment or on the people who inhabit it. Nor do assessments take into consideration the interconnections between different factors, the relationship between good design and long-term asset value being one. The 'price' of a project depends on the 'the culture of the building industry on a very local basis', but this highly unreliable figure is then 'the target to which the organization aims rather than a true description of real costs' (Groak, 1992, p. 103).

During the late 1990s the value of design had a powerful champion in the form of New Labour Deputy Prime Minister John Prescott (under Tony Blair), who believed that 'in the broadest sense [good design] is the key to respect for people whether they be users of the building or passers-by' (Macmillan, 2004, p. 4). One result was the foundation of CABE, its aim being to bring about a real improvement in design quality, while its creation was in fact a thinly disguised ploy to temper the damaging excesses of enterprise culture, in other words the prioritizing of financial value above everything else ushered in by the Egan Report (Punter, 2011). At the same time the then government's Better Public Buildings Group made a commitment to improving the design of publicly funded buildings, notably housing (Punter, 2011). Such developments existed in parallel with an expanding interest in the health benefits of a good environment, a narrative which continues to gain momentum (The King's Fund, 2017).

The 2006 CABE *Value Handbook* appears to mark a pinnacle in the organization's optimism, the authors advising local authority planners to 'use value rather than cost when making the business case' (CABE, 2006, p. 10), a sentiment that seems to have been largely ignored for reasons that will emerge in this book. CABE's research team played a pivotal role in developing an evidence base for good design across an extensive field of activity including health, education, housing, public space, commercial properties, the value of design, sustainability and inclusive design. It published over 80 reports and developed an online resource that documented almost 400 case studies. Its projects were classified by theme across sectors including public space and building, homes, neighbourhoods and cultural change, and also according to the types of research they entailed. A further strand attempted to influence the research of organizations such as the Royal Institute of British Architects (RIBA), Department of Trade & Industry, the Building Services Research and Information Association (BSRIA) and the Town and Country Planning Association through collaborative projects (Warwick, 2014). These CABE outputs were accompanied by an 'unprecedented flow of policy pronouncements and plans, monitoring reports and evaluation studies' and the 'bewildering' initiatives that came into being during this period' (Punter, 2011, p. 2). At the same time CABE had to navigate a difficult political line between the innovative capitalist deregulatory vision of the New Right and the egalitarian community ideals of the Old Left (Punter, 2011). As the CABE team negotiated a cocktail of resource reduction and political pressure, their research became variable in its quality (Macmillan, 2005). CABE's work is characteristic of 'corporate social science', which is subject to very different strictures than those of the academy (Taylor, 2016). However, documents such as *What It's Like to Live There: The Views of Residents on the Design of New Housing* (CABE, 2005) and *People and Place: Public Attitudes to Beauty* (Ipsos Mori and CABE, 2010) remain unparalleled. As design lost its hold on the British government with the waning of New Labour, it gained strength in the devolved administration of Scotland, where it became more embedded in national strategies for wellbeing than over the border (Scottish Executive, 2006). The work of CABE has been the subject of a research project based at University College London, 'Design Governance: The CABE Experiment' (Natajaran and Carmona, 2016).

CABE were not the only ones to champion design quality. One of the major achievements during this period was the creation of the Design Quality Indicators tool (Construction Industry Council, 1999) under the leadership of Sunand Prasad

(RIBA President 2007–2009 and founding CABE commissioner), conceived to create a shared language of design as well as a tool for post-occupancy evaluation (POE) to influence the course of what Prasad described as the 'mediocre and worse-than-mediocre architecture and design in both the public and private sector[s]' (Odgers and Samuel, 2010, p. 50). The Design Quality Indicators (DQI), a digital tool for use by project teams, was structured around a framework of three headings: functionality (encompassing use), access and space; build quality (encompassing performance, engineering and construction); and impact (encompassing character and innovation, forms and materials, and internal environment, as well as urban and social integration) (Odgers and Samuel, 2010, p. 43). The DQI seems to have had various teething problems: the briefing stage was problematic as it required the team to imagine the building when it had not yet been designed and it became mandatory for the government Building Schools for the Future programme before it was really ready. Despite the strong advocacy of those who put it to the test, it hasn't achieved prominent uptake across the construction industry. It has, however, continued in another form within the National Health Service as the DQI for Heath (CIC, 2016) and provides an important basis for future action in this area (Whyte and Gann, 2003).

Conclusion

Auditing has changed the way in which professionals conceptualize themselves – 'the audited subject is recast as a depersonalized unit of economic resource whose productivity and performance must constantly be measured and enhanced' (Shore and Wright, 2000, p. 62). With reference to the literature of organizational metaphor (Morgan, 2006), audit culture lends itself to organizations that have a mechanistic self-image, not to a profession that sees itself as a vocation, as does architecture, which often relies on 'bodily kinesthetic' and tacit forms of intelligence (Gardner, 1993).

'The social processes of classification, equivalence and standardization are the basis of any form of numerical valuation and evaluation which they both shape and constrain' (Nowotny, 2015, p. 113). Part of the problem for architects is that they have not played an adequate role in the making of the bald statistics through which their value is perceived. At the same time the field lacks the adequate knowledge base to form a convincing counter-attack against others.

Research is important here as it 'permits a better understanding of different orders of worth and their logics, as well as unveiling the evaluation criteria that bring forth the institutions and social structures that support and enable them' (Nowotny, 2015, p. 113). Questions of 'wellbeing' and its relationship to the built environment need to be faced head on despite all the complexities 'related to data availability, methodologies, selection of variables and, in the case of indexes, weighing of the variables'. Rather than be defeated by the challenge, it is vital to develop research to communicate a message about the impact of the built environment on people's lives to both policymakers and civil society (Brandon and Lombardi, 2010). Architects need to play an active role in the creation of this formula in evolution. Whatever one's political convictions, if we are to see any improvements in the quality of our built environment, there is an urgent need to bridge the gap between the financial models of policy, public perception and the practices of architects in the UK context.

References

ACE, 2014. *The Architectural Profession in Europe*. Architects Council of Europe, Brussels.

Adams, D., Watkins, C., 2014. *The Value of Planning*. RTPI.

Ahlfeldt, G.M., Holman, N., 2015. 'Distinctively Different: A New Approach to Valuing Architectural Amenities', www.spatialeconomics.ac.uk/textonly/SERC/publications/download/sercdp0171.pdf (accessed 18.7.17).

AIA, 2016. 'Practicing Architecture: Economics'. www.aia.org/practicing/economics/index.htm

ARUP, 2016. 'Economics and Planning'. www.arup.com/services/economics_and_planning

Battle, G., 2016. 'Social Value Portal: Where Community Speaks & Business Listens'. http://socialvalueportal.com/ (accessed 9.12.16).

Benedikt, M. (ed.), 1997. *Center/10 Value*. Center for American Architecture and Design, Austin, TX.

Bowker, G.C., Leigh Star, S., 1999. *Sorting Things Out: Classification and Its Consequences*. MIT Press, Cambridge, MA.

Brandon, P.S., Lombardi, P., 2010. *Evaluating Sustainable Development in the Built Environment*. Wiley, Oxford.

BSI, 2000. 'Value Management'. BS EN 12973:2000. British Standards Institute/Centre for the Protection of National Infrastructure, London.

Bunting, C., 2008. 'What Instrumentalism? A Public Perception of Value'. *Cultural Trends*, 17, 4, pp. 323–328.

Burke, C., King, A., 2015. 'Generating Social Value through Public Sector Construction Procurement: A Study of Local Authorities and SMEs'. Presented at the ARCOM, Lincoln.

CABE, 2006. 'The Value Handbook: Getting the Most from Your Buildings and Spaces'. http://webarchive.nationalarchives.gov.uk/20110118095356/http://www.cabe.org.uk/files/the-value-handbook.pdf#page=1&zoom= auto,36,643

CABE, 2005. 'What It's Like to Live There: The View of Residents on the Design of New Housing'. http://webarchive.nationalarchives.gov.uk/20110118095356/http://www.cabe.org.uk/publications/what-its-like-to-live-there

Cadman, E., 2016. 'Services close to 80% of UK economy'. *Financial Times*. www.ft.com/content/2ce78f36-ed2e-11e5-888e-2eadd5fbc4a4 (accessed 9.12.16).

CIC (Construction Industry Council), 2016. 'DQI – Healthcare'. www.dqi.org.uk/case-studies/healthcare/ (accessed 24.11.16).

Colander, D., Holt, R., Barkley Rosser Jr., J., 2004. 'The Changing Face of Mainstream Economics'. *Review of Political Economy*, 16, 4, pp. 485–499. doi:10.1080/0953825042000256702

Construction Industry Council, 1999. Design Quality Indicators. www.dqi.org.uk (accessed 8.9.15).

Crossick, G., Kaszynska, P., 2016. *Understanding the Value of Arts and Culture: The AHRC Cultural Value Project.* AHRC, Swindon.

Darke, J., 1984. 'Architects and User Requirements in Public-sector Housing: 2. The Sources for Architects' Assumptions', *Environment and Planning B: Planning and Design*, 11, 4, pp. 405–416.

DCMS, 2016. 'Creative Industries Economic Estimates'. www.gov.uk/government/statistics/creative-industries-economic-estimates-january-2016

DCMS, 2012. *Report 5: Post-Games Evaluation: Meta-Evaluation of the Impacts and Legacy of the London 2012 Olympic Games and Paralympic Games.* UK Gov, London.

Design Council, 2007. *The Value of Design Factfinder Report.* Design Council, London.

Designing Buildings Wiki, 2017. 'Value in Building Design and Construction'. www.designingbuildings.co.uk/wiki/Value_in_building_design_and_construction (accessed 3.1.17).

Donovan, C., 2013. 'A Holistic Approach to Valuing our Culture'. www.gov.uk/government/publications/a-holistic-approach-to-valuing-our-culture (accessed 15.1.14).

Fujiwara, D., 2014. *The Social Impact of Housing Providers.* HACT, London.

Gardner, H., 1993. *Multiple Intelligences: The Theory in Practice.* Basic Books, New York.

Gibson, L., 2008. 'In Defence of Instrumentality'. *Cultural Trends*, 17, 4, pp. 247–257. doi:10.1080/09548960802615380

GLA Economics, 2017. 'London's Architectural Sector' (Working paper 86). www.london.gov.uk/business-and-economy-publications/londons-architectural-sector

Green, B., 2016. 'Designers by numbers'. *RIBAJ*, 9 September.

Groak, S., 1992. *The Idea of Building: Thought and Action in the Design and Production of Buildings.* Taylor & Francis, Oxford.

Ipsos Mori, CABE, 2010. 'People and Place: Public Attitudes to Beauty'. Commission for Architecture and the Built Environment, London.

Kelly, J., Male, S., Graham, D., 2010. *Value Management of Construction Projects.* Wiley, Oxford; Malden, MA.

King's Fund, The, 2017. 'Health and Spatial Planning'. www.kingsfund.org.uk/projects/improving-publics-health/health-and-spatial-planning

LEK Consulting, 2009. *Construction in the UK Economy.* UK Contractors Group, London.

Loe, E., 2000. *The Value of Architecture: Context and Current Thinking.* RIBA Future Studies, London.

Macmillan, S. (ed.), 2005. 'Design Quality Needs Conscious Values', in: *Designing Better Buildings: Quality and Value in the Built Environment.* Taylor & Francis, Oxford, pp. 135–144.

Macmillan, S., 2004. *Designing Better Buildings: Quality and Value in the Built Environment.* Spon, New York.

Morgan, G., 2006, *Images of Organisation.* Sage, London.

Myers, D., 2008. *Construction Economics: A New Approach.* Routledge, London.

Natajaran, L., Carmona, M., 2016. *Design Governance: The CABE Experiment.* Taylor & Francis, Oxford.

Nowotny, H., 2015. *The Cunning of Uncertainty.* Polity, London.

Odgers, J., Samuel, F., 2010. 'Designing in Quality', in: Dutoit, A., Odgers, J., Sharr, A. (eds), *Quality Out of Control.* Routledge, London, pp. 41–54.

Pels, P., 2000. 'The Trickster's Dilemma: Ethics and the Technologies of the Anthropological Self', in: Strathern, M. (ed.), *Audit Cultures.* Routledge, London, pp. 136–172.

Phillips, A., 2015. 'The Problem of Value within the Regime of Art', presentation at *Transvaluation conference.* Chalmers University, Gothenburg.

Punter, J., 2011. 'Urban Design and the English Urban Renaissance 1999–2009: A Review and Preliminary Evaluation'. *Journal of Urban Design,* 16, 1, pp. 1–41.

Reinmuth, G., Horton, T., Burke, A., Edwards, D., Foley, C., Scerri, M., Horn, Z., 2016. *Measuring Up; Innovation and the Value Add of Architecture.* NSW Registration Board. doi:http://dx.doi.org/10.13140/RG.2.1.1583.3845

Saunders, W.S., 2007. *Judging Architectural Value.* University of Minnesota Press, Minneapolis.

Schumacher, E.F., 1993 [1973]. *Small Is Beautiful: A Study of Economics as if People Mattered.* New edition. Vintage, London.

Scottish Executive, 2006. 'A Literature Review of the Social, Economic and Environmental Impact of Design'. www.scotland.gov.uk/Resource/Doc/137370/0034117.pdf

Shore, C., Wright, S., 2000. 'Coercive accountability', in: Strathern, M. (ed.), *Audit Cultures.* Routledge, London, pp. 57–89.

Simmons, R., 2015. 'Constraints on Evidence-based Policy: Insights from Government Practices'. *Building Research and Information,* 43, 4, pp. 407–419.

Spierings, N., 2012. 'The Inclusion of Quantitative Techniques and Diversity in the Mainstream of Feminist Research'. *Eur. J. Women's Stud.* 19, pp. 331–347.

Taylor, P.J., 2016. 'Corporate Social Science and the Loss of Curiosity'. Social Science Research Council. http://items.ssrc.org/corporate-social-science-and-the-loss-of-curiosity/

UK Gov, 2016. 'Launch of the Procuring for Growth Balanced Scorecard'. www.gov.uk/government/news/launch-of-the-procuring-for-growth-balanced-scorecard (accessed 4.8.17).

UK Gov, 2013a. 'The Green Book: Appraisal and Evaluation in Central Government'. www.gov.uk/government/publications/the-green-book-appraisal-and-evaluation-in-central-governent (accessed 16.1.14).

UK Gov, 2013b. 'CASE Programme: Understanding the Drivers, Impacts and Value of Engagement in Culture and Sport'. www.gov.uk/government/publications/case-programme-understanding-the-drivers-impacts-and-value-of-engagement-in-culture-and-sport (accessed 16.1.14).

UK Gov, 2012. 'Social Value Act: Information and Resources'. www.gov.uk/government/publications/social-value-act-information-and-resources/social-value-act-information-and-resources (accessed 7.11.16).

van Toorn, R., 2007. 'No More Dreams? The Passion for Reality in Recent Dutch Architecture'. www.roemervantoorn.nl/Resources/Toorn,%20van_%20No%20More%20Dreams.pdf

Waite, R., 2014. 'UK Ministers Snub British Pavilion at the Venice Biennale'. *Architects' Journal*, 5 June. www.architectsjournal.co.uk/news/uk-ministers-snub-british-pavilion-at-venice-biennale-2014/8663652.article

Warwick, E., 2014. 'CABE's Approach to Research', in: Sakai, A., Koide, K. (eds), *CABE and the Processes of Design Evaluation in Architecture and the Built Environment*. Kajima, Tokyo.

Watkins, C., McMaster, R., 2011. 'The Behavioural Turn in Housing Economics: Reflections on the Theoretical and Operational Challenges'. *Housing Theory and Society*, 28, 3, pp. 281–287.

Watson, K.J., 2016. 'Learning Loops in Sustainable Design: Applying Social Return on Investment to Buildings'. Unpublished PhD thesis, University of Manchester.

Whyte, J., Gann, D., 2003. 'Design Quality Indicators: Work in Progress'. *Building Research and Information*, 31, 5, pp. 387–398.

Wigglesworth, S., 2006. 'Critical Practice'. *Journal of Architecture*, 10, 3, pp. 335–346.

Part II

The value of architects

Chapter 6

So what is an architect?

> *I believe that failure is less frequently attributable to either insufficiency of means or impatience of labour, than to a confused understanding of the thing actually to be done.*
>
> *(Ruskin, 1849, p. 1)*

The cover of the January 2009 edition of *Architectural Digest* shows the film star Brad Pitt and the work he has been doing on homes in New Orleans. Does this mean that Brad Pitt is an architect? Although commonly referred to as architects, neither Thomas Heatherwick or Assemble (winners of the prestigious Turner Prize for Art, Tate 2015) are qualified recipients of architectural education (Moore, 2015). Indeed it is quite possible that their success in the field is a direct result of their rejection of the cultural baggage of architectural identity and ways of working. So what then is an architect (Figure 6.1)?

This chapter begins with a discussion of the formal definitions of the term 'architect', revealing how inconsistent they are. While it may seem presumptuous, I have no alternative than to return to first principles, offering a taxonomy of architectural knowledge as a heuristic device (organizational tool) developed to give a better understanding of the value of the profession, and to begin a conversation about what it might be rather than what it is. I then attempt to set out the way this knowledge plays out in the profession in the form of particular skillsets, which can be categorized in terms of value.

That there is widespread confusion about the role of the architect is clear (Weiss and Hellman, 1999; Habraken, 2005, p. x; Potter, 2006 [1969]; Samuel et al., 2014). A survey of 2031 British adults showed that 15% didn't even know that architects design buildings. More alarmingly a large proportion were totally unaware that architects might have any role in the management of a building project, a significant number (22%) being unaware that an architect might produce detailed construction drawings (YouGov, 2012). Certainly at the level of domestic architecture the public seems largely ignorant of the subtle differences between an 'architectural designer' with no qualifications to work on their house and a registered architect (Samuel, 2008). The provision of a warm, watertight environment is not the exclusive domain of architects and is therefore not, for the purposes of this book, deemed part of the value of architects (Powell, 1996).

Figure 6.1
The Image of the Architect. © Louis Hellman.

The difference between architecture and building is often used as a means to describe the distinct skillsets of architects and builders, most usually in aesthetic terms (Ruskin, 1849). The historian Nikolaus Pevsner famously stated that:

> A bicycle shed is a building; Lincoln Cathedral is a piece of architecture. Nearly everything that encloses space on a scale sufficient for a human being to move in, is a building; the term architecture applies only to buildings designed with a view to aesthetic appeal ... this aesthetic superiority is, moreover, supplemented by a social superiority.
>
> (Pevsner, 1942, p. xx)

Although this statement might seem outdated and paternalistic, new models are lacking. Bernard Rudofsky's book *Architecture without Architects* (Rudofsky, 1987) has made it clear that you don't need to be an architect to make architecture, an idea that has gained considerable traction in some circles (Awan et al., 2011). While I am all for the democratizing of architecture, it is too important to be left entirely to non-experts.

In Chapter 4 I argued that architects are not generally artists in the traditional sense, despite aspirations to this status in the origins of the profession. Books on practice typically return to the origins of the word architect, justifying his or her place as the leader of the construction team. The word 'architect' is derived from the Greek root *arch*, meaning 'chief', and the word *tekton*, meaning 'carpenter or builder' (Chappell and Willis, 2005, p. 9). David Roochnik has devoted an entire book to the meaning of the word '*techne*' from which *tekton* is derived (Roochnik, 1998) – suffice to say that it is more than just about being a builder or carpenter. Techne, I argue, is about building with thought, with philosophical, ethical and critical awareness.

6.1 Formal definitions of architects and what they do

Architecture is part of the 'creative industries', though its size relative to the other constituent parts is small (DCMS, 2016a). Architects are paid roughly the same as other types of designer (Creative Review, 2013), but their training generally takes far longer and they carry heavier professional responsibilities. Standard Industry Classifications (SIC) and Standard Occupational Classifications (SOC) are used by the Office for National Statistics (ONS) to gather data. According to the UK Department of Culture Media and Sport, architects are SOC 2431 with 'architectural activities' covered by Standard Industry Classification SIC 71.11 (DCMS, 2016b). 'Architecture' includes 'architects, town planning officers, chartered architectural technologists and architecture and town planning technicians' (DCMS, 2016b), although each struggles to define its purpose and value (Tavistock Institute, 1966). Planners, for example, express their value (Adams and Watkins, 2014) in radically different terms to architects (Samuel et al., 2014). Gathering these varied types of impact together to make a unified case for the impact of SIC 7.11 that will impress policymakers is difficult.

According to the SIC 45 definition, architecture is not part of the construction industry, but is instead a beneficiary of investment in construction (LEK Consulting, 2009, pp. 9, 10). The 'architecture sector' includes 'architectural occupations', which are 'architectural jobs' in a wide variety of settings, 'architectural occupations in the architectural industries' – the focus of this book – and 'architectural industries', which in turn includes all jobs in this sector, such as marketing and management (GLA Economics, 2017, p. 6).

In the UK the title Architect is legally protected but there is no protection of function (Farrell, 2014). Anybody can design a building if they comply with the minimum standards. 'Even if they were to call themselves an architect, the current protection is relatively toothless. The maximum fine is £2,500 and it is difficult to justify prosecution as it requires proving it is in the public interest and has a reasonable chance of success' (Farrell, 2014, p. 68).

To be an architect carries professional legal responsibilities. Legally speaking an architect can be sued for offering erroneous advice while standing with a drink talking to acquaintances at a cocktail party, so being an architect carries certain responsibilities that are not required of the unqualified, hence the requirement by the Architects Registration Board (ARB) to have professional indemnity insurance in order to practise.

Being an architect means different things in different places. In Switzerland, for example, there is no protection of title. In the UK, as for example in the Netherlands, the profession has a registration board which is separate from the professional institution, the need for which is regularly debated. The 155 requirements listed in the UK Royal Institute for British Architects (RIBA) Validation Criteria for architectural schools are based on the much simpler European Union (EU) Directive 85/384/EEC, ostensibly allowing the transfer of qualifications across borders:

> (a) Ability to create architectural designs that satisfy both aesthetic and technical requirements;
> (b) Adequate knowledge of the history and theories of architecture and the related arts, technologies and human sciences;
> (c) Knowledge of the fine arts as an influence on the quality of architectural design;
> (d) Adequate knowledge of urban design, planning and the skills involved in the planning process;
> (e) Understanding of the relationship between people and buildings, and between buildings and their environment, and of the need to relate buildings and the spaces between them to human needs and scale;
> (f) Understanding of the profession of architecture and the role of the architect in society, in particular in preparing briefs that take account of social factors;
> (g) Understanding of the methods of investigation and preparation of the brief for a design project;
> (h) Understanding of the structural design, constructional and engineering problems associated with building design;
> (i) Adequate knowledge of physical problems and technologies and of the function of buildings so as to provide them with internal conditions of comfort and protection against the climate;
> (j) The necessary design skills to meet building users' requirements within the constraints imposed by cost factors and building regulations;
> (k) Adequate knowledge of the industries, organisations, regulations and procedures involved in translating design concepts into buildings and integrating plans into overall planning.
>
> (EU, 2005)

Just what might be considered 'adequate' depends very much on what an architect does. The criteria reflect 'the old-fashioned ideal of a well-rounded architectural jack-of-all-trades', an idea that needs to be fundamentally 'rethought' (Pringle and Porter, 2015, p. 150). A particular problem for the profession is that the teaching of innovation, research, collaboration and knowledge management is not explicitly addressed in these criteria. At the same time it is notable how little attention is given to the historical environment or to reuse, given that working on existing buildings constitutes the bread and butter work of the majority of practices. An architect, according to the International Union of Architects (UIA), is a

> person who is professionally and academically qualified and generally registered/licensed/certified to practice architecture in the jurisdiction in which he or she practices and is responsible for advocating the fair and sustainable development, welfare, and the cultural expression of society's habitat in terms of space, forms, and historical context.
>
> (UIA, 2014, p. 6)

Note here the presence of an ethical dimension not mentioned by the EU Directive but integral to being a chartered professional.

All RIBA Chartered Practices must adhere to the Code of Professional Conduct, the Continuing Professional Development (CPD) Core Curriculum and the RIBA Chartered Practice accreditation criteria and standards. These include using an appropriate quality management system, a health and safety policy, an employment policy, an appropriate CPD framework and an appropriate environmental management policy. However, these safeguards don't seem to have safeguarded society from an epidemic of narchitecture.

6.2 Services

Yet another document that has a say in what architects do and when they will do it is the *RIBA Plan of Work* (RIBA, 2013). It was first published in 1963 and has been revised on a regular basis ever since. The *Plan of Work* is frequently used as a basis for project programming, management and costing and there are multiple versions available from different institutions across the globe. The *RIBA Plan of Work 2013* organizes the process of briefing, designing, constructing, maintaining, operating and using building projects into eight Work Stages, but it has also been subject to various overlays, updates and extensions, for example the Building Information Modelling (BIM) overlay. The current digital version invites bespoke additions and changes, but very few architects have exploited this potential. Until this happens the true complexity and value of research practice that underpins the *Plan of Work* will remain hidden in its interstices.

Many architects see their job as a vocation, something that sits uneasily with their role as commercial service providers (Grönroos, 2000). Services, commodities and goods are categories commonly used within economics to discuss value. Gilmore and Pine 'discern' two more important categories, which, I argue, are fundamental to architecture: 'experiences and transformations':

> *Commodities* are extracted from the earth – raised, mined or harvested … and then exchanged in the marketplace as raw fungible offerings

> *Goods* are the tangible things manufactured from commodities
> *Services* are intangible activities delivered on behalf of individual customers
> *Experiences* are memorable events that engage individuals in an inherently personal way
> *Transformations* are effectual outcomes that guide customers to change some dimension of self.
>
> (Gilmore and Pine II, 2007, pp. 46–47)

Seen in this light the *RIBA Plan of Work* misses out some really important aspects of working with an architect, the transformational possibilities of the experience. Architects create 'integrating devices' that translate knowledge across boundaries, creating models, drawings and so on that form the basis of action. This can be a service, but it can also be an experience and even a transformation. Architects also design experiences and transformations for others, an important subject that I will return to.

6.3 Defining the core skills and knowledge of architects

Categorization, the clustering of information, is the infrastructure of our 'built moral environment' (Bowker and Leigh Star, 1999). Information becomes knowledge when sifted in a systematic way. Knowledge theoretically is things you know and skills are things you do, putting knowledge into action. Knowledge is generally categorized as tacit or explicit, the latter type being knowledge that has been expressed in formal languages that can then be introduced into processes such as search engines, economic models and so on. Explicit knowledge is 'manifested in drawings, specifications and other artefacts produced for architectural projects' (Bashouri and William Duncan, 2014, p. 170). Tacit process-based knowledge dominates the field of architecture, starting with the socialization that occurs in education. The creation of new knowledge is described as having four phases: 'socialisation', 'externalisation', 'combination' and 'internalisation' (Nonaka and Takeuchi, 1995; Lu and Sexton, 2009, p. 14). Essentially this is a journey from converting tacit knowledge into new explicit knowledge and then back into tacit knowledge at the levels of both individuals and groups. Theories of knowledge management have been displaced by theories of organizational learning that give full recognition to the fact that knowledge is fluid, dynamic and constantly changing. However, I place emphasis on knowledge management to make the point that architectural knowledge is something of value and to attempt to disaggregate what knowledge might be in the context of knowledge-based organizations such as architectural practices, a subject I will return to in Chapter 15.

Knowledge can in theory be subdivided into: 'human knowledge' (often tacit); 'relationship/social knowledge' arising from the process of working collaboratively; and 'structure/structural knowledge', which is at the heart of organizational processes and is very often explicit (De Long and Fahey, 2000; Lu and Sexton, 2009, p. 16). What happens when you try to apply these theories of knowledge to the complex and shifting knowledge economy of architects? Below is a proposal for a taxonomy of knowledge in twenty-first-century architectural practice developed out of a literature review and in consultation with the Research Practice Leads group convened as part of the Evidencing and Communicating the Value of Architects project. I have clustered the knowledge to indicate whether it is common to all professional design-related practices, whether it is generic to the built environment or whether it is specific to architects. The list is not exhaustive by any means; that such a list cannot do justice to tacit and embodied aspects of architectural knowledge is clear. It does, however, represent a very tentative step towards classifying architectural knowledge and is intended as a provocation to others to continue this process.

Human knowledge

People (field-specific)

Management and leadership skills

In-house knowledge 'stocks'

Practice culture

Ethical practice

Relationship/social knowledge

Networks (field-specific)

Potential clients

Favoured local collaborators

Collaborators overseas

Potential research funders

Advocates

Mentors

Talent-spotters

Influencers

Favoured clients

Favoured contractors

Favoured consultants

Favoured subcontractors

Fablabs

Contact database

Local knowledge

Knowledge (field-specific)

Horizon-spotting

New markets

Knowledge security

Knowledge sources

Knowledge development

Knowledge management

Research project development

In-house library

Contribution to shared bodies of knowledge

Understanding of competitors
Awareness of competitor industries

Service design (transferable)
The experience of the client
Problem solving
Consultation
Briefing
Design studio and the making of boundary objects
Handover, user guides and post-occupancy
Methodologies for pitching for work
Office layout, look and atmosphere

Communications (transferable)
In-house communication
Marketing – website, social media, brand strategy
Archive – past people, projects, awards and knowledge
Writing and representation

Creative industry design research knowledge (transferable)
Design research
User experience
Catalysing networks
Resourcefulness
Long-term value
Conceptual design
Representation
Modelling
Ethical procedures
In-house design review
Intellectual property
Patents and routes to market
Different types of research representation, including writing
Infographics

Architectural design research knowledge (field-specific spacecraft)
Building typologies and historical precedent
Architecture studio research methodology
The design of spaces, experiences and details for particular ends
Resourcefulness at multiple scales
Boundary-spanning between widely diverse constituencies
Adding value (social, cultural and environmental knowledge as well as financial)
Briefing (helping clients establish their requirements)
Sustainable design
Ethical practice
Inclusive design

Favoured materials (sometimes held within a material library)
Favoured products
Favoured construction systems
Knowledge to develop and implement new construction systems
Digital design
How to enter architectural competitions
How to apply for frameworks
Mapping
Architectural writing and representation

Construction knowledge (built environment-specific)
Financial appraisal
Post-occupancy evaluation
Sustainability and life-cycle costings
Facilities management
Estates management
Value management
Surveying
Engineering (structural, environmental and civil)
Procurement
Laws and codes
Planning procedure
Project management
Supply chains
Digital construction
Construction design management (CDM)
BIM

Structure/Structural knowledge (transferable)

Business planning and finance
Risk assessment
Business planning
Financial planning
Human resources
Insurance

Technology
Software and hardware
Model-making, printers and laser cutters
Digital strategy
Data management

Space use
Facilities management
Evaluation
Spatial design for organizational performance benefits

This list suggests the important mediating role architects should play between the creative industries and the construction industry. The marginalization of architects from the process of building may be impacting on the ability of the construction industry to engage with the creative industries and hence its ability to innovate.

It is notable that only design research and service design really require subject-specific knowledge. The other areas are generic to all creative industry service providers and even a large proportion of businesses. While a change of context might require some adjustment, people with these generic skills regularly skip across industries and fields. This is why I believe that architectural education needs subdivision into subject-specific and transferable skills and why architects could be offering so much more than just building designs.

Definitions are needed so that the activities of architects can be found on search engines, and analysed by ever more intelligent Artificial Intelligence systems, programmed into models and, ultimately, evaluated. If we don't offer categorizations which align with those of other disciplines, the things that architects do will be left out of the algorithms and variables upon which the world is currently being constructed, for example as part of Google's mission to 'organize the world's information and make it universally accessible and useful' (Burkeman, 2014).

6.4 Defining types of architects and their skillsets

If non-architects are to engage with architects, they need to know with whom they are dealing. It is helpful in this context to reframe the activities of architects in terms of the benefits that they bring in a language that non-architects can use. While definitions may be limiting (Baydar, 2004), they are necessary at this point in time to 'externalize' our knowledge. Bowker and Leigh Star note that orderings are always culturally and temporally specific and therefore need to be constantly under review. They call for a new form of information science that mixes 'formal and folk classifications' (Bowker and Leigh Star, 1999, p. 32). Such is the ordering that is posited here.

Building on Higgin's observation, over fifty years ago, that: 'A categorization is needed that gets to the heart of the practice's values, includes the diversity of potential future services and gives potential clients a real sense of what they might be about' (Higgin, 1964, p. 139), several attempts have been made to define the activities of architects. Bentley, for example, characterizes the relationship between designer and developer in terms of power relations: 'heroic form giver'; 'master and servant'; 'market signals', in essence a passive response to what the market wants (Bentley, 1999). Carmona identifies 'three distinct traditions': 'creative, market driven and regulatory' (Carmona, 2009, p. 2644). Winch subdivides practices in terms of 'strong delivery', 'strong experience', 'strong ambition' and 'strong ideas' (Winch, 2008). Eraut recognizes the role of money, subdividing professional practice in terms of users: patronage 'by wealthy and powerful clients' in which confidentiality and social acceptability play an important role; a 'commercial relationship' in which agreement over fees is key; and 'a welfare relationship' for clients 'perceived as needy', funded largely by the state (Eraut, 1994, p. 4). Cohen et al. work from the bottom up, by asking architects how they account for 'the purpose and process of their work', identifying three dominant discourses in the process: 'architecture as creative endeavour, architecture as business activity and architecture as public service' (Cohen et al., 2005, p. 782). Seidel et al. define the roles of architects as: 'Fashionistas', for example starchitects; 'Life Improvers', making evidence-based improvements to wellbeing; and 'Object-service packagers', providing an ongoing service as well as objects (buildings) to profitable and innovative ends (Seidel et al., 2012, p. 242). A more recent Design Commission survey has explored how the built environment fosters 'healthy behaviours; environmentally sustainable behaviours; socially cohesive behaviours'; and 'productive, innovative and creative behaviours' (Design Commission, 2017, p. 1). There is an emerging pattern here that I will build on.

As an aside, it is also worth noting the meaning of heritage values, for example Historic England's 'Conservation Principles', as these embody reasons for valuing the built environment in the long term. For English Heritage, heritage value is defined as: evidential, 'the potential of a place to yield evidence about past human activity'; historic, connecting past to present; aesthetic, deriving 'from the ways in which people draw sensory and intellectual stimulation from a place'; and communal, which 'derives from the meanings of a place for the people who relate to it, or for whom it figures in their collective experience or memory' (English Heritage, 2008, pp. 27–32). These seem to be very helpful in delineating some of the more intangible impacts of the built environment.

While undertaking a formal review of 120 'grey literature' industry and academic report documents pertaining to the value of architects for the Arts and Humanities Research Council (AHRC) funded Cultural Value of Architecture (CVoA) project it became apparent that value, as the word suggests, has different meaning depending on the value system that is being used. It has already been seen that one of the reasons architecture is so opaque is that it contains several, often apparently conflicting, value systems (McNeill, 2006; Bunting, 2008), which need to be disaggregated (Foxell, 2003; McClean, 2009) if they are to be better understood.

One of the notable findings of the CVoA team was that most attempts to demonstrate the value of architects are flawed largely because they focus on the finished product, the building, which is always the result of a diverse set of 'actors' – including the building itself if you are an aficionado of Actor Network Theory (Beauregard, 2015). This means that the particular contribution of architects is difficult, if not impossible, to discern. Another problem was that the word architect is rarely, if ever, used, perhaps because its meaning is so fuzzy. It soon became apparent that in order to establish value it is necessary to focus on the 'actions of architects' (CABE, 2005, p. 1), what it is that they do, rather than try to extrapolate their value from a built project, which is always the result of team effort. Their value is in what they add to the process.

Clients and architects work together best when they share the same values and have a shared sense of desirable outcomes. The team therefore posited a series of architect types, based on their value systems (cultural, social, and commercial) and a definition of their skillsets. The types and skillsets then became an 'artefact of knowing' which was developed and negotiated with clients, non-architect academics and industry experts both within and without architecture through the industry press, the teaching of an 'Architecture 101' module at the University of Sheffield, the structure of the book *Demystifying Architectural Research*

(Samuel and Dye, 2015) and through the restructuring of the RIBA President's Medals for Research in 2016. One of the casualties of this period was the category 'Commercial Architect', lost as the category 'Knowledge Architect' began to come into focus, partly because of the growth of this term in the information technology (IT) sector, partly inspired by the writings of Frank Duffy and partly because few UK practices we spoke to wanted to be identified with the word 'commercial', despite the seeming dominance of this sector globally. Reflecting backwards the architects that were included in the 'commercial architect' section of *Demystifying Architectural Research* were all 'knowledge architects', people who were gathering intelligence in a strategic way in order to bring about business advantage.

The category 'Technological Architect' was included in *Demystifying Architectural Research* as a means to disseminate specifically technological research but it is omitted here. All architectural problems are socio-technical. An improvement in environmental performance cannot be regarded as sustainable if a user's quality of life is negatively impacted by factors such as layout, restrictions, lack of natural lighting or by the need to move to a different home if their circumstances change (Prochorskaite et al., 2016). Technology we argue is a means to an end and is not an end in itself.

The role of architects in the spatializing of change should not be underestimated (Davies, 2013). The 'artefacts of knowing' produced by architects are in themselves symbols of change, triggering responses in all those that engage with them. The activities of starchitects and their impact on cities desperate to up their distinctive cultural value in the face of global competition for business, investment and tourism have been subject to extensive analysis by geographers and sociologists. The concept of the 'imaginary', is set out by Cornelius Castoriadis in his 1975 book *The Imaginary Institution of Society* (Castoriadis, 1987) is useful here. According to his logic, architecture becomes 'a totem, a performative entity for constituting new authority or new social relations as real or naturalised' (Kaika, 2011, p. 972). Architects create new imaginaries – signs, symbols, processes and indeed buildings that prepare people for change.

The CVoA types and skillsets are an imaginary of good practice going forward, a fresh view of the enabling capability of architects. It is important to stress that the architect types and skillsets set out below and developed in Chapters 7, 8 and 9 are *not mutually exclusive*. There will always be overlaps and grey areas. There are moments when a particular practice will foreground a particular value system based on the client or the situation and then switch to another for another situation. One client the team spoke to, a property developer, believed that high-quality design should be a 'given' for architects, and indeed it is an assumption for the types and skillsets. While they have been developed around the value added by architects, they could equally be inverted to suggest the damage that they can do.

Skillset of social architects

- Create environments for wellbeing that change the way we feel and think;
- Create places for community interaction;
- Co-create places to foster a sense of identity;

- Deliver learning experiences;
- Map and record community assets.

Skillset of cultural architects

- Use a strong conceptual framework to create novel environments with high cultural value often derived from art-based practice;
- Confer cultural capital to client and project through practice brand;
- Carefully choreograph the experience of working with the practice, giving added value to the client;
- Market the practice and its work to inspire debate and media coverage;
- Use innovation in technology and representation to the benefit of brand identity.

Skillset of knowledge architects

- Make frameworks for the development of knowledge;
- Order space for the development of knowledge;
- Design user experiences to promote knowledge generation;
- Design interfaces to make large bodies of knowledge and big data accessible, including parametric design and digital construction;
- Make rigorous judgements about the validity of knowledge.

It is worth noting that all the skillsets described here require the socially nuanced processing of extremely complex bodies of knowledge. Many of them also require face-to-face contact with clients, user groups and others and are very unlikely to be provided by a robot or an app any time soon. Such skills are therefore key to the development of a resilient profession that can ride out the uncertainties of technological and societal change.

Conclusion

In order to be a profession it is necessary to have custody of a body of knowledge and to be able to delineate that body of knowledge, yet the formal definitions of architectural knowledge are both inconsistent and outdated. In this chapter I have posited a taxonomy of the baseline knowledge of architects in practice for the twenty-first century. This exercise suggests that a substantial segment of architectural knowledge is generic to professional practice across the board. There is, however, an important pocket of catalysing knowledge specific to architects, which is core to their value.

Architects use their knowledge to generate value in different ways. The architect types and skillsets, developed with the CVoA team, constitute an organizing device for gathering data on the social, cultural and knowledge value of architects, negative or positive. They are based more on a vision of how practice might be – research-led and innovative – rather than how it is in reality. The rest of Part II of this book is devoted to fleshing out the different architect types. This includes a review of what little is known about their value from related research. This can be reframed to suggest potentials areas of value, while also revealing gaps in our knowledge base. While the data appear here in narrative form, the systematic literature reviews on which they are based can be found as a database on the website www.valueofarchitects.org.

Research for this chapter was undertaken with the AHRC Cultural Value of Architecture team, Nishat Awan, Carolyn Butterworth, Sophie Handler and Jo Lintonbon, and Rowena Hay, Research Assistant for the AHRC Value of Architects project.

References

Adams, D., Watkins, C., 2014. *The Value of Planning*. Royal Town Planning Institute, London.

Awan, N., Schneider, T., Till, J., 2011. *Spatial Agency: Other Ways of Doing Architecture*. Routledge, Oxford.

Bashouri, J., William Duncan, G., 2014. 'A Model for Sharing Knowledge in Architectural Firms'. *Construction Innovation*, 14, 2, pp. 168–185.

Baydar, G., 2004. 'The Cultural Burden of Architecture'. *Journal of Architectural Education*, 57, 4, pp. 19–27.

Beauregard, R., 2015. 'We Blame the Building! The Architecture of Distributed Responsibility'. *International Journal of Urban and Regional Research*, 39, 3, pp. 533–549.

Bentley, I., 1999. *Urban Transformations: Power, People and Urban Design*. Routledge, Oxford.

Bowker, G.C., Leigh Star, S., 1999. *Sorting Things Out: Classification and its Consequences*. MIT Press, Cambridge, MA.

Bunting, C., 2008. 'What Instrumentalism? A Public Perception of Value'. *Cultural Trends*, 17, 4, pp. 323–328.

Burkeman, O., 2014. 'Death, Drones and Driverless Cars: How Google Wants to Control Our Lives'. *The Guardian*, 22 September. www.theguardian.com/technology/2014/sep/22/what-does-google-want-glass-drones-self-driving-cars

CABE, 2005. 'What Its Like to Live There: The View of Residents on the Design of New Housing'. http://webarchive.nationalarchives.gov.uk/20110118095356/http://www.cabe.org.uk/publications/what-its-like-to-live-there

Carmona, M., 2009. 'Design Coding and the Creative, Market and Regulatory Tyrannies of Practice'. *Urban Studies*, 46, 12, pp. 2643–2667.

Castoriadis, C., 1987 [1975]. *The Imaginary Institution of Society*. MIT Press, Cambridge, MA.

Chappell, D., Willis, A., 2005. *The Architect in Practice*. Blackwell, Oxford.

Cohen, L., Wilkinson, A., Arnold, J., Finn, R., 2005. '"Remember, I'm the Bloody Architect!": Architects' Organizations and Discourses of Profession'. *Work, Employment and Society*, 19, 4, pp. 775–796.

Creative Review, 2013. 'On the Money: Are Designers Badly Paid?' www.creativereview.co.uk/on-the-money/

Davies, R., 2013. 'Healthcare Built Environment Impacts, Construction Projects and Organisational Change', in: *ARCOM Conference Proceedings*, Reading, pp. 167–177. www.arcom.ac.uk/-docs/proceedings/ar2013-0167-0177_Davies.pdf

DCMS, 2016a. 'Creative Industries Economic Estimates'. www.gov.uk/government/statistics/creative-industries-economic-estimates-january-2016

DCMS, 2016b. 'Creative Industries Focus on Employment'. UK Gov. www.gov.uk/government/statistics/creative-industries-2016-focus-on

De Long, D.W., Fahey, L., 2000. 'Diagnosing Cultural Barriers to Knowledge Management'. *Academy of Management Executive*, 14, 4, pp. 113–127.

Design Commission, 2017. 'People and Places'. www.policyconnect.org.uk/apdig/research/design-commission-people-and-places-design-built-environment-and-behaviour

English Heritage, 2008. *Conservation Principles, Policies and Guidance*. https://content.historicengland.org.uk/images-books/publications/conservation-principles-sustainable-management-historic-environment/conservationprinciplespoliciesguidanceapr08web.pdf/

Eraut, M., 1994. *Developing Professional Knowledge and Competence*. Routledge, London; Washington, D.C.

EU, 2005. *Directive 2005/36/EC of the European Parliament and the Council*. European Commission, Brussels.

Farrell, T., 2014. 'The Farrell Review of Architecture and the Built Environment'. www.farrellreview.co.uk/

Foxell, S., 2003. 'The Professionals' Choice'. *Building Futures*, London.

Gilmore, J.H., Pine II, J., 2007. *Authenticity: What Consumers Want*. Harvard Business School, Boston, MA.

GLA Economics, 2017. 'London's Architectural Sector' (Working paper 86). www.london.gov.uk/business-and-economy-publications/londons-architectural-sector

Grönroos, C., 2000. *Service Management and Marketing: A Customer Relationship Management Approach*. Wiley, Chichester.

Habraken, N.J., 2005. *Palladio's Children*. Taylor & Francis, Oxford.

Higgin, G., 1964. 'The Architect as Professional'. *RIBA Journal*, 71, 1, pp. 139–145.

Kaika, M., 2011. 'Autistic Architecture: The Fall of the Icon and the Rise of the Serial Object of Architecture'. *Environment and Planning D: Society and Space*, 29, 6, pp. 968–992.

LEK Consulting, 2009. *Construction in the UK Economy*. UK Contractors Group, London.

Lu, S., Sexton, M., 2009. *Innovation in Small Professional Practices in the Built Environment*. Wiley Blackwell, Oxford.

McClean, D., 2009. 'Embedding Learner Independence in Architecture Education: Reconsidering Design Studio'. Unpublished PhD thesis, Robert Gordon University, Glasgow.

McNeill, D., 2006. 'Globalization and the Ethics of Architectural Design', *City*, 10, 1, pp. 49–58.

Moore, R., 2015. 'Assemble: The Unfashionable Art of Making a Difference', *The Guardian*. 29 November.

Nonaka, I., Takeuchi, H., 1995. *The Knowledge Creating Company: How Japanese Companies Create the Dynamics of Innovation.* Oxford University Press, Oxford.

Pevsner, N., 1942. *An Outline of European Architecture.* Penguin, London.

Potter, N., 2006 [1969]. *What is a Designer?* Hyphen, London.

Powell, C., 1996. *The British Building Industry since 1800: An Economic History.* Routledge, Oxford.

Pringle, J., Porter, H., 2015. 'Education to Reboot a Failed Profession', in: Harriss, H., Froud, D. (eds), *Radical Pedagogies.* RIBA Publishing, Newcastle-upon-Tyne, p. 146.

Prochorskaite, A., Couch, C., Malys, N., Meliene, V., 2016. 'Housing Stakeholder Preferences for the Soft Features of Sustainable and Healthy Housing in the UK'. *International Journal of Environmental Research and Public Health,* 13, 1, pp. 1–15.

RIBA, 2013. 'RIBA Plan of Work'. www.ribaplanofwork.com/

Roochnik, D., 1998. *Of Art and Wisdom: Plato's Understanding of Techne.* Penn State Press, Pennsylvania.

Rudofsky, B., 1987. *Architecture Without Architects: A Short Introduction to Non-pedigreed Architecture.* University of New Mexico Press, Albuquerque.

Ruskin, J., 1849. *The Seven Lamps of Architecture.* John Wiley, New York.

Samuel, F., 2008. 'Suburban Self-build'. *Field,* 2, pp. 111–124.

Samuel, F., Awan, N., Handler, S., Lintonbon, J., 2014. 'Cultural Value of Architects in Homes and Neighbourhoods'. University of Sheffield/AHRC. www.sheffield.ac.uk/polopoly_fs/1.384071!/file/CuluralValueReport.pdf

Samuel, F., Dye, A., 2015. *Demystifying Architectural Research: Adding Value and Winning Business.* RIBA Enterprises, Newcastle-upon-Tyne.

Seidel, A.D., Kim, J.T., Tanaka, I.B.R., 2012. 'Architects, Urban Design, Health and the Built Environment'. *Journal of Architectural and Planning Research,* 29, 3, pp. 241–268.

Tate, 2015. 'Turner Prize 2015 Artists: Assemble'. www.tate.org.uk/whats-on/tramway/exhibition/turner-prize-2015/turner-prize-2015-artists-assemble (accessed 25.2.16).

Tavistock Institute, 1966. *Interdependence and Uncertainty (Digest of a Report from the Tavistock Institute to the Building Industry Communication Research Project).* Tavistock Institution, London.

UIA, 2014. 'UIA on Recommended International Standards of Professionalism in Architectural Practice'. www.uia-architectes.org/sites/default/files/UIAAccordEN.pdf

Weiss, B., Hellman, L., 1999. *Do It with an Architect: How to Survive Refurbishing Your Home.* Mitchell Beazley, London.

Winch, G., 2008. 'Internationalisation Strategies in Business-to-business Services: The Case of Architectural Practice'. *The Service Industries Journal,* 28, 1, pp. 1–13.

YouGov, 2012. 'An Archi-what?' https://yougov.co.uk/news/2012/09/03/archi-what/

Chapter 7

The value of social architects

Social architects, as an ideal, work for the good of people and the planet. Social architects tend to prioritize process over buildings but, if they do build, the results are often quiet, the product of hard-won consensus and ethical probity, and they do not lend themselves to celebration in glossy magazines. This requires a degree of humility and self-effacement that is not generally associated with architects.

> Socially motivated practices aim to transform the spaces and buildings people care about. Often they have a strong commitment to equality, sustainability and social justice, and research in this field supports these aims, valuing lived experiences and non-professional forms of expertise.
>
> (Udall, 2015, p. 44)

Social architects can often be found in housing practice. They are active in Community Land Trusts, community participation projects, participatory practice and where there are community share offers, self-builders, co-operative ownership models, and public sector building. In the USA they are sometimes known as 'public interest' practices' (Quirk, 2012) which is interesting since all architects are supposed to be working in the public interest. Socially motivated architects also abound in more mainstream practice, but their activities are less visible. 'Good old participatory design' (Bjogvinsson et al., 2012, p. 101) is not the sole terrain of architects, but architects have a particular way of doing it.

Social architects are in the business of creating social value. There is, however, no easy definition of social value; hence the 'extremely varied' ways in which it is demonstrated (Wilkes and Mullins, 2012, p. 5). Social practice and ethical practice are not necessarily the same thing. Multiple indicators of wellbeing and quality of life can be found on the internet, most notably from bodies like the European Union (EU), the Office for National Statistics (ONS) and think tanks such as the New Economics Foundation (Jeffrey and Michaelson, 2015). Watson et al.'s literature review of 'building users in their social context' provides a useful starting point for a consideration of the very different ways in which social value can be manifested and analysed (Watson et al., 2016b). A recognition of social value is becoming widespread in business – see for example the social life-cycle work of British Land (McCarthy, 2015) – and is an opportunity for architects. In this context it is worth noting discussions around Building Information Modelling (BIM) Maturity Level 4, which involves the demonstration of 'Better Outcomes for Society'. The profession needs to be ready to demonstrate those outcomes.

In Chapter 4 it was seen that architects have been criticized for overstepping the mark in terms of claims of social impact. The resultant accusations of determinism have contributed to the hesitancy of architects in developing its knowledge in this area. The social research of the past was, in the opinion of Jane Darke, 'positivistic, functionalistic, biased and particularistic' and did not meet architects' need for in-depth knowledge of how people use their buildings (Darke, 1984, p. 413). Since then, drawing methodological inspiration from geographers, anthropologists and others, research methods have developed and we are better able to develop robust knowledge on a wide range of important built environment issues. It is here that architects have much to learn from other disciplines that have been more astute in developing their evidence base, most notably planners. This is why there is more research into urban design and impacts on wellbeing – personal space: a human dimension, views from within and outside, pedestrian access, comfort, rest, social interaction, engagement with the senses, travelling and walking at street level – than there is at the building scale (Seidel et al., 2012).

New methods of developing and indeed monetizing social impact are being developed across the globe. An important development in this area is the HACT project, an online resource for measuring social value which was launched in March 2014 (Fujiwara, 2014). The project is in response to the deregulatory approach of the current government, making new ways of defining and evidencing social value ever more important (Fujiwara, 2014). It uses a 'wellbeing valuation' method which examines how people state that their level of wellbeing has been affected by their housing and then ascribes a financial value to this impact (Fujiwara, 2014, p. 11). Another method for monetizing social value is Social Return on Investment (SROI), based on traditional cost–benefit analysis developed in the USA in the mid-1990s and used by the New Economics Foundation (NEF) in the UK, as well as by an increasing number of local authorities and charitable organizations. It is a complex process requiring the development of definitions of shared outcomes with stakeholders, as well as extensive qualitative and quantitative research, breaking down user groups into different typologies and analysing the time each one spends in the building. The data is then monetized using a range of 'financial proxies' already in existence. An example of a financial proxy is the annual cost of relieving one person of depression (currently somehow set at £44,000). As an organization starts to develop its own financial proxies, it becomes better able to compare projects over time and to assist in the process of improving the financial proxies already in existence. Watson et al. (part funded by Arup) have used SROI to demonstrate the social value of three non-clinical health buildings over a sixty-year period (Watson et al., 2016a). Their provisional findings indicate that the additional cost of employing an architect to deliver a high-quality environment is very worthwhile in the long term.

7.1 Create environments for wellbeing that change the way we feel and think

For as long as architects have existed they have been thinking about ways in which they can enhance the connection between people and nature. There is now quite a convincing body of evidence to show the positive impact of the direct experience of 'nature' – daylight, views and sounds of water, plants inside and out, connection with the weather and natural cycles, landscapes and ecosystems – on people. Access to green space can even affect the coping ability of those living in poverty in inner cities (Kuo, 2001), while views of nature improve both student learning and satisfaction (Benfield et al., 2013). Even the perception of greenness can impact on quality of life (Hipp et al., 2016). More robust evidence is, however, needed on the impact of the indirect experience of nature through images, natural materials, natural geometries, and so on, on cultural and ecological attachment to place (Gillis and Gatersleben, 2015). 'Becoming cosmically conscious' is a theme underpinning some extremely exploratory architectural investigations (Armstrong, 2016, p. 383). It isn't, however, necessary to make a leap of faith to grasp the impact of the built environment on people.

The concept of wellbeing is gaining increasing traction in built environment discourse (Jones and Grigoriou, 2014). It is usually associated with mental health, but can also be linked to the health aspects of environmental comfort. Watson notes two significant strands of wellbeing discourse: 'hedonic', which relates to 'happiness and perceived quality of life'; and 'eudaimonic', which relates to 'a fuller psychological concept of one's life having purpose' and the ability to strive to fulfil that purpose (Watson, 2017, p. 122; see also Deci and Ryan, 2006). The 'eudaimonic' has of course long been fundamental to the lived experience of formal religion and spirituality of every sort and needs greater recognition in education, to be discussed in Chapter 10. The very best architecture reinforces eudaimonic wellbeing, but this kind of value has been, very largely, edited out of contemporary architectural culture.

Whatever the indicators used, the key role of personal and community autonomy in creating a sense of wellbeing quickly becomes clear. 'Well-being is conditioned by the balance between the life challenges people face and their capabilities for coping with them' (Nowotny, 2015, p. xiii). It is therefore unsurprising that the positive impact of involving people in the design of their environments has gained wide evidence-based acceptance (Halpern, 1995; Jones et al., 2005). In this context it is worth mentioning the efficacy of community art practice on health (MacPherson et al., 2012). Lawson has set out some of the many ways in which 'the language of space' can be used to impact on people:

> Through it we can express both our individuality and our solidarity with others. We can indicate our values and lifestyles, allegiances and dislikes. We can use it to help generate feelings of excitement or calm. We can communicate our willingness or otherwise to be approached, interrupted, greeted and engaged in social intercourse. We can control the proximity of others. We can demonstrate our dominance or submission and our status in society. We can use it to bring people together or keep them apart. We can use it to

> convey complex collections of rules of acceptable behavior. We can also use it on occasion to signal our intention to break those rules!
>
> (Lawson, 1999, p. 2)

Researchers in material culture give full recognition to the impact of 'stuff' on ourselves and create a 'setting' for what we do (Miller, 2009, p. 50), so why not architects?

Much of the social impact of architects may be intangible, but this doesn't mean that it doesn't matter. This brief summary of the way in which the built environment can change the way we feel and think begins with healthcare environments, which, being well regulated, lend themselves to research. It then moves into the more diffuse realm of education, homes and neighbourhoods. The impact of design on gaining competitive advantage through working environments and retail will be discussed in Chapter 9.

The impact of the built environment on health, both physical and mental – while not perhaps as tangible as medicine or surgery – is widely acknowledged (Guite et al., 2006; Design Commission, 2017). A pivotal moment in the development of evidence-based design was Roger Ulrich's ground-breaking article in *Science*, which suggested that patients recovering from gall bladder surgery needed fewer painkillers and stayed for a shorter time in hospital if they had a view of nature (Ulrich, 1984). Medicine has traditionally overlooked the role of the physical environment in patient wellbeing (Devlin and Arneill, 2003) and as a 'source of coping resources' for stressed patients and families (Leather et al., 2003), but we now have a very convincing body of research on its impact on the healing process (Ulrich et al., 2008) and on the wellbeing of healthcare workers (CABE/PricewaterhouseCoopers, 2004; Ulrich et al., 2004). Patients with access to daylight and external views require less medication and recover faster (Beauchemin and Hays, 1996), while views of nature can have a direct impact on reducing stress and pain and speeding up recovery (Ulrich and Delani, 1999). A robust case has also been made for the value of good design – including participatory design and the integration of art – in the context of hospitals (Hutton and Richardson, 1995; Scher and Senior, 2000) and there is a growing body of research on the cost savings therein, but much more research is needed to tease out the impact of design for dignity, particularly in hospices (Clarke, 2009). At the beginning of life the design of maternity facilities can significantly improve the process of labour and birth (Jenkinson et al., 2014), and presumably therefore infant mortality. Lighting, disposition of space and quality of materials act as frames for these treasured and painful memories. Adolescents in particular are sensitive to the symbolic aspects of hospital design and need to be included in discussions about healthcare space (Ullan et al., 2012). The built environment also impacts on the wellbeing of people with mental health problems (Marcheschi et al., 2014). As with birthing spaces, institutional atmospheres should be avoided (Chrysikou, 2015). Involving people in the process of shaping their healthcare environments is crucial to success (Stern et al., 2003; Van der Linden et al., 2016), but this can be very difficult when the user population is in constant flux.

There is an extensive and growing body of research on the effect of design on older people. An understanding that the physical environment of care homes impacts on both residents and staff is gaining currency (Barnes, 2002; Joseph et al., 2016). Views of nature and greenery are unsurprisingly important in the design of care homes and facilities for older people (Sugiyama and Ward Thompson, 2007), as are practical, accessible and open-plan layouts (Burton and Sheehan, 2010). Design can impact on the experience of dementia both for those afflicted and for carers (Mitchell et al., 2003): 'Although they play an important role in such people's orientation, interventions such as signage, furnishings, lighting, and colours cannot compensate for an adverse architectural design' (Marquardt, 2011, p. 87).

Social interaction is key for wellbeing – the less able a person is the more extreme the impact of the surroundings can be on his or her life (Campbell, 2015). Bouts of exercise and brief walks from one place to another need to be made manageable, meaningful and desirable (Zhipeng et al., 2015). Design plays an important role in creating a balance between autonomy and a sense of security through spatial layout and the relationship between private and public spaces, materials and building proportions (Steenwinkel et al., 2012). Housing design can facilitate healthy and active ageing (Torrington et al., 2004; Ahrentzen and Tural, 2015). Architects can play an important role in making communities that not only facilitate healthy lifestyles, but also project that image into the wider world, for example the new forms of intergenerational living celebrated in Lorraine Farrelly's review of design for active ageing (Farrelly, 2014).

The principles of good design deriving from Judy Torrington's HAPPI work (HAPPI, 2012) are growing in traction for people of all ages and types. Inclusive or universal design according to the British Standards Institute is 'The design of mainstream products and/or services that are accessible to, and usable by, as many people as reasonably possible ... without the need for special adaptation or specialised design' (BSI, 2005). Generally there is a strong case for supporting the tenets of universal design in the home to improve the wellbeing of a wide range of people with special needs (Nagib and Williams, 2016).

Research also shows what we all know, that the home, its neighbourhood atmosphere and connectivity have a profound effect on lives (Halpern, 1995; Carmona, 2001; Scottish Executive, 2006). People will forgive their environment for some of its shortcomings if they are happy with how it looks (Groak, 1992; CABE, 2010; Cranz et al., 2014). At the same time, buildings that fulfil all the right regulatory codes may be aesthetically ugly and even cause stigma to those who live in them (Imrie, 2005). In this complex terrain perceptions of beauty, security and belonging can make a huge overall difference to whether a person feels able to venture out of their home. Even the simple configuration of a door has important practical and symbolic impacts (Kaup, 2011). 'How residents feel about their neighbourhood, and how they perceive *others* to view their neighbourhood are related to both their perceptions of home quality, and their feelings of status and control' (Clark and Kearns, 2012, p. 934). Clare Cooper-Marcuse and Wendy Sarkissian's *Housing as if People Mattered*, research based on nearly 100 post-occupancy evaluations (POEs) in the UK and elsewhere came to the, perhaps obvious, conclusion that the overall impression of homes had a considerable effect on the way that people felt about them (Cooper-Marcuse and Sarkissian, 1986). Further, if a person perceives the place that they are in to be beautiful, it can have a radical impact on their sense of wellbeing (Aspinall et al., 2010; Ipsos Mori and CABE, 2010). The word 'beauty', despite its fascination for philosophers over millennia, has been ruled out in debates about the built environment because of its elitist connotations, yet as the Commission for Architecture in the Built Environment (CABE) has shown, different people have different ideas of beauty, it is a word that the public understands and relates to. Further, beauty is something that people need, satisfying some inherent aspect of what it means to be human. Beauty in place is also seen as part of a cycle of respect: it can make people respect an area more and, by being respected, an area can retain its beauty. People's overall ability to appreciate beauty is affected by whether they feel comfortable, safe and included in a place. Hence, when there is a shared history, feeling of community and pride in a place, people are more likely to say they experience beauty there (Ipsos Mori and CABE, 2010).

Research has shown the importance of building distinctive features into housing, a sense of identity being important for neighbourhood satisfaction (CABE, 2005) as well as real estate value (Forrest et al., 1997). 'Historical associations and character' are important for homeowner satisfaction – 'The patina and mellowness of building components: robustness, aesthetic appeal, emotional connections' are important. People want building materials that 'age well' (Nordwall and Olofsson, 2013, p. 19). Whether buildings are in a modern or pseudo vernacular style is less important to homeowners than the care that is visible in their detail (Horn, 2018). 'Care' has also been shown to be important in the design of religious buildings, alongside 'visual richness' (Mazumdar and Mazumdar, 2009; Herzog et al., 2011). Interestingly there is a growing body of evidence that the blandness of our urban environment is impacting on mental health (Urist, 2016). Diversity is important (Steemers and Steane, 2004).

A sense of autonomy and feelings of security relate directly back to the experience of space (Steenwinkel et al., 2012). Design can play a very important role in the reduction of crime and perceptions of safety (Armitage, 2013). Design against crime works at different scales, from the layout of streets to the design of front doors. Perceptions of safety, for example relating to levels of street lighting, can impact on feelings of wellbeing (Suzy Lamplugh Trust, 2013) and on children walking to school. Findings suggest that

> neighbourliness – including reciprocal relationship and trust of neighbours as well as neighbourly knowledge and contacts – increases with the cumulative presence of physical-environment characteristics that provide semi private space for informal interaction, including front porches, continuous sidewalks, and freedom from high-traffic streets, bars on windows and doors, and litter and graffiti.
>
> (Wilkerson et al., 2012, p. 606)

The health benefits of place-making have in recent years received increasing recognition at even the highest levels of government (Barton and Tsourou, 2000;

Marmot, 2010; UK Gov, 2010). The quality and form of the built environment has a profound impact on physical activity (Aminian et al., 2015; Burney and Claflin, 2015) and obesity (Kate et al., 2014), but studies vary in quality (Sivam et al., 2012). In terms of wellbeing there are some quick fixes that can be done by planners and architects to improve physical wellbeing at the scale of urbanism through the provision of green space and safe green routes for walking and bicycling (Hillsdon et al., 2011), as well as consideration of the needs of different user groups, particularly older people (Aspinall et al., 2010). Access to green space is beneficial to people's health, regardless of their economic circumstances. The extent to which it is used directly relates to its quality (Mitchell and Popham, 2008). Perhaps unsurprisingly large open spaces do not promote positive community feelings as much as smaller natural areas close to housing. A sense of community cohesion can be further promoted by providing a range of uses including private and public activities that keep the area animated throughout the day for the enjoyment of a wide range of users (Kaplan, 1985, 1984). Research is proving what we innately know, that design can have a profound impact on the way people feel and think and hence upon wellbeing (Pfeiffer and Cloutier, 2016).

7.2 Create places for community interaction

The democratic design studio approach of architects lends itself to work with communities in supporting bottom-up development and helps resist the negative impact of regeneration. There are many examples the world over but R-Urban, the work of Atelier d'Architecture Autogérée (AAA) in Paris, is notable, not only for its achievements but also for its ability to evidence and disseminate them (Figure 7.1). 'R-Urban provides tools and resources to facilitate citizen involvement in this project, including accompanying emerging projects at

Figure 7.1 **Agrocité R-Urban in Colombes, France (2016). Photo © Atelier d'Architecture Autogérée.**

local and regional levels that are working to meet the same ends' (R-Urban, 2016). Its first pilot unit at Colombes in France, comprising urban agriculture, residential space, recycling and community gardens, explores the development of community resilience through the co-production of community assets and provides a good example of the way in which 'architects and researchers could play an important role in designing and creating new conditions for resilient living through communing' (Petrescu et al., 2016, p. 17). The recent book *The Social (Re)Production of Architecture* brings together a wide range of projects in a similar vein (Petrescu and Trogal, 2017).

Community involvement in urban design can enrich social networks with direct benefits for social value and wellbeing (Semenza and Tanya, 2009). David Halpern has noted that 'the form of the built environment can strongly influence friendship and group formation (Halpern, 1995, p. 119). Choreographing the degree of interaction between neighbours is a complex issue, particularly in high-density settings (CABE, 2005) and in situations in which neighbours have no desire for interaction (CABE, 2005). There has over recent years been a drive towards mixed development (Joseph and Chaskin, 2010). While mixed use may create diverse communities, it doesn't necessarily foster social inclusiveness (URBED, 2000). The choreography of the mix takes considerable skill and needs to be developed over time.

7.3 Co-create places to foster a sense of identity

As mentioned already, there is very broad agreement about the importance of involving people in the conception of their own places. The architecture/planning co-operative URBED provides an excellent exemplar of a practice that focuses on participatory work and the 'visioning' of community (URBED, 2000) (Figure 7.2), another underexplored aspect of architecture. As John Punter notes 'it has a particularly important role to play in conveying desirable urban futures and building public consensus to deliver them' (Punter, 2011, p. 29). A NEF study based in Peckham in London found that

> the use of local designers and artists in the development of the streetscape in the Bellenden neighbourhood roused curiosity in residents and bestowed the place with a uniqueness and distinctiveness, features which are thought to be important for a shared sense of belonging.
>
> (NEF, 2012)

Interestingly a research project based in Hull revealed that residents derived 'comfort' even from the predictability of 'kitsch' place-branding exercises put in place by developers (Atkinson, 2007) – for example a nautical theme – so imagine how much more powerful a community generated vision might be, especially if the Hawthorne Effect (the way human subjects in experiments change their behaviour because they know they are being observed) is taken into consideration.

(a) 

(b) 

(c) 

Figure 7.2
Consultations with URBED in Anfield, Liverpool with Debbie Fuller (2006), in Old Trafford, Manchester with David Rudlin (2011) and in Rochdale with Shruti Hemani (2005).
Photo © URBED.

Designing the identity of a place, sometimes known as place branding (Hall, 2013), makes most sense when it is done with the community, for example the 'anti-*tabula rasa*' work by Crimson with Fashion Architecture Taste (FAT) at Hoogvliet in the Netherlands (Crimson Architectural Historians and Rottenberg, 2007). 'We wanted to show what the inhabitants themselves had to offer. We wanted to exploit their creativity and make them responsible for projects we developed with them' (Crimson Architectural Historians, 2017).

Heritage of course plays a vital role in the creation of identity (Neill, 2004). Conservation architects traditionally deal with the conservation of built fabric, but more and more they are being asked to consider the intangible social fabric of the environment (English Heritage, 2006, 2011; Heritage Alliance, 2011). The process of assigning significance to buildings is a socio-cultural activity rather than a purely technical one (De La Torre and Mason, 2002).

> In a world that is increasingly subject to the forces of globalization and homogenization, and in a world in which the search for cultural identity is sometimes pursued through aggressive nationalism and the suppression of the cultures of minorities, the essential contribution made by the consideration of authenticity in conservation practice is to clarify and illuminate the collective memory of humanity.
>
> (ICOMOS, 1994)

There is an opportunity to communicate a 'long view' of design processes to the general public and to policymakers, and to demonstrate the value that can be accrued through professional design skills in the careful editing and accretion of existing spaces throughout the management-of-change model of conservation practice (Samuel et al., 2014, p. 42). Such is the complexity of this issue that a diverse skillset is needed.

7.4 Deliver learning experiences

One of the mantras that runs through this text is that architects are not making enough of the user experiences that they offer. NEF observes a need for a 'new skills base within the sector in engagement and coaching techniques' (NEF, 2012), but these are intrinsic to social architecture. Architects facilitate learning through co-design, through the process of consultation, working with clients and end users to distil a variety of needs into a brief or built solutions. This can be at the level of a family home (Burnside, 2015) or a larger community (Sampson, 2015). 'Boundary objects' such as mood boards, Pinterest posts, models, plans and drawings are tweaked and refreshed as the collective vision is developed. New technologies offer new formats for consultation including the crowd-sourcing of ideas (see for example stickyworld.com) and the development of open-source architecture. According to Ratti and Claudel, 'so-called "participatory design" is an almost one-way street of endless questionnaires and begrudging stakeholder responses, whereas the magnetic energy of people coming together is a viral, powerful, unconstrained force that accretes as it accelerates, beyond the limits of top down initiatives' (Ratti and Claudel, 2015, p. 82). Their arguments for the power of new digital technologies in creating open-source architecture is a compelling one, but not everyone has the necessary access to technology.

Following on from its Peckham studies, NEF made a series of recommendations for future work in this area including a 'co-production approach' in which professionals share information and experiences with local people from the very beginnings of any project. They found that 'being actively involved in the development process through choosing street-level designs or helping to manage community gardens was important for stimulating social interaction and strengthening social networks' (NEF, 2012). In other words, the very act of co-design had a positive impact. 'This sense of "neighbourliness" was sustained long after the renewal work ceased and was identified as one of the core neighbourhood assets in Bellenden that supported people's individual well-being' (NEF, 2012). It can make financial sense to work in this way. An example is the case of a £2.2 million housing redevelopment project for the Shoreditch Trust in North London where savings due to community engagement were estimated to be in the region of £500,000. It was also noted that, compared with other projects, there were fewer delays and associated costs caused by responding to residents' complaints, reworking designs at a late stage to meet user needs, and on-site events such as vandalism and crime (Kaszynska and Parkinson, 2012).

Even better than involving people in the design of their buildings is involving them in the building of their buildings. How best to support non-experts in the construction of space has been the subject of a series of projects led by Piers

Figure 7.3 **Volunteer assisting with frame fabrication of Mess Building, Westonbirt Arboretum, Gloucestershire, Invisible Studio (2016). Photo © Piers Taylor.**

Taylor and Invisible Studio, starting with the construction of Room 13, a classroom for children in difficult circumstances, left purposely unfinished to allow them to take ownership of the space. In 2006 in collaboration with the carpenter Charlie Brentall, Taylor set up Studio in the Woods with the particular aim of making a space for novices to build on the potentials inherent in timber, the only rules being no waste, no tools and no measurements with drawings negotiated on the hoof. Most recently the Wolfson Foundation funded the construction of the acclaimed Wolfson Tree Management Centre at Westonbirt Arboretum in Somerset on the condition that it was constructed by students from the local college (Figure 7.3). While the buildings produced by Invisible Studio may be delightful, their real merit is in the process that drove their inception, a process that clearly can be transformative for those involved. The collective act of building can reap considerable community rewards (Mazumdar and Mazumdar, 2009).

It is really important to involve children in the design of their space (Yucel, 2008), not least so that they can be informed clients in the future. The remarkable Leverhulme Trust-funded project 'Children Transforming Spatial Design: creative encounters with children' shows just how much reciprocal learning between children and architects is possible (Birch et al., 2016). Despite government rhetoric to the contrary, a compelling case has also been made for the impact of good design on learning outcomes in schools and other learning environments (Barrett, 2015). Architype's work on a series of primary schools in Wolverhampton (Thoua and Hines, 2016) is remarkable for being built on an extremely creative and mutually beneficial partnership with their staff and children, who then become advocates for building in this way. The headmistress of the Willows School, Tina Gibbon, spoke at the RIBA Design Quality Proposition (17.11.15) of the 'high level of sympathy' between her staff and Architype and described the way the spaces of her school 'prepare children for the 21st century'. It 'has transformed the way I teach my students' and of the very general consensus that the building promoted 'active social learning' (Figure 7.4). The success of the schools has been tested through regular POE involving users (Hay et al., 2017), the result being a high degree of

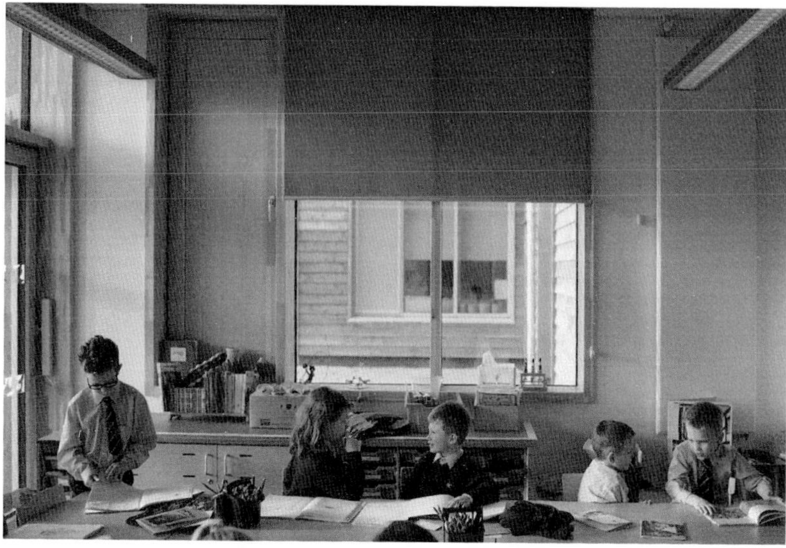

Figure 7.4 **Willows School by Architype. Photo © Leigh Simpson.**

ownership from pupils and teachers alike, exemplified by a short educational film made in collaboration with the pupils, *Passivhaus Explained* (Architype, 2016). A no less important issue is the ameliorating effects of a good environment on teacher stress (Uline, 2009).

Not only should the built environment be conducive to wellbeing, but it should also prompt intellectual development and personal growth. For Nowotny:

> More than anything, it is a democratic challenge, a question of societal participation and of responsible innovation in which citizens are not expected to only accept the future as it has been designed for them. Rather, they must be enabled to appropriate the future in the making.
>
> (Nowotny, 2015, p. 30)

7.5 Map and record community assets

As Bentre Frost, mayor for city planning in Copenhagen, stated in 1996: 'Without the many studies from the School of Architecture, we politicians would not have had the courage to carry out the many projects to increase the city's attractiveness' (Gehl and Svarre, 2013, p. 157). He is referring here to the work of Gehl Architects, who have played such an important role in making Copenhagen the 'best city to live in' (Metropolis, 2016). An example in the UK context that builds on the work of Gehl is Dinah Bornat's work on the way in which space on estates is used for children to 'play out' (Bornat, 2017). Mappings which record the movement and activities of people provide an important evidence base for space use over time as the starting point for future changes.

Tools of mapping are invaluable to make manifest aspects of spatial experience rarely addressed by other fields (Awan and Langley, 2013). Sarah

(a)

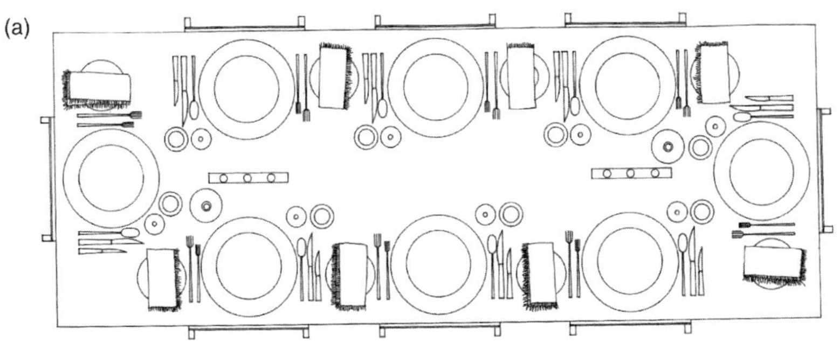

(b)

(c)

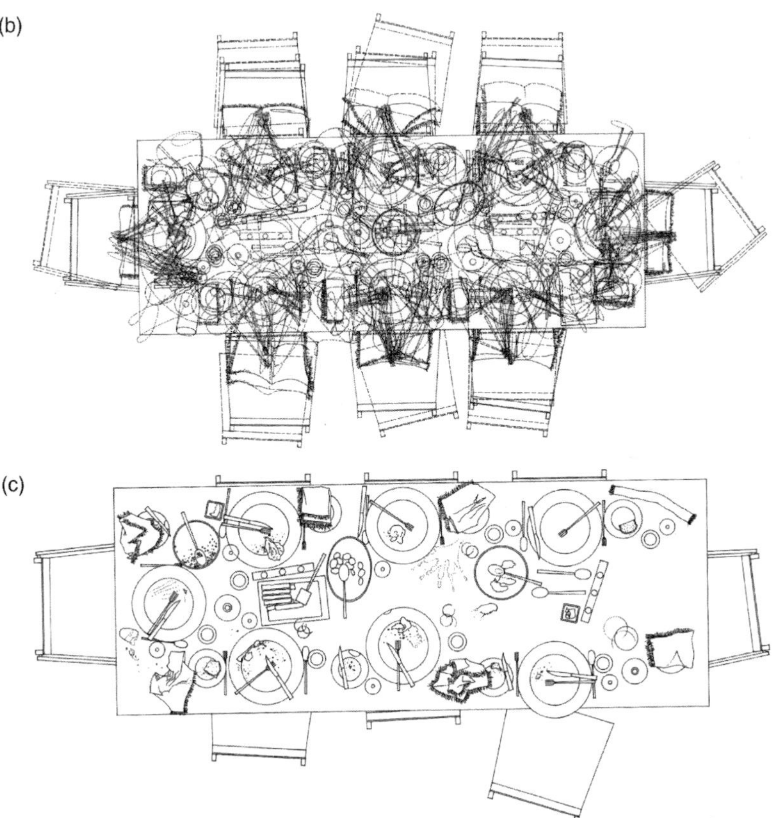

Figure 7.5 **Increasing Disorder of the Dining Table: Stock Orchard Street. © and authorship Sarah Wigglesworth, 1998.**

Wigglesworth's evocative plans of the dining table in her house tell a temporal story through the simple mapping of stuff (Figure 7.5). Nishat Awan's mapping of the social networks of a Turkish café in London indicates some of the intangible aspects of experience that might be included in such maps (Figure 7.6). Social asset mapping, the spatial mapping of social value, is a very undeveloped field (CABE, 2006), but such maps provide an important counterpoint to those that favour more concrete aspects of experience. Collaboratively 'mapping' the

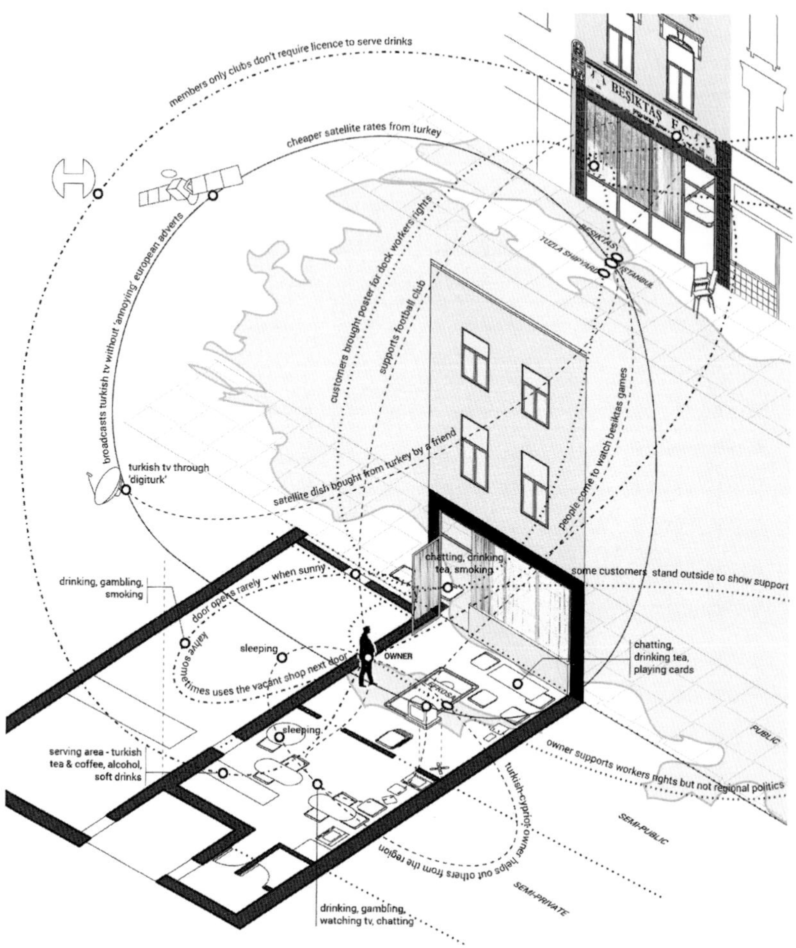

Figure 7.6
The Social Networks of a Turkish Café in London (2008).
© Nishat Awan.

assets of places is a process that could bring policymakers and service providers together with the wider public, creating platforms for genuine discussion about the shared aspirations for places (Alexiou et al., 2012, p. 8).

Some very specialized architects have taken mapping to new heights with the use of digital technologies (Yaneva, 2012). There is growing recognition of the impact of new technologies on perceptions of place (Tierney, 2013). Coyne points to the importance of drawing and mapping to make sense of the potential of these technologies: 'Digital devices are pervasive, but spatial understanding and the means to express it are not' (Coyne, 2010, p. x). With new research techniques and new technologies, such mappings seem set to get far more sophisticated. New GPS systems, Wi-Fi occupancy monitoring (which detects the presence of phones) and locative media have made the tracing of people alarmingly easy (Schaick and Spek, 2008). Computers too can be used to map social logistics (Hillier and Hanson, 1984). I look forward to the time when social value and the more intangible aspects of experience are integrated into digital models such as BIM, assisted perhaps by social media.

Conclusion

This chapter has set out a range of ways in which architects can and could support communities in the development of social value: changing the way people feel and think; creating frameworks for community interaction; co-curating places to foster a sense of identity; delivering learning experiences; and mapping and recording community assets. This is a range of services with much potential. With the growth of overtly ethical businesses there should be a growing market for ethical practices wishing to share a vision of 'good work' and the 'feel-good' factor that it can bring (Gardner, 2002, p. 5), particularly in a local context.

Unfortunately design for exclusion is common nowadays, not least in the form of gated communities (Atkinson and Blandy, 2006). In the UK the Social Value Act 2012 has been put in place to ensure that public monies are spent on activities that foster social value. The extremely complex question faced by professionals is how to develop the best 'conditions' to channel collective creativity in a manner that includes others in choices about societal risk and its impact on wellbeing (Rosenblatt et al., 2009). Architects should be well placed to help with this agenda (Jenkins and Forsyth, 2010) if only they can persuade others that they are capable of more than just pretty pictures.

References

Ahrentzen, S., Tural, E., 2015. 'The Role of Building Design and Interiors in Ageing Actively at Home'. *Building Research and Information*, 43, 5, pp. 582–601.

Alexiou, K., Zamenopoulos, T., Alevizou, G., 2012. 'Valuing Community-led Design' (Summary report for AHRC Connected Communities). http://oro.open.ac.uk/39646/

Aminian, S., Hinckson, E.A., Stewart, T., 2015. 'Modifying the Classroom Environment to Increase Standing and Reduce Sitting'. *Building Research and Information*, 43, 5, pp. 631–645.

Architype, 2016. 'Passivhaus Explained'. www.youtube.com/watch?v=TTUbsKPkKPo

Armitage, R., 2013. *Crime Prevention through Housing Design: Policy and Practice*. Palgrave Macmillan, Basingstoke.

Armstrong, R., 2016. *Star Ark: A Living, Self-sustaining Spaceship*. Springer, London.

Aspinall, P.A., Ward Thompson, C., Takemi, S.A., Brice, R., Vickers, A., 2010. 'Preference and Relative Importance for Environmental Attributes of Neighbourhood Open Space in Older People'. *Environment and Planning B: Urban Analytics and City Science*, 37, 6, pp. 1022–1039.

Atkinson, D., 2007. 'Kitsch Geographies and the Everyday Spaces of Social Memory'. *Environment and Planning A*, 39, 3, pp. 521–540.

Atkinson, R., Blandy, S., 2006. *Gated Communities*. Routledge, Taylor & Francis, London.

Awan, N., Langley, P., 2013. 'Mapping Migrant Territories as Topological Deformations of Space'. *Space and Culture*, 16, 2, pp. 229–245.

Barnes, S., 2002. 'The Design of Caring Environments and the Quality of Life for Older People'. *Ageing and Society*, 22, 6, pp. 775–789.

Barrett, P., 2015. 'Clever Classrooms'. www.salford.ac.uk/cleverclass rooms/1503-Salford-Uni-Report-DIGITAL.pdf (accessed 22.2.16).

Barton, H., Tsourou, C., 2000. *Healthy Urban Planning: A WHO Guide to Planning for People*. Taylor & Francis, London; New York.

Beauchemin, K., Hays, P., 1996. 'Sunny Hospital Rooms Expedite Recovery from Severe and Refractory Depressions'. *Journal of Affective Disorders*, 40 (1–2), pp. 49–51.

Benfield, J.A., Rainbolt, G.N., Bell, P.A., Donovan, G.H., 2013. 'Classrooms with Nature Views: Evidence of Differing Student Perceptions and Behaviours'. E*nvironment and Behaviour*, 47, 2, pp. 140–157.

Birch, J., Parnell, R., Patsarika, M., Šorn, M., 2016. 'Participating Together: Dialogic Space for Children and Architects in the Design Process'. *Children's Geographies*, 15, 2, pp. 224–236.

Bjogvinsson, E., Ehn, P., Hillgren, P.-A., 2012. 'Design Things and Design Thinking: Contemporary Participatory Design Challenges'. *Design Issues*, 28, 3, pp. 101–116.

Bornat, D., 2017. 'The Benefits for Research for a Small Practice', in: Hay, R., Samuel, F. (eds), *Professional Practices in the Built Environment*, University of Reading, pp. 139–146. www.reading.ac.uk/architecture/soa-professional-practices-conference.aspx

BSI, 2005. 'BS7000-6 Guide to Managing Inclusive Design'. British Standards Institute.

Burney, D., Claflin, A., 2015. 'Practical Considerations for Implementing Research on the Indoor Built Environment'. *Building Research and Information*, 44, 3, pp. 342–344.

Burnside, J., 2015. 'Co-design for New Lifestyles', in: Dye, A., Samuel, F. (eds), *Demystifying Architectural Research*. RIBA Enterprises, Newcastle-upon-Tyne, pp. 55–61.

Burton, E.J., Sheehan, B., 2010. 'Care-home Environments and Well-being: Identifying the Design Features that Most Affect Older Residents'. *Journal of Architectural and Planning Research*, Volume 27, 3, pp. 237–256.

CABE, 2010. 'Ordinary Places'. http://webarchive.nationalarchives.gov.uk/20110118095356/http://www.cabe.org.uk/publications/ordinary-places

CABE, 2006. 'Mapping Value in the Built Environment'. https://placealliance.org.uk/mapping-value-in-the-built-environment/

CABE, 2005. 'What It's Like to Live There: The View of Residents on the Design of New Housing'. http://webarchive.nationalarchives.gov.uk/20110118095356/http:/www.cabe.org.uk/publications/what-its-like-to-live-there

CABE/PricewaterhouseCoopers, 2004. *The Role of Hospital Design in the Recruitments, Retention and Performance of NHS Nurses in England.* CABE, London.

Campbell, N.M., 2015. 'Third Place Characteristics in Planned Retirement Community Social Spaces', *Journal of Interior Design*, 39, 4, pp. 1–14.

Carmona, M., 2001. 'Bibliography of Design Value'. CABE. http://webarchive.nationalarchives.gov.uk/20110118095356/http:/www.cabe.org.uk/publications/bibliography-of-design-value

Chrysikou, E., 2015. *Architecture for Psychiatric Environments and Therapeutic Spaces.* IOS Press, Amsterdam.

Clark, J., Kearns, A., 2012. 'Housing Improvements, Perceived Housing Quality and Psychosocial Benefits from the Home'. *Housing Studies*, 27, 7, p. 915–939.

Clarke, I., 2009. 'Design and Dignity'. Irish Hospice Foundation. http://hospice-foundation.ie/wp-content/uploads/2013/04/Ian-Clarke-Design-Dignity-Essay.-October-2009.pdf

Cooper-Marcuse, C., Sarkissian, W., 1986. *Housing as if People Mattered.* University of California Press, Berkeley.

Coyne, R., 2010. *The Tuning of Place: Sociable Spaces and Pervasive Digital Media.* MIT Press, Cambridge, MA.

Cranz, G., Lindsay, G., Morhayim, L., Lin, A., 2014. 'Communicating Sustainability: A Post-occupancy Evaluation of the David Brower Centre'. *Environment and Behaviour*, 7, pp. 46, pp. 826–847.

Crimson Architectural Historians, 2017. 'Happy Hoogvliet'. www.crimsonweb.org/spip.php?article51

Crimson Architectural Historians, Rottenberg, F., 2007. *WIMBY! Hoogvliet.* NAi, Rotterdam.

Darke, J., 1984. 'Architects and User Requirements in Public-sector Housing: 3. Towards an Adequate Understanding of User Requirements in Housing'. *Environment and Planning B*, 11, pp. 417–433.

Deci, E.L., Ryan, R.M., 2006. 'Hedonia, Eudaimonia and Well-being: An Introduction'. *Journal of Happiness Studies*, 9, 1, pp. 1–11.

De La Torre, M., Mason, R., 2002. *Assessing the Values of Built Heritage Research Report.* The Getty Conservation Institute.

Design Commission, 2017. 'People and Places'. www.policyconnect.org.uk/apdig/research/design-commission-people-and-places-design-built-environment-and-behaviour

Devlin, A., Arneill, A., 2003. 'Health Care Environments and Patient Outcomes: A Review of the Literature'. *Environment and Behaviour*, 35, 5, pp. 665–694.

English Heritage, 2006. 'Heritage Counts: Communities and Heritage'. c.english-heritage.org.uk/content/pub/HC_2006_NATIONAL_20061114094800.pdf

English Heritage, 2011. 'Heritage Counts: Heritage and the Big Society'. https://historicengland.org.uk/research/heritage-counts/2011-big-society/

Farrelly, L., 2014. 'Designing for the Third Age: Architecture Redefined for a Generation of "Active Agers"'. *Architectural Design*, 84.

Forrest, R., Kennett, T., Leather, P., 1997. *Home Owners on New Estates in the 1990s*. Joseph Rowntree Foundation. www.jrf.org.uk/report/home-owners-new-estates-1990s

Fujiwara, D., 2014. 'The Social Impact of Housing Providers'. HACT, London. www.hact.org.uk/sites/default/files/uploads/Archives/2013/02/The%20Social%20Impact%20of%20Housing%20FINALpdf.pdf

Gardner, H., 2002. *Good Work*, Reprint edition. Basic Books, New York.

Gehl, J., Svarre, B., 2013. *How to Study Public Life*. Island Press, London.

Gillis, K., Gatersleben, B., 2015. 'A Review of the Psychological Literature on the Health and Wellbeing Benefits of Biophilic Design'. *Building: An Open Access Journal for the Built Environment*, 5, 3, pp. 948–963.

Groak, S., 1992. *The Idea of Building: Thought and Action in the Design and Production of Buildings*. Taylor & Francis, Oxford.

Guite, H.F., Clark, C., Ackrill, G., 2006. 'The Impact of the Physical and Urban Environment on Mental Well-being'. *Public Health*, 120, 12, pp. 1117–1126. doi:10.1016/j.puhe.2006.10.005

Hall, P., 2013. *Good Cities, Better Lives: How Europe Discovered the Lost Art of Urbanism*. Routledge, London.

Halpern, D., 1995. *Mental Health and the Built Environment: More than Bricks and Mortar?* Taylor & Francis, London; Bristol, PA.

HAPPI, 2012. 'HAPPI 2 – Housing our Ageing Population: Plan for Implementation'. www.housinglin.org.uk/_assets/Resources/Housing/Support_materials/Other_reports_and_guidance/Housing_our_Ageing_Population_Plan_for_Implementation.pdf

Hay, R., Bradbury, S., Dixon, D., Martindale, K., Samuel, F., Tait, A., 2017. *Building Knowledge: Pathways to POE*. RIBA/University of Reading.

Heritage Alliance, 2011. *Strengthening Civil Society: The Role of Heritage*. Heritage Counts. https://content.historicengland.org.uk/content/heritage-counts/pub/2011/strengthening-civil-soc-summary.pdf

Herzog, T.R., Gray, L.E., Dunville, A.M., Hicks, A.M., Gilson, E.A., 2011. 'Preference and Tranquility for Houses of Worship'. *Environment and Behaviour*, 45, 4, pp. 504–525.

Hillier, B., Hanson, J., 1984. *The Social Logic of Space*. Cambridge University Press, Cambridge; New York.

Hillsdon, M., Jones, A., Coombes, E., 2011. 'Green Space Access, Green Space Use, Physical Activity and Overweight' (Natural England Commissioned Reports 067). http://publications.naturalengland.org.uk/publication/40017

Hipp, J.A., Gulwadi, G.B., Alves, S., Sequira, S., 2016. 'The Relationship Between Perceived Greenness and Perceived Restorativeness of University Campuses and Student Reported Quality of Life'. *Environment and Behavior*, 48, 10, pp. 1292–1308.

Horn, G., 2018. 'The Actions of Taste in Volume House Building'. PhD Thesis, University of Sheffield.

Hutton, J.D., Richardson, L.D., 1995. 'Healthscapes: The Role of the Facility and Physical Environment on Consumer Attitudes, Satisfaction, Quality Assessments, and Behaviors'. *Health Care Management. Review*, 20, 2, pp. 48–61.

ICOMOS, 1994. 'The Nara Document on Authenticity'. whc.unesco.org/document/116018

Imrie, R., 2005. *Accessible Housing: Quality, Disability and Design: Disability, Design and the Home Environment*, New edition. Routledge, London; New York.

Ipsos Mori, CABE, 2010. 'People and Place: Public Attitudes to Beauty'. www.designcouncil.org.uk/sites/default/files/asset/document/people-and-places.pdf

Jeffrey, K., Michaelson, J., 2015. *Five Headline Indicators of National Success*. NEF (New Economics Foundation), London.

Jenkins, P., Forsyth, L., 2010. *Architecture, Participation and Society*. Routledge, London; New York.

Jenkinson, B., Josey, N., Kruske, S., 2014. *Birthspace: An Evidence-based Guide to Birth Environment Design*. Queensland Centre for Mothers & Babies, St Lucia, QLD.

Jones, P.B., Petrescu, D., Till, J., 2005. *Architecture and Participation*. Routledge, Oxford.

Jones, S., Grigoriou, E., 2014. *Wellbeing Matters: Assessing Views on the Impact of the Built Environment on Wellbeing*. Feeling Good Foundation, London.

Joseph, A., Choi, Y., Quan, X., 2016. 'Impact of the Physical Environment of Residential Health, Care and Support Facilities (RHCSF) on Staff and Residents: A Systematic Review of the Literature'. *Environment and Behaviour*. 48, 10, pp. 1203–1241.

Joseph, M., Chaskin, R., 2010. 'Living in a Mixed-income Development: Resident Perceptions of the Benefits and Disadvantages of Two Developments in Chicago'. *Urban Studies*, 47, 11, pp. 2347–2366.

Kaplan, R., 1985. 'Nature at the Doorstep: Residential Satisfaction and the Nearby Environment'. *Journal of Architecture and Planning Research*, 2, 2, pp. 115–127.

Kaplan, R., 1984. 'Impact of Urban Nature: A Theoretical Analysis'. *Urban Ecology*. 8, 3, pp. 189–197.

Kaszynska, P., Parkinson, J., 2012. *Rethinking Neighbourhood Planning*. RIBA and ResPublica. www.bl.uk/collection-items/rethinking-neighbourhood-planning-from-consultation-to-collaboration

Kate, R., Veatch, M., Huang, K., Sackes, R., Lent, M., Gall, P., Goldstein, M., Lee, K., 2014. 'Developing Built Environment Programmes in Local Health Departments'. *American Journal of Public Health*, 104, 5, pp. 10–18.

Kaup, M.L., 2011. 'The Significance of the Door in Nursing Homes: A Symbol of Control in the Domestic Sphere'. *Home Cultures*, 8, 1, pp. 25–41.

Kuo, F.E., 2001. 'Coping with Poverty: Impacts of Environment and Attention in the Inner City'. *Environment and Behavior*, 33, 1, pp. 5–34.

Lawson, B., 1999. *The Language of Space*. Architectural Press, New York.

Leather, P., Beal, D., Santos, A., Watts, J., Lee, L., 2003. 'Outcomes of Environmental Appraisal of Different Hospital Waiting Areas'. *Environment and Behavior*, 35, 6, pp. 842–869.

MacPherson, H., Hart, A., Heaver, B., 2012. *Building Resilience through Collaborative Community Arts Practice*. AHRC, Swindon.

Marcheschi, E., Johansson, M., Brunt, D., Laike, T., 2014. 'Physical-environment Qualities of Supported-housing Facilities for People with Severe Mental Illness'. *Journal of Architectural and Planning Research*, 31, 2, pp. 128–142.

Marmot, M., 2010. *Fair Society Healthy Lives: The Marmot Review 2010: Strategic Review of Health Inequalities in England Post 2010*. Institute of Health Equity, London.

Marquardt, G., 2011. 'Wayfinding for People with Dementia: A Review of the Role of Architectural Design'. *HERD*, 4, 2, pp. 75–90.

Mazumdar, S., Mazumdar, S., 2009. 'Religious Placemaking and Community Building in Diaspora'. *Environment and Behavior*, 41, 3, pp. 307–337.

McCarthy, S., 2015. 'Delivering Real Social Value – Apprenticeships, Procurement and Employment'. www.britishland.com/sustainability/blogs/articles/2015/delivering-real-social-value-apprenticeships-procurement-and-employment

Metropolis, 2016. 'The Ten Best Cities to Live in 2016'. www.metropolismag.com/cities/the-best-cities-to-live-in

Miller, D., 2009. *Stuff*, Polity, Cambridge.

Mitchell, M., Burton, E., Raman, S., Blackman, T., Jenks, M., Williams, K., 2003. 'Making the Outside World Dementia-friendly: Design Issues and Considerations'. *Environment and Planning B*, 30, 4, pp. 605–632.

Mitchell, R., Popham, F., 2008. 'Effect of Exposure to Natural Environment on Health Inequalities: An Observational Population Study'. *The Lancet*, 372, 9650, pp. 1655–1660.

Nagib, W., Williams, A., 2016. 'Towards an Autism-friendly Home Environment'. *Housing Studies*, 32, 2, pp. 140–167.

NEF, 2012. 'Good Foundations: Towards a Low Carbon, High Well-Being Built Environment'. http://neweconomics.org/2012/02/good-foundations/

Neill, W.J.V., 2004. *Urban Planning and Cultural Identity*. Psychology Press, Hove.

Nordwall, U., Olofsson, T., 2013. 'Architectural Caring: Architectural Qualities from a Residential Property Perspective'. *Architectural Engineering and Design Management*, 9, 1, pp. 1–20.

Nowotny, H., 2015. *The Cunning of Uncertainty*. Polity, London.

Petrescu, D., Trogal, K. (eds), 2017. *The Social (Re)Production of Architecture*. Routledge, London.

Petrescu, D., Petcou, C., Baibarac, C., 2016. 'Co-producing commons-based resilience: lessons from R-Urban'. *Building Research and Information*, 44, 7, pp. 714–736.

Pfeiffer, D., Cloutier, S., 2016. 'Planning for Happy Neighborhoods'. *Journal of the American Planning Association*, 82, 3, pp. 267–279.

Punter, J., 2011. 'Urban Design and the English Urban Renaissance 1999–2009: A Review and Preliminary Evaluation'. *Journal of Urban Design*, 16, 1, pp. 1–41.

Quirk, V., 2012. 'After the Meltdown: Where Does Architecture Go from here?' ArchDaily. www.archdaily.com/226248/after-the-meltdown-where-does-architecture-go-from-here/

Ratti, C., Claudel, M. (eds), 2015. *Open Source Architecture*. Thames and Hudson, London.

Rosenblatt, T., Cheshire, L., Lawrence, G., 2009. 'Social Interaction and Sense of Community in a Master Planned Community'. *Housing Theory and Society*. 26, 2, pp. 122–142. doi:10.1080/14036090701862484

R-Urban, 2016. 'R-Urban: About'. http://r-urban.net/en/sample-page/

Sampson, J., 2015. 'Visioning Brentford Lock West', in: Dye, A., Samuel, F. (eds), *Demystifying Architectural Research*. RIBA Enterprises, Newcastle-upon-Tyne, pp. 62–66.

Samuel, F., Awan, N., Handler, S., Lintonbon, J., 2014. *Cultural Value of Architects in Homes and Neighbourhoods*. University of Sheffield/AHRC.

Schaick, J., Spek, S.C., 2008. *Urbanism on Track: Application of Tracking Technologies in Urbanism*. IOS Press, Amsterdam.

Scher, P., Senior, P., 2000. 'Research and Evaluation of the Exeter Health Care Arts Project'. *Medical Humanities*, 26, 2, pp. 71–78.

Scottish Executive, M., 2006. *A Literature Review of the Social, Economic and Environmental Impact of Design*. Scottish Executive. www.gov.scot/Publications/2006/07/21095819/0

Seidel, A.D., Kim, J.T., Tanaka, I.B.R., 2012. 'Architects, Urban Design, Health and the Built Environment'. *Journal of Architectural and Planning Research*, 29, 3, pp. 241–268.

Semenza, J.C., Tanya, L., 2009. 'An Urban Community-Based Intervention to Advance Social Interactions'. *Environment and Behavior*, 41, 1, pp. 22–42.

Sivam, A., Karuppannan, S., Koohsari, M.J., Mohammed, A., 2012. 'Does Urban Design Influence Physical Activity in the Reduction of Obesity? A Review of Evidence'. *Open Urban Studies Journal*, 5, pp. 14–21.

Steemers, K., Steane, M.A., 2004. *Environmental Diversity in Architecture*. Spon, London.

Steenwinkel, I.V., Baumers, S., Heylighen, A., 2012. 'Home in Later Life'. *Home Cultures*, 9, 2, pp. 195–217.

Stern, A.L., MacRae, S., Gerteis, M., Harrison, T., Fowler, E., Edgman-Levitan, S., Walker, J., Ruga, W., 2003. 'Understanding the Consumer Perspective to Improve Design Quality'. *Journal of Architectural and Planning Research*, 20, 1, pp. 16–28.

Stevenson, F., Baborska-Narozny, M., Chatterton, P., 2016. 'Resilience, Redundancy and Low-carbon Living: Co-producing Individual and Community Learning'. *Building Research and Information*, 44, 7, pp. 789–803.

Sugiyama, T., Ward Thompson, C., 2007. 'Outdoor Environments, Activity and the Well-being of Older People: Conceptualising Environmental Support'. *Environment and Planning A*, 39, 8, pp. 1943–1960.

Suzy Lamplugh Trust, 2013. 'Street Lighting and Perceptions of Safety Survey'. www.suzylamplugh.org/street-lighting

Thoua, C., Hines, J., 2016. 'Post-occupancy Evaluation of Five Schools by Architype'. *Architects' Journal*, 7 April.

Tierney, T., 2013. *The Public Space of Social Media: Connected Cultures of Network Society*. Routledge, New York.

Torrington, J., Barnes, S., McKee, K., Morgan, K., Tregenza, P., 2004. 'The Influence of Building Design on the Quality of Life of Older People'. *Architectural Science Review*, 47, 2, pp. 193–197.

Udall, J., 2015. 'Demystifying Social Research Methods', in: Dye, A., Samuel, F. (eds), *Demystifying Architectural Research*. RIBA Enterprises, Newcastle-upon-Tyne, pp. 43–50.

UK Gov, 2010. 'Healthy Lives, Healthy People'. www.gov.uk/government/publications/healthy-lives-healthy-people-our-strategy-for-public-health-in-england

Uline, C.L., 2009. 'Building High-quality Schools for Learners and Communities'. *J. Educ. Adm.*, 47, 3, pp. 400–426, www.emeraldinsight.com/doi/full/10.1108/jea.2009.07447caa.002

Ullan, A.M., Belver, M.H., Fernandez, E., Serrano, I., Delgado, J., Herrero, C., 2012. 'Hospital Designs for Patients of Different Ages: Preferences of Hospitalised Adolescents, Non-hospitalised Adolescents, Parents and Clinical Staff'. *Environment and Behavior*, 44, 5, pp. 668–694.

Ulrich, R., 1984. 'View through a Window May Influence Recovery from Surgery'. *Science*, 224, 4647, pp. 420–421.

Ulrich, R., Delani, A. (ed.), 1999. 'Effects of Gardens on Health Outcomes', in: *Design and Health: Proceedings of the Second International Conference on Health and Design*. Svensk Byggtjanst, Stockholm.

Ulrich, R., Quan, X., Zimring, C., Joseph, A., Choudhary, R., 2004. 'The Role of the Physical Environment in the Hospital of the 21st Century: A Once-in-a-Lifetime Opportunity'. Report to The Center for Health Design for the Designing the 21st Century Hospital Project.

Ulrich, R., Zimring, C., Zhu, X., DuBose, J., Seo, H.B., Choi, Y.S., Quan, X., Joseph, A., 2008. 'A Review of the Research Literature on Evidence-based Healthcare Design'. *HERD*, 1, 3, pp. 61–125.

URBED, 2000. 'Living Places – Urban Renaissance in the SE'. www.rudi.net/books/10433

Urist, J., 2016. 'The Psychological Cost of Boring Buildings'. http://nymag.com/scienceofus/2016/04/the-psychological-cost-of-boring-buildings.html?mid=facebook_nymag

Van der Linden, V., Annemans, M., Heylighen, A., 2016. 'Architects' Approaches to Healing Environment in Designing a Maggie's Cancer Caring Centre'. *Design Journal*, 19, 3, pp. 511–533.

Watson, K.J., 2017. 'Developing Wellbeing Valuation Practices in the Built Environment', in: *Professional Practices in the Built Environment Conference, University of Reading*, pp. 120–130.

Watson, K.J., Evans, J., Karvonen, A., 2016a. 'Capturing the Social Value of Buildings: The Promise of Social Return on Investments (SROI)'. *Building and Environment*, 103, pp. 289–301.

Watson, K.J., Evans, J., Karvonen, A., Whitley, T., 2016b. 'Re-conceiving Building Design Quality: A Review of Building Users in Their Social Context'. *Indoor Built Environment*, 25, 3, pp. 509–523.

Wilkerson, A., Carlson, N.E., Yen, I.H., Michael, Y.L., 2012. 'Neighborhood Physical Features and Relationships with Neighbors: Does Positive Physical

Environment Increase Neighborliness?' *Environment and Behavior*, 44, 5, pp. 595–615.

Wilkes, V., Mullins, D., 2012. 'Community Investment by Social Housing Organisations: Measuring the Impact'. HACT, London. www.hact.org.uk/sites/default/files/uploads/Archives/2012/03/Survey_Report_for_HACT_-_Community_investment_for_social_housing,_Wilkes_and_Mullins,_March_2012.pdf

Yaneva, A., 2012. *Mapping Controversies in Architecture*. Ashgate, Burlington.

Yucel, S., 2008. 'The Effects of Children's Participation in Planning and Design Activities on Their Place Attachment'. *Journal of Architectural and Planning Research*, 32, 4, pp. 271–293.

Zhipeng, L., Rodiek, S., Mardelle, M., Shepley, G., Louis, G., 2015. 'Environmental Influences on Indoor Walking Behaviours of Assisted Living Residents'. *Building Research and Information*, 43, 5, pp. 602–612.

Chapter 8

The value of cultural architects

Cultural architects, as an ideal, often take the shape of charismatic leaders. Their practice name is often that of a single person whose skill at design and marketing cultural cachet, designer clothes and strong personality sweeps the practice along in its wake, often with the help of a highly skilled business sidekick. They are not generally known for ethical sensitivity.

Given the visibility of their buildings, cultural architects form by far the most prominent category of architects in the mind of the public, usually for their role in the creation of 'icons', but in reality they make up only a small proportion of the profession as a whole. Cultural architects confer cultural capital to people, places and things (they sometimes have strong connections to the fashion industry), often backed up by the architectural canon as described in Chapter 3.

Of particular use in considering the activities of cultural architects is Pierre Bourdieu's concept of 'symbolic' or 'cultural capital', which Ceridwen Owen and Kim Dovey describe as 'a form of honour that accumulates in buildings and people' (Owen and Dovey, 2008, p. 10). In the past, high culture was very often associated with beauty and the highest levels of taste. It wasn't until the early nineteenth century that culture developed the artificially elevated meaning that I use in this chapter: 'the training and refinement of mind, tastes, and manners; the condition of being thus trained and refined; the intellectual side of civilisation' (Temple, 2012, p. xxiv). Art and aesthetics are repeatedly called upon by architects to justify their existence, to define their worth (Saint, 1983) and, some might argue, to obscure their collusion with the neo-liberal agenda (Jones, 2009). The focus of this chapter, then, is high culture, high art, the 'key market niche' of the cultural architect.

It is important in this context to remember that 'art is a fungible hedge' (Joselit, 2013, p. 1), in other words a good investment. Websites such as Artfacts.net rank the cultural value of artists on the basis of the 'attention economy' of exhibitions since 1996, including numerous architects in their rankings. Another website is the Mei Moses Fine Art Index, which rates art on secondary market sales. On the 'Beautiful Assets Index' art is tracked as an investment according to emotional appeal, enjoyment from acquisition/possession, the excitement of the chase and the chance to 'meet the maker', as well as longevity and financial performance. Art ultimately is 'quite a robust alternative asset class' (Phillips, 2015) and architectural exhibitions in art galleries and museums are a powerful medium for developing the cultural value of the highest echelons of the profession, a value which is then conferred on the client in both financial and cultural terms. There are a number of architects in these rankings. Impact assessment has now become so much a part of public life that 'it is only a matter of time, then, before the revenue-earning merits and demerits of branded buildings, and branded architects, are measured and consolidated into performance league tables' (Woudhuysen and Abley, 2004, p. 175).

The discourse of architecture is led by 'intelligentsia-managed institutions' (Olds, 2002, p. 155) which have a financial stake in developing cultural capital. High art/cultural capital comes into play in transactions of high-culture architecture; why else would multi-millionaire Peter Palumbo take ownership of Le Corbusier's Maisons Jaoul, to name but one example? The house, then, becomes a part of the connoisseur's collection, as it does when contemporary connoisseurs commission a high-culture architect to add cultural and financial value to their collection through the creation of its home. Historical examples are Michael Stein's (brother of the renowned collector Gertrude) patronage of Le Corbusier for the Villa Stein de Monzie and of course his Maison La Roche, built as a gallery but also as an artefact, for Raoul La Roche in the 1920s. It is worth noting in this context that the investment bank Goldman Sachs has sponsored the construction of the Serpentine Pavilion over the last three years (Goldman Sachs, 2017), one of the most prestigious opportunities currently available to an architect. In 2017 Diébédo Francis Kéré, an architect who cut his teeth doing some very remarkable socially motivated projects in Burkina Faso, was the recipient of this high-profile commission.

Heritage status and cultural value are of course very important factors for investment by highly mobile transnational elites not known for 'place loyalty' (Kaika, 2010, p. 467). These people are participants in a 'world culture' which is then overlaid on 'local culture' (King, 1991) of the place where they settle, casuing divisions in the process.

Of course art is not a monolithic entity, and some artists position themselves in active resistance to the commoditized situation described above, yet both kinds of art have become a tool of global finance and 'bureaucratized, patronized, professionalized, and commercialized, culture' (Nowotny et al., 2001, p. 27), a situation that has ironically left a generation of young artists dispossessed, deprived of funding, unable to rent studios, unable to find jobs. As with architecture, there is little collective solidarity. Not-for-profit artists such as those that work in communities (Alexiou et al., 2012) rely for their existence on public funding, their ability to attract that funding being related to their cultural capital.

The cultural value of art is strongly linked to designations of heritage status. Cultural heritage, sometimes blurred with 'cultural heritage values', received one of its first definitions from the Convention on the Protection of the World Cultural and Natural Heritage (UNESCO, 1972). Cultural heritage is defined in terms of 'monuments', 'groups of buildings' and 'sites' (Article 1). These need to be of 'outstanding universal value from the point of view of history, art or science'. Regularly updated 'Operational Guidelines' offer supplementary advice on the criteria for 'outstanding universal value'. A 'property' must exhibit at least one of the stated characteristics, the first, and for me most political, of which is that it must 'represent a masterpiece of human creative genius' (UNESCO, 2015, p. 15), the second that it must 'represent an important interchange of human values', the third that it is a 'unique or at least exceptional testimony to a cultural tradition', the fourth that it is 'an outstanding example of a type' ... the list goes on. A series of further documents, for example the Burra Charter (ICOMOS, 1999), set out the meaning of 'cultural significance' to include 'aesthetic, historic, scientific, social or spiritual value for past, present or future generations'. In its various iterations it has placed increased emphasis on social value and the need for public participation. Although 'the practices, representations, expressions, knowledge, skills – as well as the instruments, objects, artefacts and cultural spaces associated therewith – that communities, groups and, in some cases, individuals recognize as part of their cultural heritage' (UNESCO, 2003, p. article 2) are achieving greater recognition, the designation of heritage value is enhanced through the intervention of cultural architects and the value that they represent. The aim of this chapter is to develop a framework through which the 'cultural' contribution of architects might be described and ultimately evaluated.

8.1 Use a strong conceptual framework to create novel environments with high cultural value often derived from art-based practice

Cultural architects are characterized by a strong, but not always articulated, conceptual framework, which often emerges from art and performance practice or the critique of that practice. These practices are described in detail by Stephen Walker in his discussion of the methods of cultural architects in the book *Demystifying Architectural Research*. In it he explores the impact of Cultural Studies on the approach of certain architects to their work, each method taking a creative response to context, whether the physical or social aspects of site, the political context of institutions, the commodifying demands of consumer society or aesthetic trends in contemporary form (Walker, 2016).

A visit to Daniel Libeskind's website reveals a series of publications including *Sonnets in Babylon* (2011), a 'Collection of 100 original hand drawings by Daniel Libeskind, published for the first time by the artist' (Libeskind, 2016). Such books, easily imaginable as coffee-table adornments in oligarch households, play a defining role in the development of cultural value. There is perhaps no better example of high culture being translated into architecture than Libeskind's Jewish Museum in Berlin, the concept for which supposedly had its origins in musicology and Libeskind's own individual take on musical notation. Significantly Bourdieu singles out taste in complex music as a major indicator of 'educational levels and social classes', it being representative of the highest form of intellectual activity (Bourdieu, 1984, p. 16).

One of the reasons for Libeskind's success is his ability to evoke atmosphere. 'Buildings are the most effective and immediate means with which to presence such absences – be they absences of origins, absences of idealized futures, or absences of people – as the intimacy between people and buildings insists upon and which destruction affirms' (Buchli, 2013, p. 172). Atmosphere in the form of absence has fungible value.

Figure 8.1 **Danish National Maritime Museum, Helsingør, Denmark by BIG (2013). Photo author.**

'Experiential consumption' is a field of research in which the provision of atmosphere, lighting and smell is linked to buyer behaviour (Platania et al., 2016). Much artistry goes into the design of theme park rides and the queuing systems that precede them, yet it is rare to find a theme park that comes under the banner of architecture despite the best efforts of Venturi, Scott Brown and Izenour to raise the profile of popular taste among architects (Venturi, Scott Brown and Izenour, 1972). What is the difference between a theme ride and one of Libeskind's charged productions? First, presumably, comes cost and longevity – truth to materials is long gone – quickly followed by cultural capital and aura. Hopefully also the theme park is more fun.

In an effort to fulfil the visitor number and satisfaction requirements of their funders, for example the UK-based Heritage Lottery Fund, museums are under increasing pressure to offer experiences as well as education. BIG's Maritime Museum at Helsingør in Denmark (2013), set beneath the surface of an old concrete dock, provides with its expressionist angular planes and exciting ramps an experience enticing enough to engage the most intransigent teenager (Figure 8.1). Here the conceptual framework, seemingly a dynamic spatial game linking back to futurism, and a conservation strategy that plays off opposites of old and new (in the manner of the Italian modernist Carlo Scarpa), evokes the asymmetric and drippy experience of being seaborne, cleverly eliciting thought (Turkle, 2011) in connoisseur and child alike.

8.2 Confer cultural capital and power to client and project through practice brand

In his well known 1936 essay 'The Work of Art in the Age of Mechanical Reproduction' Walter Benjamin reflected on the 'aura' of the original art work and its subsequent transformation through reproduction (Benjamin, 2008 [1936]). The work of prized cultural architects undoubtedly retains aura, which becomes diluted as formulaic projects are rehashed, often without the input of the original instigator. There is a long tradition of paintings and ceramics being produced en masse by large studios full of apprentices in the name of a particular artist, a tradition that Andy Warhol played on in calling his studio the Factory, and one that continues today, for example in the studio of Damien Hirst. The point at which authorship is so diluted as to be non-existent is extremely blurry. The same goes for architecture, where inexperienced architects may be set to work on projects, often in less high-profile cities, that are low on the priority list of a busy practice.

The aura of fame contributes to 'iconicity' and the so-called 'Bilbao Effect', the economic benefits purported to have been generated as a result of Gehry's Guggenheim Museum in the north of Spain. The museum optimistically reported in 2004 that the initial investment of $183.8 million was recovered within the first six years of the museum's operation but everything depends on how such figures are calculated (Plaza, 2006). It seems that Bilbao even contributed to the overall 'brand' of Spain itself (Gilmore, 2002). Evidence for the economic impact of cultural buildings is growing (Scottish Executive, 2006), but we suffer from the lack of a systematic way of calculating such impact or defining its spatial limits. Will, for example, the impact of the new Museum of London end at the borders of the City? At the same time there is increasing recognition of the damage such buildings can do to local communities through gentrification (Bennet, 2017). Profit that is generated in one place may well be lost in another.

Iconic buildings 'are the cultural objects of cities par excellence' (Kaika, 2010, p. 454). For Steven Miles 'the iconic' is used by crumbling cities across the world as 'a sort of instant chemical high intended to, artificially, bring them out of a slumber which simply cannot go on, or more accurately cannot appear to go on' (Miles, 2010, p. 7). In this context he notes the significance of the annual European Capital of Culture, 'creating a kind of class hierarchy across cities' (Miles, 2010, p. 2). It isn't uncommon for city councils to specify that what they want from a new building is an 'icon'. A research consultancy employed by the City of London Corporation to report on the impact of its infrastructure noted that 'If one piece of iconic infrastructure were missing, the perception of the power of the centre would be significantly diminished' (Bourse, 2007, cited in Kaika, 2010, p. 471). However, as Maria Kaika notes, more criticism is needed of 'the dominant view that culture alone can save the city, intellectually, politically or economically' (Kaika, 2010, p. 471).

Architects create seductive symbols of change (Perez-Gomez, 2006) that are used by those who commission them to bring about new realities. Kaika uses Castoriadis's work on societal imaginaries (Castoriadis, 1987) as 'the basis for developing a concrete analytical framework within which to interpret the overproduction of aesthetic symbols at moments of institutional and economic crisis' (Kaika, 2010, p. 456). Architecture then becomes 'an instrument of statecraft'

Figure 8.2 **Dongdaneum Design Plaza, Seoul (inaugurated 2014), Zaha Hadid Architects and SAMOO. Photo author.**

(Sudjic, 2006). Through the creation of 'an imaginary institution' it can facilitate the transition of collective identity from a 'potential' to a new existence (Castoriadis, 1987, p. 187). An example might be the opera houses that are built, many in China, to symbolize cultural transformation, some of which are now underused white elephants (Eichler, 2014). New buildings provide very persuasive evidence that change is in the air. Architects can also re-programme buildings with positive new associations, an extreme example being the transformation of the Sultanahmet Prison in Istanbul (1917) into the Four Seasons Hotel (Arnold and Ballantyne, 2004).

The added cachet of a cultural architect can help authorities fight for a better quality of build than otherwise, as was the case with Zaha Hadid Architects' Dongdaneum Design Plaza in Seoul (Figure 8.2), though the constructional demands of such cutting-edge construction can be too much for some, as was the case with their Guangzhou Opera House, which has been literally falling apart since its completion in 2010 (Moore, 2011). The cultural capital that an architect brings to a project can have a significant impact on rental values (Fuerst et al., 2011) and can also be used quite cynically by developers to neutralize dissent against regeneration. The charismatic creator architect can transcend practical and social objections to their work through recourse to ineffable arguments and higher powers, hence their popularity with unsavoury regimes. According to Lang's examination of fifty international urban design projects, artistic arguments have often been used to make the case for anti-social designs (Lang, 2005). The majority of urban planning, certainly in the UK, is built by short-termist governments and impecunious local authorities to encourage consumption – shopping – with all the environmental and psychological problems that it brings. Such developments are not built for wellbeing or for the people who don't have money to buy (McNeill, 2006; Miles, 2010).

Internationally oriented but locally based clients may gain status for their project by involving an internationally renowned architect, deliberately ignoring local suppliers in the process (Winch, 2008). A recent case is the commissioning of Norman Foster and Partners by Cardiff Council for the redevelopment of part of its station area, a decision that caused upset to local professionals, with the apparent intention of putting Cardiff on the map. Whether the building currently emerging from the ground can do this remains to be seen.

Not only do cultural architects present seductive images of change for cities; they also present people with aspirational possibilities of other, more glamorous, ways of being. I find it impossible not to return to Daniel Libeskind at this point and the 2016 launch of his perfume for men Scent of Life, produced by Ferragamo, the design of his chess set for Swarovski, the crystal manufacturer, and his 'Time Maze' clock (best avoided by migraine sufferers) for Alessi. Alessi has of course also produced the famous architect-designed Michael Graves kettle and other kitchen accoutrements. It is in the design of aspirational commodities that the brand of the cultural architect is most clearly visible.

8.3 Carefully choreograph the experience of working with the practice, giving added value to the client

Cultural architects are extremely effective communicators and they go to great pains with the 'customer journey', to use the language of marketing. The clients who commission cultural architects are in many ways aspirational, keen to raise themselves or their organizations up the cultural hierarchy and into the limelight. Cultural architects cleverly position themselves in response to this desire. 'Most strong-idea firms cultivate an informal appearance: renovated lofts, art books and models lying around, the occasional piece of very fine art or the master's own creations ... open drafting rooms never too far from the principal's office' (Larson, 1993, p. 115). All this adds to the allure. At Foster + Partners' office, by the river in London, visitors are conducted past the pristine reception desk up a smooth white ramp past a bar/café where stylish young people confer, and thence into the hanger-like studio, where more young people pore over screens, surrounded by exciting models of components and buildings, all before a stunning wall of glass and the Thames beyond, and thence to gallery meeting spaces where clients can gaze back down into the creative spaces. The whole effect is overwhelmingly impressive (McNeill, 2005).

It isn't all window dressing, though. 'A key aspect of elite architects' role is in the management and motivation of a design studio that produces work of a guaranteed quality and distinction' (McNeill, 2005, p. 502). The risk to the client in employing such an architect is small and the experience of working with them is likely to be good. As Rowan Moore observes, 'Foster is popular because he supplies the look of innovation without the pain of actually changing anything; the establishment likes him because he lets it feel daring at minimal emotional expense; he is the purveyor of radical architecture for people who want no such thing' (Moore, 2002).

8.4 Market the practice and its work to inspire debate and media coverage

Cultural architects are known for having large public relations departments which exert powerful control over their own and their practice's image. Rowan Moore has written of Norman Foster:

> He exerts an extraordinary influence over British architectural critics, even the most acute of whom will give him an easy ride. When the Great Court [of the British Museum] opened, it was left to the non-specialist writers to make the sharp remarks, while the specialists (myself included) blathered about soaring roofs. It's not only because there is kudos to be had from curating Foster exhibitions, or editing his books, or because newspapers seek exclusives on the next big project. Nor is it just that the critics and Foster have been through the hard times together, when Britain seemed set against modern architecture. It is because he wants their support, more even than most architects, and the power of the Foster will is not to be underestimated.
>
> (Moore, 2002, p.52)

The media plays a central role in 'conferring agency upon contemporary buildings' and 'insinuating' an iconicity in what has yet to be built (Kaika, 2011, p. 983). As Kaika observes, it is no accident that both Libeskind and Koolhaas began their careers as journalists, only entering into practice after achieving 'international media recognition' (Kaika, 2011 p. 985). Koolhaas, for example, is purposely ironic in 'an attempt to build kudos and secure a place in history within a climate of cut-throat international competition over architectural commissions' (Kaika, 2011 p. 985). The practice brand, its cultural capital, is part of the unarticulated value of its services to the client, bringing with it a media attention which is crucial to the client in publicizing their project, raising real estate value and demonstrating their impact. However iconicity is now losing its gloss even for journalists (Dyckhoff, 2017).

The 'Gherkin', 30 St Mary's Axe, in London provides good evidence of the power of cultural capital that can be conferred by a named architect onto a building translated into cash for its client. Commissioned by the reinsurance company Swiss Re, the building was completed by Foster + Partners in 2004 with an enormous media splash based on its suggestive shape and technological wizardry, in doing so adding value to the client's brand. Three years later it was sold, 'confirming that the building's raison d'être had nothing to do with Swiss Re establishing roots in London, but served instead as a successful brand maker and a speculative real estate venture for the company' (Kaika, 2011, p. 978).

8.5 Use innovation in technology and representation to the benefit of brand identity

In the nineteenth century, the established styles – Gothic, Classical and so on – were used by architects to confer gravitas on buildings, in particular the 'secular shrines' that were built to 'assert the power' of the privately financed organizations for whom they were built – Louis Sullivan's work on office buildings, department stores and banks in and around Chicago spring to mind in this context. At the point that these secular shrines began to dominate everyday city life, people ceased to be citizens and began increasingly to be seen as consumers (Kaika and Thielen, 2006). The corporate world gradually caught on to the fact that its seeming progressiveness could be symbolized through innovative architecture (Domosh, 1992), a realization that gained momentum with the development of 'high-tech' architecture in the 1970s – Rogers' Lloyd's of London (started 1978) and Foster's Hong Kong and Shanghai Banks' (1986) headquarter buildings being early examples.

Innovative architecture has the cultural cachet and novelty to keep transnational elites interested in a city and to encourage them to keep their investments there. In a world in which novelty is valued for novelty's sake and in which selfie sites are programmed into cultural buildings to ensure their global reach through social media, it is hard to make the case for the more sustainable but expensive option of retrofit and refurbishment. Without a compelling story or image, a building will not find its way into tourist guides or airline magazines such as *High Life.* Once a successfully innovative-looking formula has been established – for example the complex angles of Gehry Partners or Studio Libeskind's architecture – they can be replayed around the world. One of Chipperfield Associates' most significant achievements is to give refurbishment an allure that is normally associated with new build in its restoration of the Neues Museum in Berlin (completed 2009).

I will only briefly touch upon one omnipresent form of cultural capital, 'bigness' (Koolhaas and Mau, 1998). The towers that, for example, are now encroaching on London's beloved skyline add novelty value to its profile, but for how long?

Conclusion

Cultural architects can add significant value to a commission but there is also government nervousness around issues of high culture, possibly because of its elitist and exclusionary associations. At the same time the demarcations between high and low culture are starting to dissolve (Nowotny et al., 2001). As a series of recent books on the demise of culture testify (Hewison, 2014; Timberg, 2015), the bewitching power of high culture is losing its sway despite the best efforts of a powerful intelligentsia. If culture is to have a sustainable base, it needs the support of the public (Holden, 2012). Most architectural practices consciously or unconsciously, position themselves — through their marketing and through their activities – as proponents of high culture, mainstream culture, low culture or even counterculture. Unusual and extremely international practices such as Zaha Hadid Architects address a 'world culture', a strategically clever move for a large practice addressing a mass audience and a mass market.

References

Alexiou, K., Zamenopoulos, T., Alevizou, G., 2012. 'Valuing Community-led Design' (Summary report for AHRC Connected Communities). http://oro.open.ac.uk/39646/

Arnold, D., Ballantyne, A., 2004. *Architecture as Experience: Radical Change in Spatial Practice*. Routledge, London.

Benjamin, W., 2008 [1936], *The Work of Art in the Age of Mechanical Reproduction*. Penguin, Harmondsworth.

Bennet, O., 2017. 'How Jaw-dropping Architecture Breathes New Life into Tired Cities'. *The Independent*. www.independent.co.uk/news/long_reads/how-stunning-architecture-like-the-guggenheim-in-bilbao-breathes-new-life-into-tired-cities-a7694756.html

Bourdieu, P., 1984. *Distinction: A Social Critique of the Judgement of Taste*. Harvard University Press, Cambridge, MA.

Buchli, V., 2013. *An Anthropology of Architecture*. Berg Publishers, London; New York.

Castoriadis, C., 1987. *The Imaginary Institution of Society*. Polity MIT, Cambridge, MA.

Domosh, M., 1992. 'Corporate Cultures and the Modern Language of New York City', in: *Inventing Places – Studies in Cultural Geography*. Langman Cheshire, Melbourne, pp. 72–88.

Dyckhoff, T., 2017. *The Age of Spectacle: Adventures in Architecture and the 21st-Century City*. Random House Books, London.

Eichler, J., 2014. 'Culture Under Construction: China's New Concert Halls'. *Interlude*, 10 December. www.interlude.hk/front/culture-construction-chinas-new-concert-halls/

Fuerst, F., McAllister, P., Murray, C.B., 2011. 'Designer Buildings: Estimating the Economic Value of "Signature" Architecture'. *Environment and Planning A*, 43, 2, pp. 166–184.

Gilmore, F., 2002. 'A Country – Can It Be Repositioned? Spain – the Success Story of Country Branding'. *Journal of Brand Management*, 9, 4, pp. 281–293.

Goldman Sachs, 2017. 'Goldman Sachs Sponsors Serpentine Pavilion 2017'. www.goldmansachs.com/citizenship/sponsorships/serpentine-pavilion/

Hewison, R., 2014. *Cultural Capital: The Rise and Fall of Creative Britain*. Verso Books, London.

Holden, J., 2012. 'Capturing Cultural Value'. www.demos.co.uk/publications/culturalvalue

ICOMOS, 1999. 'Burra Charter'. http://australia.icomos.org/publications/charters/ (accessed 9.11.15).

Jones, P., 2009. 'Putting Architecture in its Social Place: A Cultural and Political Economy of Architecture'. Urban Studies, 46, 12, pp. 2519–2536.

Joselit, D., 2013. *After Art*. Princeton University Press, Princeton, NJ.

Kaika, M., 2011. 'Autistic Architecture: The Fall of the Icon and the Rise of the Serial Object of Architecture'. *Environment and Planning D: Society and Space*, 29, 6, pp. 968–992.

Kaika, M., 2010. 'Architecture and Crisis: Re-inventing the Icon, Re-imagining London and Rebranding the City'. *Transactions of the Institute of British Geographers*, 35, 4, pp. 453–474.

Kaika, M., Thielen, K., 2006. 'Form Follows Power'. *City*, 10, 1, pp. 59–69.

King, A., 1991. *Culture, Globalisation and the World System: Contemporary Conditions for the Representation of Identity*. Palgrave, Basingstoke.

Koolhaas, R., Mau, B., 1998. *Small, Medium, Large, Extra-Large*. Monacelli, New York.

Lang, J., 2005. *Urban Design: A Typology of Procedures and Products*. Architectural Press, Oxford.

Larson, M.S., 1993. *Behind the Postmodern Facade: Architectural Change in Late Twentieth Century America*. University of California Press, Berkeley.

Libeskind, D.A., 2016. 'Studio Libeskind'. http://libeskind.com/publishing/sonnets-in-babylon/

McNeill, D., 2006. 'Globalization and the Ethics of Architectural Design'. *City*, 10, 1, pp. 49–58.

McNeill, D., 2005. 'In Search of the Global Architect: The Case of Norman Foster (and Partners)'. *International Journal for Urban and Regional Research*, 29, 3, pp. 501–515.

Miles, S., 2010. *Spaces for Consumption: Pleasure and Placelessness in the Modern Industrial City*. Sage, London.

Moore, M., 2011. 'Guangzhou Opera House Falling Apart'. *The Telegraph*. www.telegraph.co.uk/news/worldnews/asia/china/8620759/Guangzhou-Opera-House-falling-apart.html

Moore, R., 2002. 'Norman's Conquest'. *Prospect*, March. www.prospectmagazine.co.uk/magazine/norman-foster-profile

Nowotny, H., Scott, P., Gibbons, M., 2001. *Rethinking Science: Knowledge and the Public in an Age of Uncertainty*. Wiley, London.

Olds, K., 2002. *Globalization and Urban Change: Capital, Culture, and Pacific Rim Mega-Projects*. Oxford University Press, Oxford.

Owen, C., Dovey, K., 2008. 'Fields of Sustainable Architecture'. *Journal of Architecture*, 13, 1, pp. 9–21.

Perez-Gomez, A., 2006. *Built upon Love: Architectural Longing after Ethics and Aesthetics*. MIT Press, Cambridge, MA.

Phillips, A., 2015. 'The Problem of Value within the Regime of Art', in: *Transvaluation Conference*. Chalmers University, Gothenburg.

Platania, M., Platania, S., Santisi, G., 2016 'Entertainment Marketing, Experiential Consumption and Consumer Behavior: The Determinant of Choice of Wine in the Store'. *Wine Economics and Policy*, 5, 2, pp. 87–95.

Plaza, B., 2006. 'The Bilbao Effect'. *International Journal of Urban and Regional Research*, 30, 2, pp. 452–467.

Saint, A., 1983. *The Image of the Architect*. Yale University Press, New Haven, CT.

Scottish Executive, 2006. 'A Literature Review of the Social, Economic and Environmental Impact of Architecture and Design'. www.scotland.gov.uk/Resource/Doc/137370/0034117.pdf

Sudjic, D., 2006. T*he Edifice Complex: The Architecture of Power*. Penguin, London.

Temple, N., 2012. 'Prologue: Cultivating Architecture' in: Emmons, P., Hendrix, J., Lomholt, J. (eds), 2012. *The Cultural Role of Architecture: Contemporary and Historical Perspectives*. Routledge, London, pp. xix–xxvii.

Timberg, S., 2015. *Culture Crash: The Killing of the Creative Class*. Yale University Press, New Haven, CT.

Turkle, S. (ed.), 2011. *Evocative Objects: Things We Think With*. MIT Press, Cambridge, MA.

UNESCO, 2015. 'The Operational Guidelines for the Implementation of the World Heritage Convention'. http://whc.unesco.org/en/guidelines/

UNESCO, 2003. 'The Convention for the Safeguarding of Intangible Cultural Heritage'. https://ich.unesco.org/en/convention

UNESCO, 1972. 'Convention Concerning the Protection of the World Cultural and Natural Heritage'. http://whc.unesco.org/en/conventiontext/

Venturi, R., Scott Brown, D., Izenour, S., 1972. *Learning from Las Vegas*. MIT Press, Cambridge, MA.

Walker, S., 2016. 'Demystifying Cultural Research Methods', in: Dye, A., Samuel, F. (eds), *Demystifying Architectural Research*. RIBA Enterprises, Newcastle-upon-Tyne, pp. 81–87.

Winch, G., 2008. 'Internationalisation Strategies in Business-to-business Services: The Case of Architectural Practice'. *Service Industries Journal*, 28, 1, pp. 1–13.

Woudhuysen, J., Abley, I., 2004. *Why is Construction so Backward?* Wiley Academy, Chichester.

Chapter 9

The value of knowledge architects

Knowledge architects are generally quite invisible. They look like other people and they probably don't even know that they are knowledge architects. They aren't interested in the limelight. Their concern is with developing the systems and processes the profession needs to subsist, not buildings, so they are radically outward-facing and can be found on committees, think tanks and advisory groups across the globe. Their underlying motives are mostly good.

Back in the 1970s the editors of the journal *Architectural Research and Teaching* called for the recognition of a sector of the profession whose business was the study of the way in which architects worked, to reverse the focus on 'the resolution end as opposed to either the definition or solution ends of problems' (Musgrove et al., 1975, p. 43). Their activities, utilizing knowledge to improve how things are done, are celebrated by Frank Duffy in his visionary book *Architectural Knowledge* (Duffy, 1998).

In April 2016 I made a pitch to the Royal Institute of British Architects (RIBA) Council, as part of a motion on the importance of including young people within the governance of the RIBA, that the future of the profession would hinge on the way in which it organized its knowledge. I argued that 'knowledge architects', a developing professional category within Information Technology (IT) and Information Studies (librarianship), would eventually merge with 'architects' as we know them, as more and more of our activities were taken over by robots with their ever increasing ability to learn (Duncan, 2017). At that time I thought I was making a reactionary punt at predicting the future, but my continued research has convinced me of the need for knowledge architects and of the fact that they have existed for some time, largely excluded from the narratives of a discipline in which only architects who build things are deemed to be real. This chapter will give flesh to the bones of the category 'knowledge architect' as set out in Chapter 6, in doing so making the case for architecture as a spatial and temporal armature for thought and for action.

9.1 Make frameworks for the development of knowledge

Architects are generally fond of order (as opposed to chaos) and like to develop ordering systems and anti-systems (all part of the same tendency). Design projects should begin with 'The collection and ordering of information', an activity which always 'presupposes a theoretical framework of reference' (Echenique,

1970, p. 25). The odd thing is that, while most architects are unlikely to feel any kinship with scholars and librarians in 'social informatics', the first stage of developing a brief is categorization, the clustering of activities in a meaningful spatial format. This is one skill at which architects should be adept. 'The crucial issue is ... how priorities should be determined in buildings' (Canter, 1977, p. 38).

'Architects convert parts into wholes, elements into organized systems', observed John Musgrove (Editorial, 1975, p. 3). Knowledge architects use information to create frameworks for information and for people. To design is to prioritize information, functions and/or ideas to create a framework to express or house that information. Le Corbusier's obsession with categorization, ordering and taxonomies is an early case in point. Concern with building typologies is often treated with suspicion by architects protective of their right to work from first principles (Lawson, 1980), yet typologies lend themselves to the creation of templates, which can in turn be used to facilitate mass production (Imrie and Street, 2011). It is worth once again noting in this context that the pursuit of types and ordered systems did little to hinder Le Corbusier's creativity; indeed it might have been the root cause of his prolific output (Samuel, 2007).

An early example of the systematic development of an armature for the collection of knowledge is the work undertaken in the 1970s by DEGW on building typologies. With clients such as IBM, DEGW were quick to see the future impact of computers and were part of the wider systems-based way of thinking that emerged during that period. They organized their practice as a 'knowledge centre', categorizing their work in a systematic manner for future exploration. The 'database' grew in depth as the practice gained in experience and size, offering an important resource to clients, giving them confidence that their architects knew what they were doing, enabling them to undertake spatially based management consultancy and leading to DEGW's expansion into becoming an early example of a global practice, with 14 offices across the world.

Developing knowledge about and for the client was a practice priority. DEGW used sociology-based research as a basis for action, making it their business to help organizations specify the kind of space they required through developing a science of space use in relation to patterns of growth, the relationship between parts of organizations and their interface with the outside world (Duffy, 1992). In doing so they developed a knowledge of organizational behaviour that merged architecture with management consultancy and expanded the menu of architectural services way beyond anything that had gone before. A pack of DEGW 'image cards' designed to elicit ideas in a playful fashion gives a sense of their creative approach to consultation (Figure 9.1).

DEGW were among the first practices to anticipate the impact of information on the profession, on their clients and on the spaces that their clients used. At the same time they turned their lens back on their own practice to examine the development of knowledge within DEGW itself, in a continuous cycle of learning, reflection, action and dissemination through writing and leadership activities within the profession. In 2009 DEGW was bought by Davis Langdon, which itself was later bought by AECOM, one of the largest global

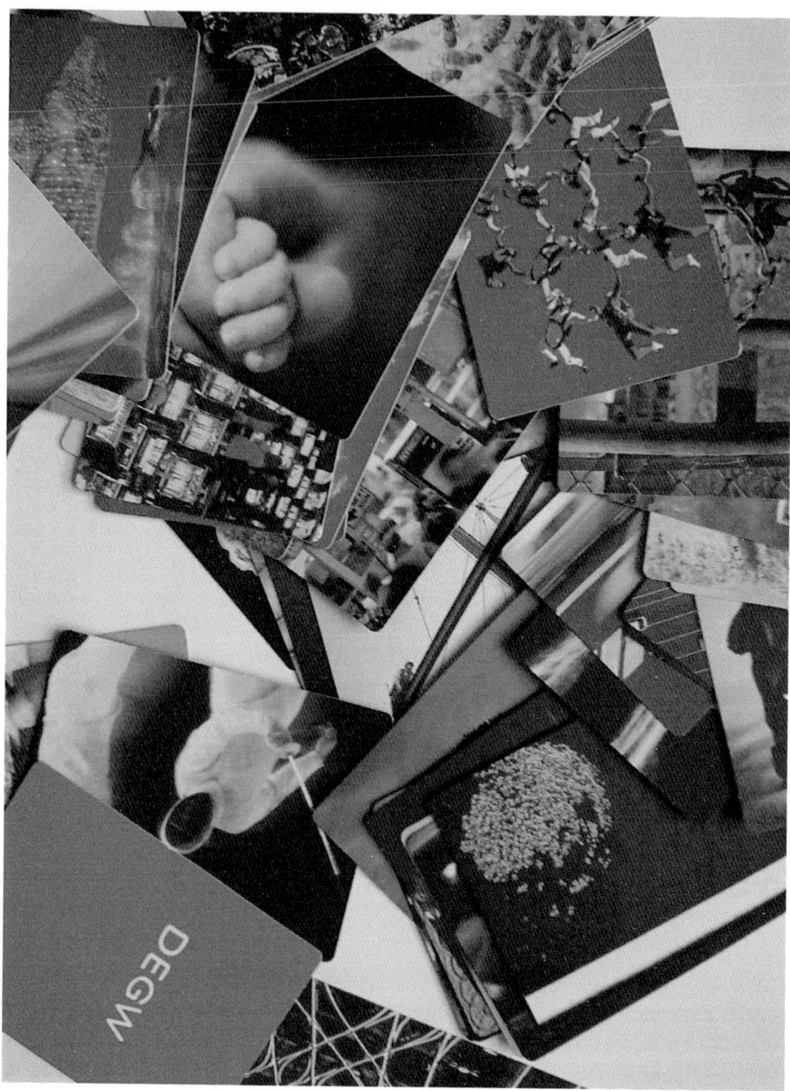

Figure 9.1
DEGW image cards from DEGW Archive Photo author.

built environment practices, with some 87500 employees. DEGW's working methods continue to influence practice across the globe (Greenberg et al., 2017). Despite the minimal extent of its built output, its influence is hidden in the fabric of cities all around us, an example being Broadgate in London. At the time of its construction (1985), marketing literature for the development of Broadgate in London celebrated the identities of the various architects involved in the construction of its individual buildings, but the name of DEGW, key advisors to the client Stuart Lipton, was nowhere to be seen. It is time to make this kind of activity much more visible.

A central problem for the profession moving forward will be the way it orders, curates and presents its services, not least to deliver mass customization and digital construction aligned with the needs and desires of people. 'A tipping point is approaching that posits architecture as information' (Ratti and Claudel, 2015, p. 96). It seems likely that in the near future architects will increasingly deliver much of their service via apps. Certainly with large projects most construction will be manufactured off site, with building sites becoming increasingly populated by robots. Integrated project delivery will be the norm and many construction teams will include data scientists, programmers, coders and computer scientists (Deutsch, 2015). It will be knowledge architects who lead on this transformation.

9.2 Order space for the development of knowledge

One way in which architects literally order knowledge and its production spatially is in the design of research facilities and libraries. OMA + LMN's Seattle Library and its play on the Dewey Decimal System makes this explicit. In their design for Biopolis, a life-science hub set into parkland in Singapore, Zaha Hadid Architects, presumably employed for their innovative reputation and brand, designed a series of key research towers named after Greek mythological figures, Helios, Chronos, Centros, Nanos, Matrix, Genome and Proteus, 'signifying the high ambition and international symbolism of the projects' (Ong, 2016, p. 2). With the spatial ordering of the towers the plans dictate which sciences interact with which and possibly the direction of travel of the global genomic research in which this institution plays such a significant role. Other examples include Knowledge City, a project that Scott Brownrigg is developing in Cairo in Egypt, and the multiple 'knowledge quarters' that are sprouting in cities across the world, Liverpool being but one example. Newcastle University has employed Hawkins\Brown Architects to design its interdisciplinary innovation wing Science Central as a learning laboratory. In such cases it makes sense to build on cutting-edge research on facilitating innovation. If academics and researchers are taken through a crafted participatory consultation process, the effects can be extremely positive (Pinder et al., 2009), not least on universities' understanding of what it is that architects do.

The use of office workspace – and its relationship with virtual space and homeworking – is a highly strategic design problem (Keeling et al., 2015). Around 90% of business operating costs are staff costs: 'therefore what may appear a modest improvement in employee health or productivity can have a huge financial implication for employers – one that is many times larger than any other financial savings associated with an efficiently designed and operated building' (UK Green Building Council, 2014). The impact of architects on knowledge work is becoming much more widely known. The design of office environments impacts on staff satisfaction and indeed on productivity (Brennan et al., 2002; Marberry, 2004; Agha-Hossein et al., 2013) and innovation (CABE and BCO, 2005), not just in terms of environment (Leaman and Bordass, 1999; Saari et al., 2006; Kato et al., 2009; Groves and Marlow, 2016). There is good evidence that the physical environment influences social behaviours and work processes and that workplaces can help or hinder collaboration, communication, workflow, coordination of activities, attention, memory and effectiveness (Kampschroer and Heerwagen, 2005). Unsurprisingly people want to work in a place that feels good (Strelitz, 2008), preferring smaller simpler buildings to large complex agglomerations, even though the latter might have more facilities (Strelitz, 2017). Such information is gathered by knowledge architects to help them develop successful design strategies.

9.3 Design user experiences to promote knowledge generation

The use of architectural knowledge to choreograph and improve client experience seems set to become a thriving area of practice if a recent report on the growth of 'Service Design' is to be believed (Madano Partnership, 2012). However, the delivery of services via apps and other scripted formats is something in which the architecture profession lags behind other disciplines. Much can be done to make the experience of working with architects more seamless, pleasurable, profitable and inspiring.

One of the great skills of architects is the choreography of movement around buildings (Groak, 1992). Architects in the heritage and leisure sector explicitly create 'scripts' for buildings that lay out the visitor journey to make it as engaging as possible. 'The script fixes and structures the story for all the members of the creative team before we start and enables us to check that the experience is working before we began to visualize it' (Greenberg, 2005, p. 231) (Figure 9.2). The experiential script then forms the basis of the curation of the collection and of learning (Nicholls, 2016). It doesn't require much imagination to translate this kind of activity into the virtual world, not least the imaginary spaces of games and films, which are morphing with experienced reality (Pavlidis et al., 2007), past and

Figure 9.2 **Story Board for the Olympic Museum by Stephen Greenberg. © Metaphor.**

present. A similar kind of choreography, albeit with rather different details, goes into the making of events, processes and information repositories such as websites. This is another skill of architects, another hole in the research and another part of their value proposition.

9.4 Design interfaces to make bodies of knowledge and big data accessible, including parametric design and digital construction

Leading on the translation of big data into useable interfaces is the innovation arm of Gehry Associates' office – Gehry Technologies – which has made a business developing formats for AEC (architecture, engineering and construction) to help clients access their big data in an intuitive way. Set up in 2002 it was bought in 2014 by Trimble, owners of the software Sketchup (Winston, 2014). A major element of Gehry Technologies' work is concerned with cybersecurity, an area of increasing importance to clients and architects alike, particularly with the development of Building Information Modelling (BIM). Architects working with highly confidential information have to commit to extreme degrees of encryption in their working practices. The dangers of neglect in this area are manifold including:

> the loss or disclosure of sensitive information which could impact on safety and security, but also the loss, theft or disclosure of commercial information and intellectual property. Any such incidents can lead to significant reputational damage, impacting through lost opportunities and the diversion of resources to handle investigation, resolution and media activities, in addition to the disruption of, and delay to, day-to-day operational activities.
>
> (BSI, 2015, p. vi)

The language of 'cyber hygiene' is martial, including 'hostile reconnaissance', 'threat' and 'risk appetite', perhaps because so many of the clients alluded to are military.

The curation of knowledge is fundamental to parametric design, a design approach in which knowledge is collected to generate objects from 'fields' of information. The process is never entirely automatic, as professional judgement is currently needed to choose the best option, quite often on the basis of looks. Architects in this field spend a great deal of time programming, but the final 'design' is at this time usually an aesthetic choice or based on highly simplified attributes of the brief or site. The possibility of a truly critical, information-based architecture is an exciting one, but it needs to be far more responsive to social and environmental needs than it is currently, one of the reasons that architects need to play catch-up on the delivery of rigorous judgements and on their digital manifestations.

Achim Menges, in his discussions of computational design, observes that architects need to move to 'the design of processes from which form, space and structure unfold' (Menges, 2016a). Computational design as delivered by the Institute for Computational Design (ICD) at the University of Stuttgart offers some inspiration in this regard with what Menges calls 'a 21st century subtext of making, wonder and production'. An example might be his team's exploration of the bubble webs of water spiders or the carapace of a shellfish. Highly sophisticated microscopes, time-lapse photography and scanners are used to describe the natural phenomenon in question, creating an algorithmic 'performance specification', then fabricated by robots.

> Through teaching, the ICD establishes a practical foundation in the fundamentals of parametric and algorithmic design strategies. This provides a platform for further exploration into the integrative use of computational processes in architectural design, with a particular focus on integrative methods for the generation, simulation and evaluation of comprehensive information-based and performance-oriented models.
>
> (Menges, 2016b)

The research process offers multiple sets of production possibilities, mass customization offering a way into a highly democratic design process.

Some knowledge architects are experts in the handling of large bodies of information, in particular big data, the morass of information that is constantly being gathered about our behaviour through, for example, the loyalty cards that record our patterns of consumption in shops, the digital tracks that we leave as we move around cities and the web, and our patterns of demand that are collated by local authorities, power stations and health services. How to make any sense of it is a central challenge of our times (Russell, 2016). The organization Urban Lens, for example, mines data generated from the use of cashpoint cards 'to discover patterns that can be used in urban planning, policy making and business decisions' (Urban Lens, 2017). Other forms of data collection include the historical information and photographs on Streetmuseum, which can be transmitted to a mobile phone to allow viewers to see present and past simultaneously, the collection of our photographs on Google maps and the collation of our contacts' opinions on restaurants and sights developed through apps such as Foursquare. These are just a few examples of the seemingly endless potential of digital interfaces (Tierney, 2013). 'Integrated cyber physical environments' should be the corollary of SMART cities (BSI, 2015, p. 5), although such developments are currently very fragmented (Dixon, 2016). Leadership is needed to make them into a collective resource for learning, another role to which the spatial problem-solving and ethical skills of architects are well suited.

9.5 Make rigorous judgments about the validity of knowledge

Architects capable of clear thinking who have a respected skillset and extensive knowledge base move into the field of expert witness consultancy. An example is Robert Tavernor, former Head of the Bath School of Architecture, who now runs a consultancy firm offering 'architectural design and heritage consultancy specializing in townscape, visual impact and conservation' issues (Tavernor, 2016). Gordon

Gibb acts as an adjudicator in construction disputes, his work 'underpinned by forensic analysis of correspondence, consultants' drawings, specifications, photographs and reports on building failure' seen through the lens of contractual obligations (Gibb, 2015, p. 128). Jane Burnside acts as an advisor on rural planning in Northern Ireland (Burnside, 2015). Richard Saxon, former Chair of the multidisciplinary practice BDP, is a client advisor and consultant. Such architects are in a prime position to slide into lucrative consultancy roles.

Some practices have made the influencing of policy agendas into a strategic priority and are recognized by other practices for their work for the good of the profession (Samuel et al., 2013). An example is PRP Architects, whose former director Andy von Bradsky was Chair of the RIBA Housing Group (2014–2016) and is now advising the UK government on housing. Policy-oriented practices tend to get involved in the crafting of the regulations, codes, guidance and laws devised to provide specific and predictable outcomes for all aspects of architectural production, from conceptual design to urban form. Participation in debate on the creation of codes is a rarely acknowledged form of co-design (Imrie and Street, 2011).

A further field of expertise is Design Review, requiring panellists known for their distinguished design knowledge to make judgements about the designs of others on behalf of such organizations as Commission for Architecture in the Built Environment (CABE) or local planning authorities. Their opinion has some sway with evolving planning decisions. Under Paragraph 55 of the UK National Planning Policy Framework, exceptions can be made to the usual planning rules for building a dwelling that is 'innovative' or of 'exceptional quality' (UK Gov, 2012). Influential Design Review members are regularly asked to make this call and are therefore powerful players in the process. Such panels generally have a sophisticated design sensibility based on extensive experience and assimilation of values in practice. As Jos Boys writes, 'both commonsense assumptions and everyday social and spatial practices are performed, reproduced and challenged through continual processes of negotiation; and this is a form of work that is both very important and goes mainly unrecognised' (Boys, 2014, p. 11). However, without an explicit framework of values, proper attention to issues of diversity and the back-up of a body of research, there is a danger that such groups are not best placed to represent civil society.

Perhaps the most obvious category of architects making rigorous judgements about the validity of knowledge is research academics, who carry out assessments for the research councils, peer review for journals, conferences and publishing houses, and sit on the assessment panel of the Research Excellence Frameworks in the UK and on equivalent bodies overseas, for example in Hong Kong. That they are called on to comment in highly charged situations such as government enquiries is evidence of the value of their accumulated knowledge.

Conclusion

Knowledge architects are kept well hidden in a profession that foregrounds and celebrates practitioners who build unexpected things. They are, however, key to the profession's future, as they will be responsible for crafting the processes and interfaces that ensure that architects stay relevant.

Knowledge architects are fully aware of the power of 'thought leadership' as a marketing tool, often using content-based marketing to attract attention to their practice and their activities. A key characteristic of knowledge architects is that they have distinct and rare transferable skills that can enable them to earn higher salaries and enjoy rewarding cross-cutting roles. This is because they know about their own value, communicate well and can hold their own in interdisciplinary environments.

I was recently contacted by an architect from a large practice who preferred employing non-architects to architects as they were better at research. This was what she was looking for:

> Ideally the person would have a degree in the built environment or social sciences e.g. architecture, urban planning, interior design, economics. Most importantly they need to think analytically, big picture and write clearly. We are looking for 5 years' plus research, briefing, and stakeholder engagement experience. Having project management skills would also be a bonus.

This is a job description for a knowledge architect and there aren't enough of them. For me it highlights the need to reconceptualize education and indeed the profession towards the way in which it frames information, the subject of the last part of this book.

References

Agha-Hossein, M.M., El-Jouzi, S., Elmualim, A.A., Ellis, J., Williams, M., 2013. 'Post-occupancy Studies of an Office Environment: Energy Performance and Occupants' Satisfaction'. *Building and Environment*, 69, pp. 121–130. doi:10.1016/j.buildenv.2013.08.003

Boys, J., 2014. *Doing Disability Differently: An Alternative Handbook on Architecture (Dis)Ability and Designing for Everyday Life*. Routledge, London.

Brennan, A., Chugh, J.S., Kline, T., 2002. 'Traditional versus Open Office Design: A Longitudinal Field Study'. *Environment and Behavior*, 34, pp. 279–299. doi:10.1177/0013916502034003001

BSI, 2015. *PAS 1192–5 Specification for Security-minded Building Information Modelling, Digital Built Environments and Smart Asset Management*. British Standards Institute/Centre for the Protection of National Infrastructure, London.

Burnside, J., 2015. 'Co-design for New Lifestyles', in: Dye, A., Samuel, F. (eds), *Demystifying Architectural Research*. RIBA Enterprises, Newcastle-upon-Tyne, pp. 55–61.

CABE, BCO, 2005. *The Impact of Office Design on Business Performance*. Commission for Architecture and the Built Environment and the British

Council for Offices, London. http://webarchive.nationalarchives.gov.uk/20110118111511/http://www.cabe.org.uk/files/impact-office-design-full-research.pdf

Canter, D., 1977. 'Priorities in Building Evaluation: Some Methodological Considerations'. *Journal of Architectural Research*, 6, pp. 38–40.

Deutsch, R., 2015. *Data-driven Design and Construction: 25 Strategies for Capturing, Analyzing and Applying Building Data*. John Wiley & Sons, London.

Dixon, T., 2016. 'Smart and Sustainable: Using Big Data to Improve People's Lives in Cities'. University of Reading.

Duffy, F., 1998. *Architectural Knowledge: The Idea of a Profession*. RIBA Publishing, London.

Duffy, F., 1992. *The Changing Workplace*. Phaidon, London.

Duncan, J. (ed.), 2017. *Retropioneers: Architecture Redefined*. RIBA Publishing.

Echenique, M., 1970. 'Models: A Discussion'. *Architectural Research and Teaching*, 1, 1, pp. 25–36.

Editorial, 1975. *Journal of Architectural Research*, 4, 2, p. 3.

Gibb, G., 2015. 'Working as an Expert Witness', in: Dye, A., Samuel, F. (eds), *Demystifying Architectural Research*. RIBA Enterprises, Newcastle-upon-Tyne, pp. 128–131.

Greenberg, S., 2005. 'The Vital Museum', in: Macleod, S. (ed.), *Reshaping Museum Space: Architecture, Design, Exhibitions*. Routledge, London, pp. 226–237.

Greenberg, S., Harrison, A., Smith, S., 2017. 'The City of Time: "Site, Structure, Skin, Services, Space, Plan, Stuff" and Then What?' in: Hay, R.F., Samuel, F. (eds), *Professional Practices in the Built Environment*. School of Architecture, University of Reading, pp. 147–154.

Groak, S., 1992. *The Idea of Building: Thought and Action in the Design and Production of Buildings*. Taylor & Francis, Oxford.

Groves, K., Marlow, O., 2016. *Spaces for Innovation: The Design and Science of Inspiring Environments*. Frame, Amsterdam.

Imrie, R., Street, E., 2011. *Architectural Design and Regulation*. Wiley Blackwell, Oxford.

Kampschroer, K., Heerwagen, J.H., 2005. 'The Strategic Workplace: Development and Evaluation'. *Building Research and Information*, 33, 6, pp. 326–337.

Kato, H., Too, L., Rask, A., 2009. 'Occupier Perceptions of Green Workplace Environment: The Australian Experience'. *Journal of Corporate Real Estate*, 11, 3, pp. 183–195.

Keeling, T., Clements-Croome, D., Roesch, E., 2015. 'The Effect of Agile Workspace and Remote Working on Experiences of Privacy, Crowding and Satisfaction'. *Buildings: An Open Access Journal for the Built Environment*, 5, 3, pp. 880–898.

Lawson, B., 1980. *How Designers Think*. Architectural Press, London.

Leaman, A., Bordass, B., 1999. 'Productivity in Buildings: The "Killer" Variables'. *Building Research and Information*, 27, 1, pp. 4–19.

Madano Partnership, 2012. *Scoping Study on Service Design*. London. www.ahrc.ac.uk/documents/project-reports-and-reviews/scoping-study-on-service-design/

Marberry, S., 2004. *Designing Better Buildings: What Can Be Learned from Offices, Factories and Schools*. Robert Wood Johnson Foundation, Princeton, NJ.

Menges, A., 2016a. 'Production'. Research-based Education AEE Conference 2016 at University College London.

Menges, A., 2016b. 'Institute for Computational Design'. http://icd.uni-stuttgart.de/?p=3343

Musgrove, J., O'Sullivan, P., Territ, C., Hillier, B., Leaman, A., 1975. 'Architectural Research: Problems of Organization and Funding in the United Kingdom'. *Journal of Architectural Research*, 4, pp. 41–43.

Nicholls, M.C., 2016. 'Digital Visualisation in Classics Teaching and Beyond'. *Journal of Classics Teaching*, 17, 3, pp. 27–30.

Ong, A., 2016. *Fungible Life: Experiment in the Asian City of Life*. Duke University Press, Durham, NC.

Pavlidis, G., Koutsoudis, A., Arnaoutoglou, F., Tsioukas, V., Chamzas, C., 2007. 'Methods for 3D Digitization of Cultural Heritage'. *Journal of Cultural Heritage*, 8, 1, pp. 93–98.

Pinder, J., Parker, J., Austin, S.A., Duggan, F., Lansdale, M., Demian, P., Baguley, T., Allenby, S., 2009. 'The Case for New Academic Workspace'. *Report*, Loughborough University. https://dspace.lboro.ac.uk/dspace-jspui/handle/2134/6037

Ratti, C., Claudel, M. (eds), 2015. *Open Source Architecture*. Thames and Hudson, London.

Russell, K., 2016. *From Big Data to Big Profits*. Oxford University Press, Oxford.

Saari, A., Tissari, T., Valkama, E., Seppanen, O., 2006. 'The Effect of a Redesigned Floor Plan, Occupant Density and the Quality of Indoor Climate on the Cost of Space, Productivity and Sick Leave in an Office Building – A case study'. *Building and Environment*, 41, pp. 1961–1972.

Samuel, F., 2007. *Le Corbusier in Detail*. Routledge, Oxford.

Samuel, F., Coucill, L., Tait, A., Dye, A., 2013. *RIBA Home Improvements: Report on Research in Housing Practice*. RIBA. www.architecture.com/knowledge-and-resources/resources-landing-page/home-improvements-housing-research-in-practice

Strelitz, Z., 2017. 'Spaces for Interaction: Empirical Evidence on Spatial Realities versus Supplier Mantra', in: Hay, R.F., Samuel, F. (eds), *Professional Practices in the Built Environment*. School of Architecture, University of Reading, pp. 131–137.

Strelitz, Z., 2008. *Buildings that Feel Good*. RIBA Publishing, Berlin; New York.

Tavernor, 2016. 'Tavernor Consultancy Architecture and Heritage'. www.tavernorconsultancy.co.uk/

Tierney, T., 2013. *The Public Space of Social Media: Connected Cultures of Network Society*. Routledge, New York.

UK Gov, 2012. 'Delivering a Wide Choice of High Quality Homes'. www.gov.uk/guidance/national-planning-policy-framework/6-delivering-a-wide-choice-of-high-quality-homes (accessed 18.7.17).

UK Green Building Council, 2014. 'Health, Wellbeing and Productivity in Offices: The Next Chapter for Green Building'. www.ukgbc.org/resources/publication/health-wellbeing-and-productivity-offices-next-chapter-green-building

Urban Lens, 2017. 'Predicting Socio-economic Indices from Big Data of Individual Bank Card's Transaction'. http://senseable.mit.edu/urban-lens/

Winston, A., 2014. 'US Firm Buys Frank Gehry's Technology Company'. www.dezeen.com/2014/09/08/trimble-buys-frank-gehry-technologies/

Part III

Making the most of architects

Chapter 10

Education for uncertainty

Perhaps the most important thing that we can teach students is how to respond to uncertainty and change, how to themselves become resilient.
(Nowotny, 2015, p. vii)

'One of the central predicaments facing the education of today's architects is that of defining the designer's expertise in relation to an industry in revolution' (Sheil, 2015, p. 112). In this third part of *Why Architects Matter* I make the case for the explicit development of transferable and interdisciplinary research skills within the architectural profession – a prerequisite for collaboration – as well as the focused development and evaluation of architects' subject-specific knowledge. Only by staking a claim to a clearly delineated and valuable territory of expertise can the profession lose the 'bogey of dispensability' and lay claim to the vital integrating role that was arguably its birth right. Architects' contribution to the construction process needs to be unpacked through the educational curriculum, illuminated through 'learning outcomes' and celebrated through assessment. The profession's reluctance to set out and explore the full complexity of the design research process, with all its setbacks and difficulties, may well have its origins in its education.

In my experience it is hard to find a more visionary, principled, talented, experimental, skilled, hard-working, useful and enthusiastic group of people than architecture students. However, architectural education in the UK is widely considered unfit for purpose by practitioners of architecture (Pringle and Porter, 2015). Sometimes it is even necessary to retrain students to make them useful for an office environment. This is costly to practice and traumatic to students, who rightly expect a smooth entry into their new roles, a transition which is key for future life chances (Schleicher, 2014).

Eudaimonic wellbeing, discussed in Chapter 7, the ability to fulfil a life-calling beyond the self, provides impetus for large numbers of underpaid and undervalued architects. In the opinion of Biesta it is the task of the educator to prepare the ground in which a student might be called to find their purpose in life (Biesta, 2014). However, the excitement and enthusiasm with which most architecture students begin their studies can leach away with alarming rapidity (Ray, 2008). A recent UK survey has shown that 25% of UK architecture students have been treated for mental health problems due to stress (Hill, 2016), suggesting that architectural programmes often make excessive and inappropriate demands upon those who they were designed to nurture. The problems of contemporary education are beautifully summed up by US architecture student Violet Whitney:

> I've spent a lot of time being overworked just to perpetuate the very things that I hate in the world. Most of the buildings I worked on after undergrad were commodity buildings for wealthy clients. When I look at my options when I graduate, the options aren't expanding. My architecture school likes to talk about inequality and social issues, and for what I have learned here I am grateful. But in order to start to chew on something as insurmountable as inequality, smaller practical tactics are necessary in combination with understanding and theory. This is where I think architecture schools are failing, and why they need to invest and innovate if they intend to have relevance. Most of my peers, including myself, will continue to prepare for the immediate demands of working in the current market because that is our reality. We will build things that are pretty, but they will not help most people. We will work long hours and talk about social aims, all while working hourly wages to make another commodified building that will make a developer a little bit richer.
>
> (Cayer et al., 2016, p. 10)

At the root of this situation is a tacitly absorbed cocktail of disrespect between practice and academia, spawned by insecurities on both sides, and a debate – often polarized – between those who believe that education should deliver graduates 'oven ready' for an outdated, cynical and unethical practice and those who teach, but rarely explicitly, architecture as a vocation (just how it will be paid for is hardly ever mentioned). Hence Violet's plaintive complaint. The expectation of high workload, unsociable working hours and unreasonable work expectations starts in schools of architecture and fuels the inward-looking and exclusive nature of the field.

The amount of time needed to become a professional is debatable (Sarfatti Larson, 1993 [1977]). In the 1990s the Royal Institute of British Architects (RIBA) put up a robust defence of the five years of university education deemed necessary (three years of undergraduate study to get RIBA Part I and a two-year postgraduate MArch to get RIBA Part II), plus two years in practice, to qualify as an architect in the UK (Duffy, 1995). At that time students were funded through their education by a system of grants, with their fees paid by government, but radical political changes to the university funding system mean that students in the UK have to take out loans to cover the cost of their education and subsistence, loans that they are unlikely to pay back given the current levels of earning within the profession (Wright, 2013). It is quite clear that more education 'does not necessarily translate into better economic and social outcomes' (Schleicher, 2014, p. 39). Many schools suffer from 'curriculum creep', in which more and more elements are added into the education with nobody having the vision (or bravery) to take anything out. It is no wonder so many architecture students feel stressed.

Architecture students are known for being remarkably versatile people. They have to be, as so very few of them actually end up being employed as architects.

The *RIBA Student Destinations Survey*, a ten-year longitudinal study of where architecture students eventually end up working, reveals that in the years immediately following their training most students try very hard to remain in practice until the realization dawns upon many that they might be able to make a more rewarding living in another field. What is most worrying is that a small but growing number regret having ever undertaken an architectural education in the first place (RIBA, 2015). While a university education might have been a good way to while away a few years during the transition into adulthood, it now comes with an extremely large debt. Unless clearly stated otherwise, universities have an ethical duty to maximize chances of employment. MacLaren and Thompson argue that 'portfolio professionals' are the future:

> She is likely to re-train for a sustained period at several points throughout her career. She is extremely unlikely to remain with a single employer for the duration of her career, and may well explore different and emerging forms of employment derived from new transactional behaviours, developed in response to market forces and digital abilities. She may find her early-career roles increasingly taken over by AI as machine learning develops, and as she moves through her career, she will seek support and direction in this rapidly-developing scenario from trusted networks and sources of knowledge.
>
> (MacLaren and Thompson, 2017, p. 89)

Such professionals will need a very particular education that enables them to work across boundaries.

The focus of this chapter is our attempts to develop a professional architectural education which embraces 'the beautiful risk of education' (Biesta, 2014), while anticipating and responding to 'the evolution of skill demand' (Schleicher, 2014, p. 39), at the new School of Architecture at the University of Reading, which opened its doors to students in 2016. Developed in close association with the existing and well established school of Construction Management and Engineering as well as key industry experts, it has collaboration in its DNA. We propose a model which explicitly addresses the skills necessary to be co-operative, versatile and resilient, a model which straddles practice and academia to productive, pleasurable, innovative and ethical ends.

We look back to the 1960s, a period when, as now, 'Interdependence and Uncertainty' were firmly on the agenda in the construction industry (Tavistock Institute, 1966). The discussion opens with a reflection on an experiment in professional education for uncertainty before moving on to a consideration of the skills and knowledge needed for the exercising of professional judgement and finishing with the learning environment we think necessary to turn students into resilient professionals sharing risk in a responsible and critical way with society.

10.1 An experiment in professional education for uncertainty

In its official guise architectural education began in the early nineteenth century as a reaction to the inadequacies of the pupillage system (Gotch, 1934; Mace,

1986; Crinson and Lubbock, 1994). 'The history of architectural education in Britain can therefore be seen as a search for an alternative to pupillage motivated by a negative perception rather than a clear ideal of something better' (Powers 2015, p. 6). As professional schools were assimilated within universities they lost 'commitment to applied work', even though they were set up to link practice with research (Boyer, 1997, p. 21). This situation was exacerbated by the introduction of the Research Assessment Exercise, which drove many architects out of practice into research. Remedial action was, and still is, needed.

Architectural education has long been used as an exemplar of the power of project-based learning (Schon, 1984), learning through problem-solving, rarely articulated in terms of research. Traditionally with an Architects Registration Board/ Royal Institute of British Architects (ARB/RIBA) based education (five years' full-time study interspersed with periods of practice) 50% of student time is spent on project-based learning, often taking the form of design projects, usually with a fairly restricted 'brief', building up in complexity across the years, each one assessed with a numerical mark and, ideally, qualitative feedback. Typically First Years might be asked to design a small house, while Third Years might focus on a small museum. It is helpful to emphasise the importance of using building 'precedents' as a jumping-off point for new investigations. For architects, precedents are just as important as 'research context' is to researchers in other fields.

From time to time design progress is tested through semi-public debate in the form of a 'crit', 'review' or 'jury'. A student or students have to stand up to present their projects in front of a panel of reviewers and colleagues. It is here that they are beginning to learn the skill of using their drawings and models as 'boundary objects' to foster co-creation with others, but these events vary greatly in their quality (Doidge et al., 2006). Students also have to take parallel 'taught' courses in subjects such as 'History and Theory', 'Environment and Construction' and, towards the end of their degree, 'Practice'. Ideally these modules should all connect, 'scaffolding' knowledge on the students' existing know-how, with assessment based on deliverable 'learning outcomes' that make clear to students exactly what they are supposed to be learning, but too often this is not the case.

An early example of 'education for change' is provided by the first paper in the short-lived journal *Architectural Research and Teaching*, founded in 1970. Diploma Project 1968–69, its generic name designed to suggest the open nature of its brief, is an account of a studio designed to: promote 'professional effectiveness'; 'encourage education for change'; 'improve skills in advanced architectural design'; 'develop effective attitudes to the professional role'; and 'prepare for team work in professional practice' (Abercrombie et al., 1970, p. 7). The evaluation of the project, a published pedagogical research piece, was structured under these same headings. Its first author – the 31 students and staff are listed as the project team – was a psychologist, Minnie Louise Johnson Abercrombie, then leader of the Architectural Education Research Unit (AERU) at the Bartlett (University College London).

The project, the latest in a series of experiments, offered a carefully choreographed educational experience lasting an entire year. Its 'intention' was to give students responsibility for their evolving education 'by involving them in planning the course, choosing their design projects and assessing their work. The 'core activity' of the unit was conceived as 'a sequence of problem-solving exercises of increasing complexity'. Following a short introductory ice-breaker exercise designed to raise a series of issues about the 'current professional scene' (Abercrombie et al., 1970, p. 7), the group was given a 'closed' task, an architectural competition for twenty-four flats for old people in Byfleet, Surrey, which led the group to broader discussions about 'social and ethical' problems of design for ageing.

North Kensington was chosen as the context for the next exploration, as it meant that the students could work with a variety of agencies interested in easing it out of its then 'twilight' state (it is worth noting that Grenfell Tower was built in North Kensington in 1967). This area then became a locus for an exploration of issues of 'social and architectural concern', individually and in groups, during the period between Christmas and Easter. The last 'term', from Easter to the summer break, was devoted to a synthesis of studies by the whole 'class', which took the form of an 'integrated proposal within the specified urban area'. This process was accompanied by an introduction to a variety of current case studies intended as 'a vehicle for understanding the application of technology, economics, contract procedure etc to design'. Within the curriculum 'Free group discussions' based on a lecture or readings happened on a weekly basis, often straying from their intended course (Abercrombie et al., 1970, p. 9).

Evaluation of the project was based on staff observations, student log books and comments made in the 'free group discussions'. The Bartlett had been pioneering new forms of assessment for some time, most notably in the work of Newton Watson. Having dispensed with a 'jury', Watson and his team wanted to recast end-of-session assessment as 'a teaching medium'. This was to take the form of a 'discussion' accompanied by a 'studio work record' (explicitly not an assessment), with comments under the headings: 'communication'; 'analysis of the problem'; 'structure'; 'materials'; 'functional planning'; 'services'; and 'inventiveness' (Watson, 1964, p. 359). The admirable aim of such initiatives was to encourage students to become less reliant on marks for validation and instead to become their own best critics.

At the end of the year some students reported 'a newly acquired confidence as self-learners and critical thinkers', while others lamented their 'turmoil, distress and uncertainty'. The AERU team are to be commended for their degree of self-critique and willingness to admit to failure. As is so often the case today, staff reported that students often experienced difficulties in making design proposals after doing extensive amounts of 'social' background research (Abercrombie et al., 1970, p. 8), an experience which was accompanied by 'frustration' and a loss of 'confidence'. In the absence of a marking scheme the students probably had difficulties deciding where to place their attention. In general there was 'a great reluctance to work as a community on mutual assessment'. The performance of one exceptional group was, however, notable:

> one member of this group contributed proposals for a mews housing scheme, the spatial organization of which fulfilled his wishes for 'participant

> democracy' by which the occupants could choose their own combination of spaces. Another member concentrated almost exclusively in provoking radical political ideas in the audience. The excessive length of the presentation (four hours with a short interval) inhibited immediate feedback, but the demonstration of skill, energy and enthusiasm made an impact which has subsequently been favourably commented on.
>
> (Abercrombie et al., 1970, p. 11)

This particular group of students exhibited a growing confidence in their ability to open the apparently closed doors of professionalism and 'to develop into the kinds of professional they wanted to be' (Abercrombie et al., 1970, p. 11).

Reading between the lines it seems that the main problems were self-organization, self-assessment and teamworking, for which the students, who came from a diverse range of educational backgrounds, were deeply unprepared. Core to this was their difficulty in making informed professional judgements both individually and collaboratively to guide their actions and manage themselves as a team. The AERU team tried to address these issues by appointing a group of external examiners to review the students' work on an ongoing basis, the aim being to enable them to examine the process not the product (Abercrombie et al., 1970). Despite their desire to provide a loose and challenging framework that would allow students to innovate in safe circumstances, the team were hindered by the university requirements for assessment, the need to fulfil professional validation criteria, the students' educational foundations and their difficulty with teamwork. Just how to counter such disincentives to innovation merits systematic investigation. It is a shame that pedagogical research has been disincentivized by the Research Excellence Framework (REF), with universities nervous to send this kind of submission to the Built Environment Panel.

10.2 Skills and knowledge for a research-based profession

The AERU students seem to have found Diploma Project 1968–69 difficult because they were not confident about making judgements, either about their own work or about that of others. Unfortunately the development of research skills to help with making those judgements, do not and did not feature highly in RIBA Validation criteria (see Chapter 6), yet those who 'can make complex inferences and evaluate subtle truth claims or arguments in written texts' have significantly better life chances (Schleicher, 2014, p. 39). A central problem of architectural education as it is framed at the moment is that it makes students dependent on their institutions and on their teachers (McClean, 2009). These dependencies on tutors are constructed or reinforced by lack of clarity of learning intention, confusion over the purpose and role of projects in relation to learning outcomes, the nature and quality of feedback, and in terms of what is assessed and valued. The formation of judgements that assimilate personal opinion with external views and information gleaned from multiple sources is key to independent learning, this process cumulatively allowing the student to develop a sense of independence over time (McClean, 2009).

Students need to be able to develop the professional judgement to ask the right questions as well as the research skills to answer them. To do this they have to practise making discerning evaluations of arguments, knowledge and indeed buildings (Mallory-Hill et al., 2012). This requires an understanding of research methodology. 'Tools', a word acceptable in architecture culture, are actually 'research methods' by another name. In our first year at Reading, students are sent out to examine the city using a range of tools, which are subsequently developed into a 'tool box' of research practice methods of increasing sophistication.

'Somehow we have to produce embedded knowledge: i.e. insights that are there for excavating later, when the context is right but not until then' (Strathern, 2000, p. 189). The diversity in learning style and intelligences that exists within student cohorts must be acknowledged in education if the profession is to become more inclusive. Inclusivity is fundamental to engendering a sense of belonging in students, as is the acknowledgement of their personal opinions, views and experiences, leading them to respect others in their turn.

Knowledge for collaboration needs to be taught explicitly as it is too important to take for granted. If the starting point for design is people, then students need to acquire professional behaviours in communicating with members of the public at the outset of their education. This includes training in listening, communications and ethical procedure. At Reading, wherever possible, students work collaboratively, with teamworking skills developed, for example, through live building projects (Figure 10.1). Tutorials in small groups encourage the development of critical skills, collaboration, shared responsibility and shared learning. The ultimate aim is an education that readies students to work across the built environment, but this is difficult within the current constraints of RIBA Validation.

Business is a form of design, one that students need to be familiar with if they are to be resilient. However, 'schools have infected a generation with an anti-business mindset' (Pringle and Porter, 2015, p. 147). It is a sad indictment of education when architectural students have to study business on the side in order to succeed as entrepreneurs when they graduate (Barton, 2016). Students usually address practice at the very end of their training, but in our case critical reflection

Figure 10.1 **University of Reading School of Architecture students constructing a gridshell with Piers Taylor (2017). Photo © Piers Taylor.**

on business starts at the very beginning, with students learning with and in practice, not least because 'skill development is far more effective if learning and work are linked' (Schleicher, 2014, p. 42). At Reading students have been fortunate in working with ACG (*Building Design* Young Architects of the Year 2017) who have been very active in the development of the curriculum and its delivery. Learning has been reinforced through the History and Theory module, which covers the histories and methodologies of practice. The aim here is to arm students with the business and critical savvy to fight the cause of their field.

Unfortunately in the current context numerical assessment can't be done away with altogether. It must, however, be possible to develop a self-audit system (probably digital) that ensures that all students take responsibility for picking up the necessary skills along the way. Currently students fill in an RIBA Professional Expertise and Development Record (PEDR) log of their developing experiences in both education and practice. A new form of curriculum is needed that allows for the custom build of education, building on a student's existing skills and predilections, which supports the development of the high level of skills and knowledge necessary for specialization.

10.3 Learning context

Context plays a major role in the development of tacit knowledge and is increasingly recognized as central to learning overall (Elton and Johnston, 2002). 'Real learning takes place between students and out in the world' (Powers, 2015, p. 17); hence the profound need for any architecture school to be permeable to practice, to the wider university, to the wider built environment industry and to society.

Building on the endeavours of Reading 2050 and the Sheffield-based Live Works (Live Works, 2016), we are creating a school of architecture as an urban Living Lab, a vital accessible space for debate and discussion around architecture and the public realm in Reading. This is simultaneously a research laboratory and a place for students to experiment in engagement with civil society in situ.

Students need to develop an in-depth range of techniques for working in their local environment. Only in this way can they develop the cultural sensitivity, ethical judgement and processes needed to work in unfamiliar contexts. The tradition of architecture schools sending students overseas to build a school or other facility, as such 'charity' work undercuts the work of local construction teams, smacks of colonialism and has questionable value in the long term (Linsell, 2017). How best to provide architectural services at a global distance is a complex ethical question (Awan, 2016). Better instead for students to try addressing the very real deprivations on our own doorsteps, at least in the beginning.

'Live projects are, if pedagogically understood and appropriately managed, a natural setting for a situated, critical and inclusive education' (Morrow and Brown, 2012, p.3). Live projects can be assessed, as they are at Sheffield University, by the client, by users, by the students and by the tutors (Figure 10.2) – each form of assessment brings into relief the different value systems at work, a critical understanding of which is vital to operation as a professional (Butterworth and Care, 2014).

Figure 10.2 **Sheffield University School of Architecture Live Project students working at Greenhill Library. Photo © Live Projects.**

In the UK 'project offices' have been used to link to the development of Live Projects in their associated schools. They take different forms and can offer academics and students opportunities to be involved in real projects, working with a real client on a real problem, modelling professionalism in the process. Whether such offices, sometimes fuelled by 'free' manpower from students and university subsidies, have a competitive advantage over local private practices is a moot point. At Reading our Project Research Unit will offer research skills, consultancy, training and student capability to practices that want to develop research with academia, providing live research training for students in the process. This builds on an important initiative currently in development in the MArch at Northumbria University, in which students add value by bringing additional research capability to a practice project and its processes.

More and more practice-based education needs to be delivered via practice. Experiments in practice-based education developed by the London School of Architecture and others have been key to raising the bar in this area (Newman, 2017), but only as yet at postgraduate (MArch) level. There is an interesting new development in the form of Trailblazer Apprenticeships, which are being paid for out of a 0.05% levy by companies with a wage bill over £3 million. Helen Taylor from Scott Brownrigg is leading on their development with a consortium of schools and practices (RIBA, 2017). A necessary part of the process will be defining competence at the end point assessment.

The responsibility for delivering a high-quality research-led practitioner education must be shared. This requires considerable adjustment on both sides, but the profession has much to gain from this kind of collaboration. It seems only a matter of time until practices become much more active in education, given the staggering levels of student debt.

A particularly interesting model is the Oxford Brookes University Office Based Exam at MArch (postgraduate RIBA Part II level). Students are charged to imagine themselves setting up their own architecture school and have to employ their own tutors. Used creatively this amounts to an amazing opportunity to select a hand-picked group of teachers in tune with student aspirations, but it requires maturity, confidence and networking ability on the part of the students, and is not perhaps suited to the average 22-year-old. A new kind of practice known for its research, its investment in people and its ethical position would be a welcome addition to the educational scene.

Professional pedagogies model the uncertainties of being a professional, hence the anxiety and excitement that surrounds them (Shulman, 2005). Nowhere is this more evident than in the 'crit', the public presentation of design work to an audience of reviewers.

> One of the mistaken arguments for the retention of the crit is that it prepares for the real world – but at what cost? Answer: the development of alien vocabularies (spoken and drawn) understood only by architects, arrogance (attack being seen as the best form of defense in a crit), are the common traits, among others, which are established in schools of architecture and which then contribute to the formation of the character of the architect.
>
> (Till, 2009, p. 8)

Crits are based on a very outdated vision of the 'real world' – aggressive confrontation is no longer seen as good management – should be reframed as collaborative research through the medium of drawings and models (Ewenstein and Whyte, 2007). The crit panel becomes more like an advisory group for a research project, offering constructive guidance and a refreshing viewpoint.

As Abercrombie et al. (1970) make clear, there is more to architectural education than working towards assessments or cramming more and more into syllabuses, 'which despite repetition are not quite grasped for lack of time and which consequently create a pathetic lack of confidence for young architects' (Groak, 1992, p. 169, quoting UK architect Martin Kenchington in 1952). It is vitally important that students have time to stop and reflect or they will not learn to trust their own instincts. Students cannot do this if they are fearful, under pressure or inundated with random information. They can do it only when they have learned how to listen and filter information – and they cannot listen to others until they have learned to listen to themselves. At the same time it is difficult for a student to playfully assemble the ingredients of an idea, or cycle through rounds of research refinement with inquisitive pleasure if he or she is stressed.

Rather than 'overteaching', at Reading we want to provide targeted teaching of skills and knowledge, leaving more time free for self-development and reflection and the accrual of other forms of specialist knowledge that will help develop a fulfilling career. In line with the old adage, often used in studio, that constrained sites offer a better foothold for creativity, carefully considered constraints, perhaps paradoxically, actually offer a degree of empowerment (Giddens, 1979; Imrie and Street, 2011, p. 282).

Conclusion

The new industry-led school of architecture at Reading aims to deliver an education for uncertainty, most notably by foregrounding research, listening, ethics, teamworking and representation skills for complex spatial problem-solving with others. Students are given ample opportunity to reflect on the nature of practice and encouraged to adjust their career plans according to their developing inclinations. That they are likely to be portfolio professionals moving across and around the built environment is acknowledged right from the start. Given the length and expense of architectural education students should be able to walk into a fulfilling job at a level of pay comparable if not better than other (less well qualified) construction colleagues.

Rather than giving sighing acceptance to RIBA statistics that suggest that only a very small minority of students who begin their studies at a UK school actually qualify as architects, we should be making sure that there are more jobs for them within architecture by raising the impact of the field as a whole. If they do choose to leave the field, it must be recognized that they are not 'drop-outs', but actually perform a very useful function in disseminating the use of architectural skills in the wider world (Sheil, 2015, p. 105), hence the importance of developing transferable skills explicitly within architectural education. Hopefully the RIBA Review of Education, begun in 2015 but stalled temporarily due to uncertainties around the UK's departure from the European Union (EU), will result in a diverse ecology of educational formats that will give students real choice.

> When we can access the world's knowledge on the internet, routine skills are being outsourced and jobs are changing, accumulating knowledge matters less and success becomes more about ways of thinking that employ creativity, critical thinking, problem solving and judgments; about ways of working using collaboration; about tools for working, including the capacity to recognize and exploit new technologies; and, lastly about the social and emotional skills that help us live and work together.
>
> (Schleicher quoted by Rubin, 2015)

We have an ethical duty to furnish students with the best possible chances of success in their own terms.

An examination of the AERU experiment shows just how much needs to change in terms of validation practices, assessment, student research skills, pedagogical culture and educational context if universities are really going to embrace uncertainty.

> Classrooms that embody education as a practice of freedom cannot be made entirely safe. These learning environments are unavoidably risky in terms of the intellectual regions they engage, the emotional experiences they engender, the verbal exchanges they facilitate, and the actions they endorse.
>
> (Glass, 2004, p. 1)

Whether students want or are ready to accept that risk is another matter (Hood et al., 2001).

The paper on which this chapter is based was developed with Lorraine Farrelly, Head of the new School of Architecture, and presented at the Association of Architectural Educators Conference at the Bartlett School of Architecture, University College London, in 2016.

References

Abercrombie, M.L.J., Forrest, A.J., Terry, P.M., 1970. 'Diploma Project 1968–69'. *Architectural Research and Teaching*, 1, pp. 7–11.

Awan, N., 2016. 'Digital Narratives and Witnessing: The Ethics of Engaging with Places at a Distance'. *GeoHumanities*, 2, 2, pp. 311–330.

Barton, G., 2016. *Don't Get a Job ... Make a Job: How to Make it as a Creative Graduate*. Laurence King, London.

Biesta, G.J.J., 2014. *Beautiful Risk of Education*. Routledge, Boulder, CO.

Boyer, E., 1997. *Scholarship Reconsidered: Priorities of the Professoriate*. John Wiley & Sons, London.

Butterworth, C., Care, L., 2014. *A Handbook for Live Projects*. University of Sheffield.

Cayer, A., Deamer, P., Korsh, S., Petersen, E., Shvartzberg, M. (eds), 2016. 'Asymmetric Labors: The Economy of Architecture in Theory and Practice'. www.academia.edu/28002267/Asymmetric_Labors_The_Economy_of_Architecture_in_Theory_and_Practice

Crinson, M., Lubbock, J., 1994. *Architecture – Art or Profession?* Manchester University Press.

Doidge, C., Sara, R., Parnell, R., Parsons, M., 2006. *The Crit: An Architecture Student's Handbook: Seriously Useful Guides*. Architectural Press, Amsterdam.

Duffy, F., 1995. *Strategic Study of the Profession, Phases 3 & 4: The Way Forward*. RIBA, London.

Elton, L., Johnston, B., 2002. *Assessment in Universities: A Critical View of Research*. LTSN Generic Centre. https://eprints.soton.ac.uk/59244/1/59244.pdf

Ewenstein, B., Whyte, J., 2007. 'Visual representations as "artefacts of knowing"'. *Building Research and Information*, 35, 1, pp. 81–89.

Giddens, A., 1979. *Central Problems in Social Theory: Action, Structure and Contradiction in Social Analysis*. University of California Press, Berkeley.

Glass, R.D., 2004. 'Moral and Political Clarity and Education as a Practice of Freedom'. *Counterpoints*, 240, pp. 15–32.

Gotch, J.A. (ed.), 1934. *The Growth and Work of the Royal Institute of British Architects*. Simson, London.

Groak, S., 1992. *The Idea of Building: Thought and Action in the Design and Production of Buildings*. Taylor & Francis, Oxford.

Hill, A., 2016. 'Survey: 25% of UK Architecture Students Treated for Mental Health Problems'. *The Guardian*. www.theguardian.com/education/2016/jul/28/uk-architecture-students-mental-health-problem-architects-journal-survey

Hood, C., Rothstein, H., Baldwin, R., 2001. *The Government of Risk*. Oxford University Press, Oxford.

Imrie, R., Street, E., 2011. *Architectural Design and Regulation*. Wiley Blackwell, Oxford.

Linsell, N., 2017. 'Architects with Borders: Developing a Sharing Economy', in: Hay, R., Samuel, F. (eds), *Professional Practices in the Built Environment*. School of Architecture, University of Reading, pp. 53–59.

Live Works, 2016. 'Live Works', Sheffield, http://live-works.org/ (accessed 4.4.17).

Mace, A., 1986. *The Royal Institute of British Architects: A Guide to its Archive and History*. Mansell, London.

MacLaren, A., Thompson, N., 2017. 'The Portfolio Professional = Education + Skills + Commercial Environment + Communications Network', in: Hay, R., Samuel, F. (eds), *Professional Practices in the Built Environment*. School of Architecture, University of Reading, pp. 80–92.

Mallory-Hill, S., Preiser, W.F.E., Watson, C. (eds), 2012. *Enhancing Building Performance*. Wiley, Hoboken, NJ.

McClean, D., 2009. 'Embedding Learner Independence in Architecture Education: Reconsidering Design Studio'. Unpublished PhD thesis, Robert Gordon University, Glasgow.

Morrow, R., Brown, J.B., 2012. 'Live Projects as Critical Pedagogies', Queen's University Belfast. https://pure.qub.ac.uk/ws/files/886353/Live%20Projects%20as%20Critical%20Pedagogies.pdf

Newman, V., 2017. 'Routes to Socially Inclusive Architectural Education', in: Duncan, J. (ed.), *Retropioneers: Architecture Redefined*. RIBA Enterprises, Newcastle-upon-Tyne, pp. 22–25.

Nowotny, H., 2015. *The Cunning of Uncertainty*. Polity, London.

Powers, A., 2015. 'The Fiction of Architectural Education', in: Harriss, J., Froud, D. (eds.) *Radical Pedagogies*. RIBA Publishing, Newcastle-upon-Tyne, p. 4.

Pringle, J., Porter, H., 2015. 'Education to Reboot a Failed Profession', in: Harriss, H., Froud, D. (eds.), *Radical Pedagogies*. RIBA Publishing, Newcastle-upon-Tyne, p. 146.

Ray, N., 2008. 'Studio teaching for social purpose'. *Open House International*, 33, 2, pp. 18–25.

RIBA, 2017. 'Apprenticeships in Architecture'. www.architecture.com/knowledge-and-resources/knowledge-landing-page/apprenticeships-in-architecture

RIBA, 2015. *RIBA Student Destinations Survey 2015*. London. www.architecture.com/-/media/gathercontent/riba-student-destinations-survey/additional-documents/reportribastudentdestinationssurvey2015pdf.pdf

Rubin, C.M. 2015. Huffington Post Blog. www.huffingtonpost.com/c-m-rubin/the-global-search-for-edu_b_6497764.html

Sarfatti Larson, M., 1993 [1977]. *The Rise of Professionalism: A Sociological Analysis*. University of California Press, Berkeley.

Schleicher, A., 2014. *Equity, Excellence and Inclusiveness in Education*. OECD, Paris.

Schon, D., 1984. *The Reflective Practitioner: How Professionals Think in Action*. Basic Books, New York.

Sheil, B., 2015. 'The After Life', in: Harriss, H., Froud, D. (eds), *Radical Pedagogies*. RIBA Publishing, Newcastle-upon-Tyne.

Shulman, L.S., 2005. 'Signature Pedagogies in the Professions'. *Daedalus* 134, 3, pp. 52–59. doi:10.1162/0011526054622015

Strathern, M., 2000. *Audit Cultures: Anthropological Studies in Accountability, Ethics and the Academy*. Routledge, London.

Tavistock Institute, 1966. *Interdependence and Uncertainty (Digest of a Report from the Tavistock Institute to the Building Industry Communication Research Project)*. Tavistock Institution, London.

Till, J., 2009. *Architecture Depends*. MIT Press, Cambridge, MA.

Watson, N., 1964. 'A Method of Assessing Studio Work of Architecture Students'. *RIBA Journal*, 71, pp. 358–360.

Wright, A., 2013. *Pathways and Gateways: The Structure and Regulation of Architectural Education*. UK Architectural Education Review Group. www.schosa.org.uk/content/pathways-and-gateways-structure-and-regulation-architectural-education

Chapter 11

Developing a shared language of research

> *What is needed now is a research paradigm, a framework of meaning and practice which derives from technology, from the process of making things, from the concept of 'know-how'. It will accept the idea of deterministic processes which are unpredictable. It will incorporate the critic as one of the participants in the building process, to help with establishing a useful meld between tacit and explicit knowledge, between information and skill. It will involve new versions of organizations, ones which are knowledge based and skill-sharing, rather than simply skill based.*
>
> *(Groak, 1992, p. 181)*

So it seems that architects need to offer very distinct knowledge and skills if they are to collaborate with others, and ultimately to diversify. The 'special features' of their discipline need to be made extremely clear: 'This means defining architectural knowledge in a way that is verifiable, open to scrutiny and sufficiently robust to distinguish it from other kinds of knowledge' (Duffy, 1998, p. xiii).

If architectural research is to develop in power and reach it must be made clear and communicable to others in normative formats that translate across disciplinary boundaries (Imrie and Street, 2014). To be a piece of research a building or a design needs to be subject to some form of 'systematic enquiry' (Archer, 1995), which should ideally be shared. As in other fields, architectural researchers must take 'personal responsibility for a narrow field of enquiry, and an ambition to be among the best of specialists' (Woudhuysen and Abley, 2004, p. 283). This chapter focuses on the way in which architects need to reframe the way they do research in order to foster collaborative research with other fields. In order to do this we have to get the message across that 'architecture is a form of knowledge that can and should be developed through research, and that good research can be identified through the triple test of originality, significance and rigour' (Till, 2011, p. 2). Architecture has its own research methodologies (EAAE, 2012), most notably design studio, but these need to be made more explicit, rigorous and ethical if they are to work successfully with colleagues in other research disciplines.

11.1 Developing a shared language

If architects in practice are guilty of 'supply side thinking', academic architects are not much better. Inward-looking 'Archispeak' is unacceptable both in contractor meetings and in universities. Architects need to become familiar during their training with the systematic language of primary research, most notably the reasonably universal stages within any research project – aims, methodology, research context, limitations, methods, testing, results, conclusion and so on. Such a structure, states Till, 'is a perfectly good way of framing a studio project' even in risky projects. 'If your method is one of risk taking then say it' (Till, 2016). These normative categories are well known across the globe and form the basis of every research grant application I have ever seen. They can, with a bit of thought, be applied to research in practice, as can be seen from the way we framed the multiple practice case studies in the book *Demystifying Architectural Research* (Samuel and Dye, 2015). Here we softened the language slightly to 'context, approach, methods, insights and lessons' for a practice audience. Another version used by Darryl Chen, who leads the Research ThinkTank at Hawkins\Brown, is 'Theory, Background, Evidence, Analysis, Speculation' (Chen, 2017). That it is perfectly possible to use such categories to describe design research has been proved through multiple submissions to the Research Excellence Framework (REF). Seemingly resisted for their restraining influence and lack of glamour, they are key to making the field and its knowledge transparent to others, key to rigorous research and key to accessing funds.

There are other adjustments to be made to make it entirely explicit that architects can and do do research. A reviewing panel on a design project is very like an advisory group on a research project. The 'theory' of architecture going forward could be reframed as 'research methodology'. Unless solely for presentation purposes, the making of an architectural model (a research method), whether built in cardboard, portrayed on a wall at a studio review or parametric is, in theory, a methodology applied to a site, form or process (Echenique, 1970). Placing a rough design model into a site model is an experiment. The form is tested visually in relationship to its surroundings, flows of people, overlooking, light, wind, heat and a range of other factors. It is in every way a form of research, though, strictly speaking, the results need to be disseminated for others to build on if such activities are to be considered proper. According to the UK REF, research is 'a process of investigation leading to new insights effectively shared' (HEFCE, 2012, p. 48). It is worth considering whether a building can be considered 'dissemination'. Within architectural culture built precedents are a key source of knowledge, but this is a way of working that is opaque to other fields.

Till has offered the provocation that 'good design does not necessarily make good research' (Till, 2011, p. 6). This of course depends on what you call good, something that requires the development of a reasonably consistent philosophical position regarding the nature of architectural expertise in the long term (Ray, 2008). I argue that good architecture should be the product of a design process, both rigorous and ethical, which builds on, and ideally disseminates, cutting-edge knowledge in the field. This has implications for the way in which the profession celebrates excellence through awards and student work. Darke noted in 1984 that 'architectural education and professional norms at present fail to penalize inadequate background research and knowledge' (Darke, 1984, p. 413). A celebrity judging panel might be entertaining to watch, but are they the best people to award the profession's highest accolades? It would be really helpful to the cause of architectural research if awards could be brought in line with what is deemed excellent design research in an academic context and indeed the context of other disciplines. Thoughtful practitioners such as Niall McLaughlin straddle these cultural divides, his work shining in both (Figure 11.1). Credible criteria are needed to enable projects to be compared on evidence rather than on aesthetic wow.

As mentioned in Chapter 4, there has been a great deal of lobbying on the part of UK architecture schools to ensure that design research – a building, an exhibition, a plan – is recognized as a valid output for the REF. While it is

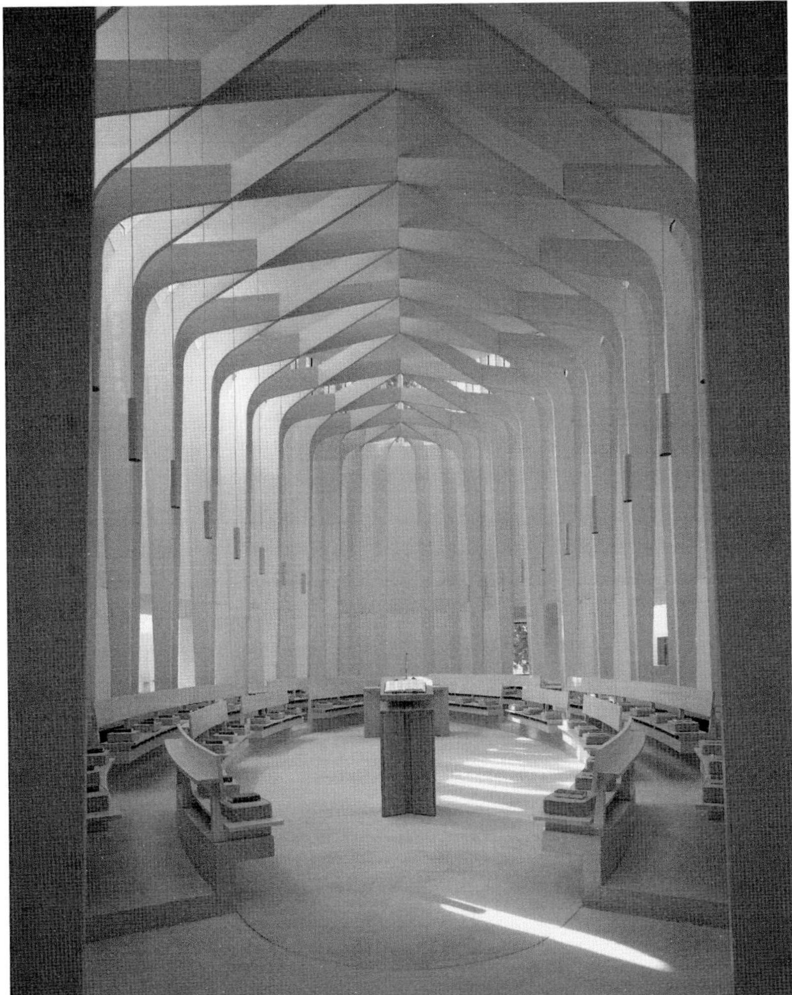

Figure 11.1 **Niall McLaughlin Architects, Bishop Edward King Chapel, Oxfordshire (2013). Photo © Nick Kane.**

really important to illustrate the unique working methodologies of architects, the creation of portfolios of design research artificially put together for submission to the REF (often with minimal dissemination, arguably a requirement of proper research) might be a quick fix, but it could just add to the impression that architects are wilfully inward-looking. When applying for academic positions, promotion and funding, such 'outputs' are unimpressive to interdisciplinary expert panels. If design research is really to stand on its own two feet, it needs to be published in rigorously vetted refereed journals, many of which are specifically interested in the relevant subject area. A recent significant example is the publication of Atelier d'Architecture Autogérée's R-Urban project in the highly respected 'indexed' journal *Building Research and Information* (Petrescu et al., 2016), with an 'impact factor' far higher than those dealing with architecture alone. In this way the work of the practice is made available to a wide construction community and its importance recognized. Only by publishing in refereed journals will design research both in academia and in practice come to be seen as the extraordinary interdisciplinary opportunity that it is. Practices themselves need to contribute to this knowledge flow, working with academics and others to publish their own findings, developing the necessary 'track record' for securing research funding and sharing ideas with colleagues in the profession.

Much more needs to be done to make it known that architectural design studio, described in detail in Chapter 3, is a distinct methodological offering that architects are keen to share. A major problem is that design studio is not taken seriously as a methodology, even by architects themselves (for an example see Gaqing and Bertin, 2013). This is ironic given that 'design thinking' has now become mainstream (Brown, 2009), both as a research methodology and as a leadership advantage, and is taught in business schools across the globe as an effective approach to innovation. Sociologist Kate Pahl has taken 'design studio' out of architecture and reused it in her work with diverse communities:

> The studio is a conceptual space where groups form and grow things which emerge from something we recognise as working already. It involves a group of people who operate beyond the structures of the university and recognises different types of expertise – all participants can emerge as 'experts'. It is adaptable and responsive to particular situations and is a space of action, process, and practice.
>
> (Pahl, 2014)

Collopy and Boland have taken it into the world of business. The 'manager is a form giver who', like architects and engineers, 'shapes organizations and economic processes' (Collopy and Bolland, 2004, p. 9). They make the significant point that 'if managers adopted a design attitude the world of business would be different and better' (Collopy and Bolland, 2004, p. 4). Architecture's 'design studio' methodology is an area of research activity that the discipline can be proud of.

11.2 A shared system of ethics

Obviously one person's idea of acceptable behaviour can be quite different from another's. Rigorous research should be undertaken within a guiding ethical framework which sets out its permissible limits. At the moment the explicit systematic consideration of the ethical dimension of design research is mechanistic at the level of funded academic projects, extremely patchy in postgraduate design studio and almost non-existent at undergraduate level, as it is in the profession. Architects regularly use images that belong to others without crediting them in presentations, in collages and in Photoshop, perhaps because they are so used to seeing their own work pass uncredited into the public realm (the appearance of an architect's name on a sign on a construction site is now a rarity).

In the USA the Architecture Lobby is fighting 'for a professional organization that feels confident to argue for what is right' (Architecture Lobby, 2017). In the UK a professional organization with a Royal Charter is required to work for the common good of society with standards 'higher than that of general law' (Lord Benson, 8 July 1992; Morrell, 2015, p. 15). David Roberts has undertaken a significant review of Codes of Conduct across the built environment and there is much more work to do in this area (Roberts, 2017).

The profession must take shared responsibility for its actions globally (UIA, 2014; Beauregard, 2015) if it 'is to be more than a professional screen for the activities of corporate and government clients' (McNeill, 2006, p. 49). This isn't only an issue for large practices developing corporate projects; it is also an issue for those doing charitable work overseas (Linsell, 2017). It is better instead to partner with local practices and universities to develop shared, respectful and reciprocal learning. The Chartered Institute of Building (CIOB) and Institute of Civil Engineers (ICE) see the promotion of ethics as a key role for their institutions. While under the leadership of Peter Oborn the Royal Institute of British Architects (RIBA) has been instrumental in putting together an international coalition for globally recognized ethics standards. This needs to become a minimum standard for Chartered Practice.

Ethical good practice in a university context can be bureaucratic, involving the filling of forms which are then policed by local ethics committees. This usually requires asking informants to give written consent to their participation in a project, a highly cumbersome process which makes people into subjects rather than co-producers of research. While some might consider these procedures managerial (Pahl, 2014) and difficult to translate into different cultural circumstances (Ong, 2016), particularly in situations of conflict (Plaza, 2016), they cannot be refined and made better without critical and considered engagement. Pels writes of the possibility of an 'emergent ethics, one which is no longer tied to a specific community (such as a professional association), but which locates ethical discussion in the negotiation of individual or communal interests that is characteristic of the practice of fieldwork'. This would replace 'quasi-legal and quasi-professional sets of standards' (Pels, 2000, p. 163) such as the RIBA Code of Conduct. This kind of negotiated ethical practice is becoming increasingly common in community research practice (CSJCA, 2012) and could therefore, I presume, become an integral part of 'studio' or indeed the project briefing process. In turn, professional ethics can impact positively on Corporate Social Responsibility, Investors in People, Great Place to Work and a wealth of other organization- and brand-enhancing measures (McElhaney, 2008).

It seems very odd that a practitioner working on a PhD involving human research must make an ethical application to their university yet they might be doing very similar research within their practice that has no such checks or balances. Governance is needed for practitioners who need an impartial outside body to check ethics applications and advise on procedure. The 'ethics toolkit' 'Just Say No' developed by the ICE for use by their members (ICE, 2015) is a promising start. The construction industry globally is known for corruption, but the black market of cash-in-hand payments to avoid tax is still widespread in the UK as, it seems, is slavery (CIOB, 2015). Although it may be difficult to implement, a clear ethical compass is vitally important for architects, whether they are research-led or not.

Conclusion

Over the five years in which I have been writing this book the research culture of architects has changed conspicuously for the better and is becoming much more open. In order to accelerate this process of change it is important that architects reframe the way they talk about their investigations into the normative, cross-cultural language and ethical values of research. The alignment between architectural research and other fields becomes all the more pressing as methodologies that span across disciplinary silos are urgently needed to address societal challenges such as climate change, rapid urbanisation and ageing.

References

Archer, B., 1995. 'The Nature of Research'. *Co-design, Interdisciplinary Journal of Design*, January, pp. 6–13. https://archive.org/stream/TheNatureOfResearch/Archer1995Codesign#page/n0/mode/2up

Architecture Lobby, 2017. 'A Response to AIA values'. https://archinect.com/features/article/149978362/architects-respond-to-the-aia-s-statement-in-support-of-president-elect-donald-trump

Beauregard, R., 2015. 'We Blame the Building! The Architecture of Distributed Responsibility'. *International Journal of Urban and Regional Research*, 39, 3, pp. 533–549.

Brown, T., 2009. *Change by Design*. HarperCollins, London.

Chen, D., 2017. Email to author 19 December 2017.

CIOB, 2015. 'Modern Slavery: The Dark Side of Construction'. https://policy.ciob.org/wp-content/uploads/2016/02/CIOB-Research-The-Darkside-of-Construction.pdf

Collopy, F., Bolland, R.J., 2004. 'Design Matters for Management', in: Collopy, F. (ed.), *Managing as Design*. Stanford Business Books, Stanford University Press, Stanford, CA.

CSJCA, 2012. *Community-based Participatory Research: A Guide to Ethical Principles and Practice*. Durham University, UK.

Darke, J., 1984. 'Architects and user requirements in public-sector housing 2: The sources for architects' assumptions, *Environment and Planning B: Planning and Design*, 11, pp. 405–416.

Duffy, F., 1998. *Architectural Knowledge: The Idea of a Profession*. Spon, London.

EAAE, 2012. *EAAE Charter on Architectural Research*. European Association of Architectural Education. www.eaae.be/about/statutes-and-policy/eaae-charter-architectural-research/

Echenique, M., 1970. 'Models: A Discussion'. *Architectural Research and Teaching*, May, pp. 25–36.

Gaqing, G., Bertin, V., 2013. *Introduction to Architectural Design*. China Architecture and Building Press, Hong Kong.

Groak, S., 1992. *The Idea of Building: Thought and Action in the Design and Production of Buildings*. Taylor & Francis, Oxford.

HEFCE, 2012. Assessment Framework and Guidance on Submissions. www.ref.ac.uk/2014/media/ref/content/pub/assessmentframeworkandguidanceon-submissions/GOS%20including%20addendum.pdf

ICE, 2015. 'Civil Engineering Ethics Toolkit – "Say No" '. www.ice.org.uk/knowledge-and-resources/best-practice/civil-engineering-ethics-toolkit (accessed 23.8.17).

Imrie, R., Street, E., 2014. 'Autonomy and the Socialisation of Architects'. *The Journal of Architecture*, 19, 5, pp. 723–739. doi:10.1080/13602365.2014.967271

Linsell, N., 2017. 'Architects with Borders: Developing a Sharing Economy', in: Hay, R., Samuel, F. (eds), *Professional Practices in the Built Environment*. School of Architecture, University of Reading, pp. 53–59.

Lord Benson, 8 July, 1992. *Criteria for a Group to be Considered a Profession*. Hansard (Lords), pp. 1206–1207.

McElhaney, K.A., 2008. *Just Good Business: The Strategic Guide to Aligning Corporate Responsibility and Brand*. Berrett-Koehler, San Francisco, CA.

McNeill, D., 2006. 'Globalization and the Ethics of Architectural Design'. *City*, 10, 1, pp. 49–58.

Morrell, P., 2015. *Collaboration for Change*. Edge, London.

Ong, A., 2016. *Fungible Life: Experiment in the Asian City of Life*. Duke University Press, Durham, NC.

Pahl, K., 2014. *Co-producing Legacy: What is the Role of Artists within Connected Communities Projects?* AHRC. http://gtr.rcuk.ac.uk/projects?ref=AH/L013185/1

Pels, P., 2000. 'The Trickster's Dilemma: Ethics and the Technologies of the Anthropological Self', in: Strathern, M. (ed.), *Audit Cultures*. Routledge, London, pp. 136–172.

Petrescu, D., Petcou, C., Baibarac, C., 2016. 'Co-producing Commons-based Resilience: Lessons from R-Urban'. *Building Research and Information*, 44, 7, pp. 717–736.

Plaza, P., 2016. ' "Oil that Harvests Culture": State, Oil and Culture in Petrosocialism (Venezuela, 2007–2013)'. Unpublished PhD thesis, City University of London.

Ray, N., 2008. 'Studio Teaching for a Social Purpose'. *Open House International*, 33, pp. 18–25.

Roberts, D., 2017. 'Ethics in the Built Environment', UCL. www.ucl.ac.uk/bartlett/research/spirit-collaboration/ethics-built-environment

Samuel, F., Dye, A., 2015. *Demystifying Architectural Research: Adding Value and Winning Business*. RIBA Enterprises, Newcastle-upon-Tyne.

Till, J., 2016. Presentation to the Association of Architectural Educators Committee, University College London, April 2016.

Till, J., 2011. 'Is Doing Architecture Doing Research?' Keynote 4th International Meeting on Urbanism and Architecture Research, Universitat Politècnica de València. https://riunet.upv.es/bitstream/handle/10251/15032/TILL%20J_Is%20doing%20architecture%20doing%20research.pdf?sequence=1

UIA, 2014. 'On Recommended International Standards of Professionalism in Architectural Practice'. http://ethics.iit.edu/ecodes/sites/default/files/UIA%20Code%20of%20Ethics-Accord_0.pdf

Woudhuysen, J., Abley, I., 2004. *Why Is Construction so Backward?* Wiley Academy, Chichester.

Chapter 12

Models of academic and practice research collaboration

Back in the 1970s the editors of *Architectural Research and Teaching* made a strong case that 'Model solutions to the problem of linking research and design should be developed' (Broadbent et al., 1970, p. 5). The need to establish routes by which 'research can be fed back into the designer's pen' was considered urgent even at that time (Musgrove et al., 1975, p. 44), and is even more so now. Slowly but steadily new ways to bring research and design together have begun to evolve, some examples of which are described below.

12.1 Academia and practice research collaboration

The public life studies of Gehl Architects, based in Copenhagen, are emblematic of what is possible when practitioners and academics work together. Their distinct research methodology for mapping city space in use, outlined in the book *How to Study Public Life* (Gehl and Svarre, 2013) and a series of other publications, was developed with students and academics at the Royal Danish Academy of Fine Arts through the process of teaching. When, in 1996, the school embarked on a study of Copenhagen as European City of Culture, several other city organizations got involved and the project snowballed. Gehl's research methodologies are now perceived by government and business as important tools to create 'user friendly urban development' (Gehl and Svarre, 2013, p. 151) and are being utilized worldwide.

12.2 Funded research projects

The best way to incentivize practice academic collaboration is through funded research projects. The chances of securing UK Research Council funding varies greatly depending on the call (in my experience the success rate varies between 7 and 35%), but experienced researchers can achieve much better odds, particularly when there is a good chance of industry impact on small and medium-sized enterprises (SMEs), perceived to be the 'backbone of the economy'. Architects who enter architectural competitions are, in any case, used to working with extremely unfavourable odds. Industry-oriented funding streams such as the Innovate UK Knowledge Transfer Partnerships, which assist in the funding of a researcher to work within a business to generate commercial benefits, have a much higher chance of success and bring about significant benefits to businesses (Regenis, 2010). The likelihood of winning funding through research competition can therefore be considerably higher and less costly than winning architectural competitions. Even if unsuccessful, the feedback from respected experts in the field can help immeasurably in the development of practice knowledge.

Competitions have long played an important role in developing innovation (de Jong and Mattie, 1994). A particularly laudable model is offered by the Netherlands' professional institute of architecture, the BNA. A research problem is identified by the institution working with stakeholders, who contribute money to a research fund for the exploration of that issue. A competition, a format that architects are familiar with (Gottschling, 2017), is then opened up to the profession for research funding and a practice or a series of practices are then paid to develop design research solutions for the matter in hand. The project calls are formulated in such a way that the competing practices need to form collaborative partnerships with others, a process that brings long-term network dividends to those involved. In this way the BNA has tackled a range of issues such as the use of dykes, the reuse of northern schools in areas of shrinking population and 'nesting in the city'. The results, written up as reports, are then made freely available to members of the BNA (van Doorn, 2014). These and other high-speed, user-friendly sources of funding suit the needs of the profession.

An example of a recent funded project by a practitioner is Sarah Wigglesworth's three-year Engineering and Physical Science Research Council (EPSRC)-funded DWELL project on design for an ageing population, a collaboration with the University of Sheffield and Sheffield City Council, which concluded at the end of 2016. Success in such a project requires a 'mature' relationship with the academic institution, so a part-time position within that University is helpful, as the complexities of winning research funding are several, and they are the kind of complexities for which the architecture profession is notably unprepared (Samuel and Dye, 2015). DWELL was strategically developed to enhance the practice's expertise in the provision of design for old people. One of its key outputs, the report *Designing with Downsizers*, is testimony to the power of research practice (Park et al., 2016). As Principal Investigator on this project, Wigglesworth had the major responsibility for sorting out the technical complexities of the bid. A more straightforward route to funding for most architects is as a co-investigator, delivering one of a number of work packages. Notably few architectural practices have benefited from the €80 billion allocated to the European Horizon 2020 funding stream, although Zaha Hadid Architects (ZHA, 2017) and Foster Associates (Foster + Partners, 2017) have enjoyed some success in the area of technical innovation, probably because these practices were large and prominent enough to be approached as collaborators by non-architect-based consortia.

Perhaps a more comfortable way of securing funding is via internal bids within bids, a process which shields practices from the alien culture of research councils and which provides a useful induction into their activities, but in reality such opportunities are rare. The Arts and Humanities Research Council-funded

Home Improvements Knowledge Exchange in the Creative Economy project was one such project, with the aim of bringing together academia, practice and the housebuilding industry to develop research solutions to some of the problems endemic to UK housing (Samuel et al., 2014a). A call for interest was posted in the *Architects' Journal* in 2012, resulting in the submission of thirty-six expressions of interest. Through careful selection nine practices were chosen to attend an 'Ideas Lab' workshop at the University of Sheffield. Feedback was also given to the unselected practices to help them apply for funding in the future. Each shortlisted practice was given an academic and industry partner to work with and together they developed a research proposal over a well received two-day 'Ideas Lab' workshop, which tested a new format for bringing practitioners, industry and academics together. The proposals were then developed into full bids and three of the practices were funded up to £45,000 each to develop a research project with their academic and industry partners. Two of them received a parliamentary launch at Portcullis House in London, one before the Secretary of State for Planning, and the other before the then Housing Minister. Architects can make a very important and distinct contribution to the research team, not least in the engaging presentation of findings, for example a film made to promote Custom Build by Ash Sakula Architects, Design for Homes and the University of Sheffield (MCCB, 2015). Another project that is currently being developed is the AHRC-funded IDAPPS, 'Information Design and Architecture in Persuasive Pharmacy Space', which includes a research competition for architects, pharmacists and typographers to work together to develop community pharmacy spaces that will help inform the public of the risks of antimicrobial resistance.

For architects to access funding it is generally necessary to partner with a research organization such as a university or an Independent Research Organization (IRO). It is, however, extremely difficult for practitioners to access academics to work with (Samuel et al., 2014b). Funders are very aware of the difficulties faced by design researchers and are keen to support them (Madano Partnership, 2012), but bids can rarely be developed at the drop of a hat. A 'mature' research relationship, often developed through a series of loss-leading activities, provides importance evidence of fitness to collaborate.

Industry and practice work at very different speeds and the degree of advance planning required by research funders is not always conducive to innovation (Nowotny, 2015). University processes can be slow and their experience of intellectual property (IP) and contract issues are, in the main, better suited to heavy industry or medicine than to small practices in the creative economy. The AHRC Creative Economy Knowledge Exchange hubs provided a much better way of funding the research of micro practices and SMEs by devolving responsibility to regional academic partners. These partners can then allocate small but important tranches of funding with relative ease while mediating between the two very different research cultures. Until practices get up to speed with their research activities, this flexible type of funding opportunity is one that the institutions should be lobbying for.

12.3 Continuing professional development (CPD)

Education does not end with qualification: it is a lifelong process. Chartered architects are required to undertake a minimum of thirty-five hours of Continuing Professional Development (CPD) a year to refresh their skills and knowledge, but innovative architects commit to far more than that. Froud and Harriss are correct in calling for 'truly meaningful CPD' (Froud and Harriss, 2015, p. 197), which I take to be CPD that takes architects away from the hustle and bustle of practice and reminds them what it means to be a professional rather than CPD which enables manufacturers to peddle their wares to architects over a 'free' lunch, as is often the case. It is perhaps worth noting that manufacturers of building products, well aware of practice inertia, categorize architects around their innovation capabilities and tailor their CPD accordingly. The result is that the profession gets the CPD it deserves rather than what it needs. It is important that institutions, both academic and professional, ensure that architects are offered opportunities to develop generic research competences such as:

Research strategy for practice
Accessing tax credits for research and development
Qualitative and quantitative research methods
Utilizing information sources
Data mining
Utilizing big data
Developing a research proposal
Understanding the need for rigorous research
Writing up research
Understanding the relationship between design and research
Accessing research funding
Undertaking literature reviews
Research impact strategy
Post-occupancy evaluation (POE)
Research methods such as ethnography for designers (Cranz, 2016)
Interdisciplinary research
Understanding research ethics
Evidence-based research
Procurement for collaborative research

Subject-specific knowledge is also needed on the current state of research in different sectors and for different building typologies. Happily the Royal Institute of British Architects (RIBA) is significantly refreshing its CPD offer in the light of its recent reorientation towards research.

At the same time an increasing number of practitioners are returning to universities to top up their training through attendance at academic conferences and enrolment for specialist master's degrees. Schools of architecture have a role to play in turn to make this flow easy, productive and inexpensive, for example in the form of massive open online courses (MOOCs), but this requires a willingness from their individual institutions to make this procedurally possible.

12.4 Research practice PhDs

A rather more laborious, but tailor-made, way of integrating practitioner and academic research is through the development of practice-based PhDs, sometimes fully funded. Architecture schools with established PhD programmes, such as the University of Sheffield or University College London in the UK, have accepted practitioner PhDs for many decades, resulting in an increasing number of PhDs 'by design' as well as other more traditional formats. A PhD programme at Sint-Lucas in Brussels specifically designed for practitioners has been going since 2006 (Verbeke, 2017) in collaboration with the well established RMIT programme based in Melbourne, Australia and has been funded through the ADAPT-r (Architecture, design and art practice training research) European Union (EU) Marie Curie Actions FP7 Fund programme (€4 million over four years, Adapt-r, 2015). The RMIT programme is a high-end offering with 'four levels of reflective research into practice': 'a base level for those leaving the academy who wish to advance their theoretical works and special skills; an invitation to reflect on peer-acknowledged mastery after ten years of practice or less; a "by publication" mode of reflection based on seminal works conducted in the following ten or so years of practice; and a capping, higher doctorate for those who are at the peak of accomplishments' (van Schaik et al., 2010, p. 74). At the University of Reading, among other things, we support practitioner PhDs that critique the nuts and bolts of practice and have an ethical dimension. A benefit of the part-time PhD route for practitioners is that it facilitates the path to a 'research track record' and hence funding. It also provides new intellectual stimulation – something sadly lacking in some practices (Smith, 2014) – and makes way for all sorts of new partnership activities.

The 'Collaborative' PhD is another format that allows industry and cultural bodies to benefit from the research developed by doctoral students. These can be partly or wholly funded by a research council or by industry. The engineering consultancy Arup has, for example, supported Kelly Watson through Manchester University in the development of her remarkable PhD research on Social Return on Investment in the built environment (Watson, 2016), conceived to inform the development of Arup's Building User Survey (BUS) POE methodology. For Arup this is just one of a series of research collaborations with the What Works Centre for Local Economic Growth, at the London School of Economics, and provides another important example (LSE, 2017).

12.5 Practice publications

An increasing number of large practices publish their research work on a regular basis, but Perkins + Will is unusual in having its research work externally reviewed (Perkins + Will, 2017). Practice monographs, if conceived with rigour, are a good way to foster collaboration between practice and academia. As reputational issues are at stake and the practice is usually paying the bill, journalists and writers are sometimes less than critical in their assessment of their subjects (Moore, 2002). However, more and more clients want robust knowledge about practice performance in a format credible to management teams and funders (Hay et al., 2017).

Academics should be well placed to support practices in the development of evidence to support this. A dialogue between practice and academia can be a creative two-way street, as I found when writing about the Berlin Chapel of Reconciliation (2000) with its architects, Reiterman and Sassenroth (Samuel and Linder-Gaillard, 2014). Bringing academics in to comment on the development of a practice's work and to support the dissemination of its research is an underutilized opportunity.

12.6 Research practice networks

Sexton and Barrett have shown the impact a single individual can have on innovation within small construction firms (Sexton and Barrett, 2003), so perhaps the first stage in changing professional culture is to ensure that all firms have a research champion or group. An example is Hawkins\Brown Architects' ThinkTank, which was instrumental in the development of the Research Practice Leads, whose first meeting took place at their offices in the summer of 2016 as part of the Evidencing and Communicating the Value of Architects research project (RPL, 2017). The team asked some twenty leading practices known to have an interest in innovation whether they had any staff members leading in this area. While some had researchers firmly in place, the expectation that they might have a named staff member responsible for research came as a surprise to others, resulting in an internal conversation which then brought forth suitable candidates – in itself a worthwhile process. The aim of the group is to lobby for practice research, sometimes seen as an 'overhead' which is likely to be dispensed with at the next recession. Conversations quickly revealed that there was much to be gained in discussing the best information sources, sharing experiences of issues such as applying for tax rebates for research and development work (RIBA, 2012), nervousness around professional indemnity insurance and research leadership across the profession. More groups are needed across the UK.

12.7 Fablabs

Universities also have an important role to play in kick-starting open source innovation by opening up their digital fabrication workshops to small businesses including the architecture micropractices which form such a large part of the profession. Practices such as Zaha Hadid Architects have a mutually beneficial relationship with schools of architecture such as University College London (UCL) and the Architectural Association (AA), which are used as both research resources and talent pipelines. Fablabs offer another opportunity for integration across practice and academia, as can be seen at the Sliperiet at Umea University in Sweden, a freely available space containing a large amount of digital kit (laser cutters, 3D printers and so on). It is open to the public, research and industry alike. Living labs for collaborative innovation and the propagation of design thinking are becoming familiar in Scandinavia: for example, Space10 in Copenhagen (Space 10, 2017) and the work of the Malmö Living Labs Project, described in wonderfully self-critical detail in the paper 'Design Things and Design Thinking' (Bjögvinsson et al., 2012).

Going forward, widely and cheaply available fablabs will play a vital role in the survival of small practices, particularly those outside major cities, where these kinds of facilities are not readily available. Without them it will be impossible to contend with large practices, some of which have fablabs of their own that rival those of the most ambitious universities.

12.8 Urban living labs

Urban living labs – spaces, both real and virtual, in which university, industry, government and citizen research can come together – are the latest thing in urban research, particularly participatory research. Architects have, however, been working, often in a voluntary capacity, on such initiatives in an activist capacity since the 1960s but are, in my experience, oddly absent from the 'Living Lab' debate, with a few notable exceptions (Evans and Karvonen, 2010). It is worth noting that the 'living lab methodology' is becoming more mainstream as a means to develop 'collaborative place-based innovation' in other fields (for example Edwards-Schachter et al., 2012). This is an opportunity for architects.

Universities can have a profound impact on the socio-economic development of cities (Winling, 2018). Hamburg in Germany is a shining example of a city that works closely with its university. This results in positive impacts on the city's economy and wellbeing, manifested in the growth of science parks – often including innovation centres for industry-based research (York, 2016). An increasing number of cash-strapped local authorities are developing research in collaboration with universities, Cardiff being one example (Invest in Cardiff, 2016). Funding opportunities such as the Future Cities Catapult incentivize engagement with research at all levels, presenting further opportunities for academics, industry and practitioners alike (Catapult, 2016). However, universities and cities need to be extremely strategic in setting up networks and projects well in advance of such project calls if they are to have any chance of success.

Conclusion

'Some organizational imagination is urgently required to invent institutions which can combine our vantage point and our action-generated enquiries with the balance and depth of academic work' (Duffy and Worthington, 1977, p. 9). The models discussed above – practitioner PhDs, collaborative projects and practice monographs, fablabs and urban living labs – represent a stop-gap, a sticking plaster over a flawed system. What is really needed is an integration of professional education, research and practice.

Fortunately universities are working hard to make it easier for academics to collaborate with practice. Techniques include part-funded PhDs, fee waivers, industry-based visiting professors and industry placements for staff and students. The process of developing research with industry has been incentivized by the inclusion of Impact in REF 2014, but the REF (Research Excellence Framework) celebrates the work of only a very few senior academic team members. The rank and file of young research academics have to deliver the highest quality publications in refereed journals, but they also need to be rewarded for knowledge exchange work, either through promotion channels or the REF (the connection between the two tends to be strong). An excellent way to begin is design studio undertaken as live projects which actually affect change in the world, however small. This kind of pedagogical endeavour is key to bringing students and part-time practitioner teachers on as active practitioner researchers and for the creation of other kinds of outward-facing relationships, but it needs to be acknowledged and rewarded (van der Hoeven, 2011, p. 185).

References

Adapt-r, 2015. 'Adapt-r'. http://adapt-r.eu/

Bjögvinsson, E., Ehn, P., Hillgren, P.-A., 2012. 'Design Things and Design Thinking: Contemporary Participatory Design Challenges'. *Design Issues*, 28, 3 pp. 101–116.

Broadbent, G., Hillier, B., Lipman, A., MacLeod, R., Musgrove, J., O'Sullivan, P., Wilson, B., 1970. 'Editorial'. *Architectural Research and Teaching*, 1, pp. 2–5.

Catapult, F.C., 2016. 'Future Cities Catapult'. http://futurecities.catapult.org.uk/ (accessed 30.11.16).

Cranz, G., 2016. *Ethnography for Designers*. Routledge, London.

de Jong, C.W., Mattie, E., 1994. *Architectural Competitions 1792–Today*. Taschen, Cologne.

Duffy, F., Worthington, J., 1977. 'Organizational Design'. *Journal of Architectural Research*, 6, pp. 4–9.

Edwards-Schachter, M., Matti, C., Alcantara, E., 2012. 'Fostering Quality of Life through Social Innovation: A Living Lab Methodology Study Case', *Review of Policy Research*, 29, 6, pp. 672–692.

Evans, J., Karvonen, A., 2010. 'Living Laboratories for Sustainability: Exploring the Politics and Epistemology of Urban Transition', in: Bulkeley, H., Castán Broto, V., Hodson, M., Marvin, S. (eds), *Cities and Low Carbon Transitions*. Routledge, Oxford, pp. 126–141.

Foster + Partners, 2017. 'Foster + Partners Looking at Novel Approaches towards Metal-based 3D Printing as Part of LASIMM Consortium'. www.fosterandpartners.com/news/archive/2017/04/foster-plus-partners-looking-at-novel-approaches-towards-metal-based-3d-printing-as-part-of-lasimm-consortium/ (accessed 8.7.17).

Froud, D., Harriss, H. (eds), 2015. *Radical Pedagogies*. RIBA Publishing, Newcastle-upon-Tyne.

Gehl, J., Svarre, B., 2013. *How to Study Public Life*. Island Press, London.

Gottschling, P., 2017. 'Where design competitions matter: Architectural artefacts and discursive events', *Journal of Material Culture*, pp. 1–18. s:O//dlo: i1.o0r. g1/107.171/1773/519351981385315717733377 4

Hay, R., Bradbury, S., Dixon, D., Martindale, K., Samuel, F., Tait, A., 2017. *Pathways to Post Occupancy Evaluation*. RIBA, London.

Invest in Cardiff, 2016. 'Invest in Cardiff'. www.investincardiff.com/gareth-harcombe/ (accessed 30.11.16).

LSE, 2017. 'Two Year Extension of What Works Centre for Local Economic Growth'. www.lse.ac.uk/News/Latest-news-from-LSE/2017/07-July-2017/What-Works-Centre-for-Local-Economic-Growth-awarded-additional-funding (accessed 4.8.17).

Madano Partnership, 2012. 'AHRC Research Programme Scoping Study'. www.designcouncil.org.uk/sites/default/files/asset/document/AHRC%20Research%20Programme%20Scoping%20Study.pdf

MCCB, 2015. 'Collective Custom Build'. www.youtube.com/watch?v=hsad6uCUlkY

Moore, R., 2002. 'Norman's Conquest'. *Prospect*, March, pp. 52–56. www.prospectmagazine.co.uk/magazine/norman-foster-profile

Musgrove, J., O'Sullivan, P., Territ, C., Hillier, B., Leaman, A., 1975. 'Architectural Research: Problems of Organization and Funding in the United Kingdom'. *Journal of Architectural Research*, 4, pp. 41–43.

Nowotny, H., 2015. *The Cunning of Uncertainty*. Polity, London.

Park, A., Ziegler, F., Wigglesworth, S., 2016. *Designing with Downsizers*. University of Sheffield. www.google.co.uk/search?q=designing+with+downsizers&ie=utf-8&oe=utf-8&client=firefox-b&gfe_rd=cr&ei=bFWgWbfcPM-N8Qe3pJaIDA

Perkins + Will, 2017. 'Research'. https://perkinswill.com/research

Regenis, 2010. 'Knowledge Transfer Partnerships Strategic Review'. http://webarchive.nationalarchives.gov.uk/20130102180151/http://www.innovateuk.org/_assets/pdf/corporate-publications/ktp%20strategic%20review%20feb%202010.pdf

RIBA, 2012. 'RIBA Tax Credit Scheme: A Guide for Architects'. www.architecture.com/files/ribaprofessionalservices/researchanddevelopment/ribataxcreditscheme-aguideforarchitects.pdf (accessed 4.2.16).

RPL, 2017. 'Research Practice Leads'. www.reading.ac.uk/architecture/soa-research-practice-leads-group.aspx

Samuel, F., Coucill, L., Dye, A., 2014a. *Home Improvements Knowledge Exchange in the Creative Economy: Final Report*. University of Sheffield/AHRC.

Samuel, F., Dye, A., 2015. *Demystifying Architectural Research: Adding Value and Winning Business*. RIBA Enterprises, Newcastle-upon-Tyne.

Samuel, F., Dye, A., Tait, A., 2014b. *SCHOSA/RIBA Review of University Located Research*. RIBA, London.

Samuel, F., Linder-Gaillard, I., 2014. *Sacred Concrete: The Churches of Le Corbusier*. Birkhauser, Basel.

Sexton, M., Barrett, P., 2003. 'Appropriate Innovation in Small Construction Firms'. *Construction Management and Economics*, 21, 6, pp. 623–633.

Smith, M., 2014. 'Why Do Women Really Leave Architecture?' *Architectural Review*. www.architectural-review.com/why-do-women-really-leave-architecture/8659000.article (accessed 14.2.14).

Space 10, 2017. 'Space 10 A Future Living Lab'. www.space10.io/#!

van der Hoeven, F., 2011. 'Mind the Evaluation Gap: Reviewing the Assessment of Architectural Research in the Netherlands'. *Architectural Research Quarterly*, 15, 2, pp. 177–187.

van Doorn, A., 2014. *BNA diestenkaarten 2014: Nieuwe rollen en verdienmodellen voor architectenbureaus*. BNA. www.bna.nl/fileadmin/user_upload/Ondernemen/BNA-dienstenkaarten-oplegger.pdf

van Schaik, L., London, G., George, B., 2010. *Procuring Innovative Architecture*. Routledge, Oxford.

Verbeke, J., 2017. 'Knowledge and Architectural Practice', in: Hay, R., Samuel, F. (eds), *Professional Practices in the Built Environment*. University of Reading, pp. 155–164.

Watson, K.J., 2016. 'Learning Loops in Sustainable Design: Applying Social Return on Investment to Buildings'. Unpublished PhD thesis, University of Manchester.

Winling, L., 2018. *Building the Ivory Tower: Universities and Metropolitan Development in the Twentieth Century*. University of Pennsylvania Press, Philadelphia, PA.

York, 2016. 'York Innovation Centre'. www.yorksciencepark.co.uk/office-space-to-rent-york/innovation-business-centre-office-space-to-rent.html (accessed 30.11.16).

ZHA, 2017. 'Creatif Consortium Smart Fabric Research Project', Zaha Hadid Architects. https://vimeo.com/219108526

Chapter 13

Incentivizing research in practice

The last chapter focused on ways in which academia can support practitioners to do research. This chapter examines industry impediments to innovation, most notably procurement. While practitioners can do much to improve the research culture within their organizations, they cannot do this without help from clients. Clients have much to gain from supporting the development of research in architectural practice and across the construction industry. The institutions have a vital role in making this known.

13.1 The role of clients in incentivizing research

A building is a piece of collaborative research. The vital role of clients in creating some of the most innovative and well-loved architecture is unquestionable, yet their role is consistently suppressed. This is particularly true of women clients, notable examples from history being Truus Schröder-Schräder, client for the Rietveld House in Utrecht (1925); Phyllis Lambert, client for Mies van der Rohe's Seagram building in New York (1958); and Heidi Weber, client for Le Corbusier's Zurich Pavilion (1967). More recently the key role of the client has been celebrated through the Royal Institute of British Architects (RIBA) Client of the Year Award, but much more needs to be done in teasing out what makes a good client and in framing projects in terms of reciprocal learning and shared risk. It can only be hoped that, as architects start to be rated on Airbnb-type apps, they get a chance to rate their clients in return.

These same clients are of course absolutely key to the incentivization of research in practice. Clients derive significant benefits from knowing how their environment impacts on their morale, identity, organizational performance and energy use but, 'unless they are prepared to collaborate, not simply by a share of sponsorship but by participating in the sometimes uncomfortable experiments and examinations which the research will involve, the changes which are necessary in some of the long-established procedures of the industry will not occur' (Tavistock Institute, 1966, p. x). Key to all this is procurement, the way in which the project team comes together. One of the single biggest problems of the construction industry is the bidding process (Flanagan, 2017). Lack of professionalism in this area leads to the inappropriate formulation of briefs, 'overt gold plating' and excessive complication.

Many large clients have 'frameworks', typically reviewed every four years, which include a select corpus of practices vetted long in advance and ready to jump at the opportunity of a new project. Walter Menteth has highlighted the considerable damage caused by such frameworks, as they often require practices to have unrealistic amounts of experience, finance and business capability in an area before they are able to bid for work (Menteth, 2015). As the requirements of frameworks tend to be generic, the bar is set high for any eventuality.

In reality frameworks exclude new and hungry practices, providing clients with very limited choice, preventing them from having the tenderly crafted architecture that they deserve while squashing innovation and adding to the homogeneity of our environment. Some client bodies require practices to have disproportionately high, and therefore expensive, levels of professional indemnity insurance. Directors of Estates (who put such frameworks in place), in my experience, vary wildly in their conservatism and creativity, something that their employers need to be fully aware of. Instead, Menteth offers G-Cloud, a digital marketplace for information technology (IT) services, as an exemplar of an alternative approach to how architects' services could be procured on a much fairer and more accessible basis (UK Gov, 2013).

With its competition for the design of West Green Place Nursery and Community Centre, Pocket Living have worked against this tendency (Edwards, 2016). They know it makes sense to call upon emerging practices, as they come full of ideas and are keen to impress. Pocket tries to ensure it achieves its desired outcome by using a bespoke appointment contract with a highly detailed brief and a standard specification – something that is easier to achieve if you are repeatedly delivering the same kinds of spaces (Edwards, 2017).

The forced marriages that are currently imposed upon so many construction teams result in multiple agendas, each pulling a project away from its original design intention. Team empathies are more important than contractual complexities. Procurement can, however, be used creatively to encourage collaboration, learning and sustainability, for example the use of Project Partnering Contract (PPC) 2000, 'the standard form of contract for project partnering' (Designing Buildings Wiki, 2017) for the Centre for Alternative Technology at Machynlleth (started 2006).

Another serious problem is that there is rarely any continuity in the make-up of a construction team, nor is there any reflection on past collaborations. This results in a loss of shared learning improvement (UK Gov, 2015). Few clients appear to have picked up on the importance of this for their organizations in the long term, perhaps because they themselves suffer from so much churn. Ways of ensuring continued learning – and therefore innovation – across projects include the use of consortia bidding by a cross-disciplinary design team (now usually led by a contractor), nominated subcontractors, partnered supply chains (Christos, 2013) and integrated project delivery.

Contracts and specifications can never fully describe what is intended. It would be better instead to pay for the achievement of pre-identified outcomes. Performance-based contracts, contracts that pay for functionality rather than materials or labour, common outside the construction industry (Hughes et al., 2015), present the industry with an opportunity to develop a collective culture of post-occupancy evaluation (POE) and monitoring. Performance-based partnering, in which the next contract is awarded on the basis of the first, provides a real incentive for collective working, quality and research. Propositions such as this are alarming to many as they are frequently associated with financial performance, but imagine what might happen if other kinds of value, including long-term value, came to the fore under such arrangements. Contracts based on social and sustainable performance are something to which we should aspire.

While experienced clients may be aware of the opportunities inherent in good procurement practice it is hard for inexperienced clients to know where to begin. In such, architects can play an important role in induction. Complex spatial problems cannot be solved with financial spreadsheets alone.

> Today, rather than enlist designers to make an already developed idea more attractive, the most progressive companies are challenging them to create ideas at the outset of the development process. The former role is tactical; it builds on what exists and usually moves it one step further. The latter is strategic; it pulls 'design' out of the studio and unleashes its disruptive, game-changing potential.
>
> (Brown, 2009, p. 7)

That architectural practices, particularly SMEs, have difficulty in aligning themselves to the procurement context is not surprising given the complexity of international issues in this area. Indeed some architects are driven to paying private consultants to translate procurement opportunities into a legible form. It is, however, salutary to see what can be done when architects work together for the common good of the profession, as is the case with Project Compass, established in 2014 by Menteth (winner of the 2015 RIBA President's Medal for Research) as a voluntary organization developed to address an extraordinarily wasteful and slow competition context in the UK under the banner 'Better Procurement, Better Design'. Project Compass is a useful digital resource for framework notices and UK architectural competitions, collecting data under standardized headings for easy use and comparison. The 'Compass' service on the website contains a range of resources including information about European Union (EU) Directives, guidance on their application, national regulations, government guidance, international competition portals, and guidance on challenging poor procurement practices. In over ten other specific architectural competitions Project Compass has intervened to seek amendments (Project Compass, 2017), reporting on flawed practice in this area – for example in London's notorious Thames Garden Bridge project, now shelved. Together with Architectuur Lokaal in the Netherlands the Project Compass team is developing a portal to give free, transparent and intelligible access to architectural competitions and to help with the streamlining of procurement procedures (TheFulcrum.eu, 2017).

It is worth noting how strategic clients with very large budgets such as Anglian Water and Heathrow Airport Holdings are about the way in which they build teams to work together as one on their large infrastructure projects, involving billions of pounds spent over perhaps fifteen years. Practitioner Andrew Wright's project 'Constructive Collaboration' (Wright Associates, 2017) is examining the way wide-ranging multidisciplinary, inter-practice experts have delivered collaborative success by forming broad alliances that encourage overlap and help spread risk and reward.

Procurement can be a highly creative activity designed to foster innovation. In Japan, contracts, even for large buildings, can be minimal (Buntrock, 2014), but Japanese culture deals with non-performance in very different ways from the UK. In the course of writing this book I have consulted with many procurement experts, none of whom could offer a tidy solution to the problem of fostering collaborative innovation, but it has to be possible to create contracts in which mutual objectives are formalized, methods for resolving problems are agreed and measurable improvements are actively sought without paying lawyers excessive fees. Long-term personal relationships that build up across construction teams are extremely important, but these relationships have largely been edited out of current practices. New creative relationships will not happen without the intervention of knowledgeable clients and a return to first principles.

The government can do much to incentivize improved processes through the administration of its own contracts. Indeed 'improving technical solutions and reducing costs by challenging the existing roles of consultants, contractors and suppliers' has become a key government objective (UK Gov, 2015, p. 10). Complexity in procurement reduces the industry's ability to change (Clegg, 2012).

13.2 Incentivizing post-occupancy evaluation

The 'creation of a cultural environment which is co-operative [and] seeks to learn and share' has never been so important (UK Gov, 2015, p. 6). POE is a very important place to begin. I have found that architects are quite shy about asking their clients if they would support or benefit from additional research services, assuming that they will say no. Yet many of these same clients are immersed in the world of research and of strategic evidence-based management and would have much to gain from knowing more about their buildings and their relationship with organizational performance. Professor Tim Helliwell, client for the Royal College of Pathologists in London, observes:

> A lot of effort goes in to researching the client's needs and desire at the planning stage, but for us post-occupancy evaluation would provide the opportunity to reflect on the whole process, celebrate successes and learn from any aspects that were less than successful. A rounded research project would not be complete without an assessment of the results of the 'experiment' of constructing a new building. Common sense would suggest that for a substantial project of this nature, an evaluation of what was achieved or not achieved and the reasons why would be expected by our membership and should form part of our annual report.
>
> (Hay et al., 2017, p. 13)

An example is the retail company Marks & Spencer, which understands the power of research, using POE in its Ellesmere Port store in Cheshire Oaks to help reduce running costs, strengthen reputation and create spaces that are more comfortable and enjoyable for shoppers and workers alike while at the same time reinforcing its brand strapline 'Spend well'. POE enables stakeholders, including customers, to play a part in the development of its facilities, but it entails a rather different take on what it is to be an architect (Hay et al., 2017). The 'old demarcations between producer, supplier and user have broken down' (Nowotny et al., 2001, p. 26). In the case of Ellesmere Port, consumers become part of the project team.

The 'greening of business' is a growth area among enlightened companies, which have discovered that it makes financial as well as moral sense (Esty and Winston, 2009). Company premises have a major impact on sustainability and ways of working (Edwards and Naboni, 2013). The environment is, for example, taken into account in the Great Places to Work scheme, an important accolade for business brands. More mileage needs to be made of these kinds of alignments.

'POE is an extremely valuable tool which helps organisations like ourselves understand how we can optimise our buildings and spaces', observes John Davies of the major property developer Derwent in London (Davies, 2016). Clients are waking up to the importance of POE for the development of management strategies within their organizations. The focus on evidencing improvement through POE has also led to the development of new contracts with clients based on performance. For example, one architect we interviewed had developed a long-term partnership with a developer which included a profit-sharing relationship if building performance is improved from one development to the next:

> In these ongoing projects we are creating a complete feedback loop with outputs on building performance including energy and user feedback fed into future work. If we achieve more and push the performance further we share in profit with the developer for delivering on all aspects – performance and innovation as well as commercial. We invest a lot of time on these projects in thinking, discussion and reflecting but it is worth it and not too risky because our fees are guaranteed because of the ongoing work with this particular client.
>
> (Hay et al., 2017a)

Stability in teams of clients, designers and contractors with a proven track record, experience of working well together and the ability to learn from project to project as part of a 'conscious process' has 'huge benefits' (Hay et al., 2017a) and would seem to be the way forward.

POE serves a very important role in organizational learning (Hay et al., 2017b). At the very least a practice should regularly evaluate the impact of its own premises on the effectiveness and cost of its own operation (Roszynski and Keeling, 2017). In Part II of this book I described a range of ways in which architects can add value – social value, cultural value and knowledge value – but extensive POE is needed to develop this evidence base. With the development of new research methods there is real potential to explore with rigour a range of complex and sensitive phenomena, 'atmosphere' being a case in point (Wieczorek, 2017). POE can take a variety of forms – light touch in the form of a building walkabout and user interviews or more detailed, the Arup BUS (Building User Survey) tool being a popular choice (ARUP, 2016). The freely available research report *Building Knowledge: Pathways to Post Occupancy Evaluation*, developed with the RIBA, makes the business case for POE through a series of practice POE case studies from CZWG, AHMM, Hawkins\Brown, Anne Thorne Architects, Cullinan Studio, JDDK Architects, Aukett Swanke, Architype and Urbed. It sets out a clear path for the development of POE in practice (Hay et al., 2017b), which does not need to be duplicated here. As POE becomes more common, those practices that have a long track record in this area will be ahead of the game with refined processes and data that will make guarantees of performance possible while at the same time reducing risk.

POE is currently being incentivized in a number of ways. In the UK the incorporation of the principles of Government Soft Landings into Building Information Modelling (BIM) Level 2 through Building Standard 8536-1 gives a clear indication of a wider recognition of the value of the integration of POE in the procurement process. Another example is the development of new and existing international standards such as the WELL Building Standard and Passivhaus, which both depend upon POE for certification. BREEAM, LEED, SKA (Royal Institute of Chartered Surveyors) and the Green Building Council of Australia, Green Star, all give credit for the use of POE. Market and regulatory emphasis on performance in rating tools such as the National Australian Built Environment Rating System (NABERS) for energy efficiency, water usage, waste management and indoor environment quality forces building owners to undertake partial or comprehensive POE studies of their buildings.

Owner-occupier clients have much to gain from POE, but there are unfortunately many other types of client who have a vested interest in not knowing how badly the buildings that they commission perform. It is helpful that the UK operations and facilities management (FM) industry is becoming increasingly large and influential 'with an output of £106.3Bn in 2013, forecast to grow by 2% pa to 2017' (UK Gov, 2015, p. 12). This is a sector that has much to gain from good design. As an aside it is worth mentioning the company Creative Space Management, which provides an innovative take on FM by designing the user experience of the spaces it looks after (CreativeSpaceman, 2017).

POE provides an important opportunity for architects to work closely with facilities managers on refining buildings in use and on demonstrating long-term value. An interesting development, one in which practices such as Woods Bagot and Chapman Taylor are active, is the build-to-rent market, in which tenants rate developments through TripAdvisor-like social media channels, in this way forcing those who own the building to give greater focus to quality (Saint, 2016). The volatile world of social media rankings is one that the construction industry ignores at its peril and could even be a force for good.

13.3 The role of insurers

'Fail fast, fail often' may be a guiding precept for tech start-ups, but failure is less easy when a huge investment has been made in a project or building and issues of reputation are at stake. Nonetheless, the acknowledgement of failure is essential for the development of architecture's research culture (Leaman and Bordass, 1999; Fedoruk et al., 2015). However, this will require a profound shift in working practices from university onwards. 'The linear model of innovation' as 'a straight process leading from scientific discovery, through application to successful commercial uptake on the market' is unrealistic (Nowotny, 2015, p. 106). Iteration and failure are now acknowledged as key to the development of new creative ideas (Leski, 2015) and, as digital models become more and more sophisticated, iteration and failure will be possible in the relative safety of the virtual world.

Architects are nervous about discovering errors because of their impact on professional indemnity insurance (Samuel et al., 2013), hence the considerable work that the RIBA has been doing on showing that professional indemnity (PI) insurance should not be a disincentive to research (RIBA, 2016b). Responsible research practice should really be rewarded by lower premiums, as is sometimes the case in other industries. For example, the National House Builder Confederation's (NHBC) housing warranties fall in price relative to performance. Failure needs to be faced so that learning can happen before loss of life. Integrated project insurance, in which the whole team shares risk and cost, is another way to incentivize research. It is perhaps worth noting that the insurance industry is experiencing radical changes with the introduction of new technology and that in the future data analysed by machines will be key to setting premiums and handling claims. While architectural PI insurance may currently be a relatively small and specialized field, it may have to change to fulfil the demands of its underwriters. In such a world the ability to provide performance data seems set to become more and more important, and failure may become much more public.

13.4 The role of institutions

Institutions such as the RIBA set the tone of what is expected of a professional. The profession needs to be bullish about its knowledge and its value. This is especially important when professional knowledge is so contested. Nobody has understood this better than Frank Duffy. A significant 1980 'Space Study' of the RIBA by his practice DEGW, 'Making the Best of 66 Portland Place', in the DEGW Archive at the Special Collections at the University of Reading, provides clear evidence of the marginalization of research both spatially and culturally within the RIBA – an observation which must have contributed to Duffy's unsurpassed *Strategic Study of the Profession: The Way Forward* (1995). For Duffy, knowledge should be the foundation of the profession and the foundation of the RIBA. The institute's library, perhaps the foremost architectural library in the world, is an amazing resource but requires investment. As a priority its journals need to be freely available online to its members. I suggest that the focus of the RIBA should be the development and dissemination of its knowledge, reflected in its structure, which could be built on the following lines:

- Development (horizon-spotting, strategy, knowledge management, consultations, policy, awards);
- Dissemination (PR, marketing);
- Outreach (exhibitions, schools, public engagement);
- Education (validation, CPD);
- Protection (Chartered status, procurement, competitions, conduct, ethics, intellectual property, spin-outs and copyright);
- Knowledge community (membership, global network);
- Knowledge bank (library, website, member knowledge, institutional knowledge).

Only in this way, I argue, can the RIBA achieve its full potential as a learning organization enabling architects to move into this increasingly interdisciplinary world confident in what they know and its value. In this context it is perhaps worth reflecting on the simple structure of the Institution of Civil Engineers (ICE), which has three main elements: External Affairs and Policy; Engineering Knowledge; and Members.

It seems likely that in future the construction institutions will bifurcate rather like practice, with some specialist institutions supporting more 'boutique' specialist offerings and others becoming very large and supporting 'portfolio professionals' regularly moving across professional territories (MacLaren and Thompson, 2017). Variations between the two might be achieved with careful use of different types of membership. The institutions need:

> to improve the 'guarantee' of a particular quality of individual – by appropriate control of qualifications and entry to the profession; benchmarking the expertise of members; here too through increased transparency of sanctions, again increasing client and public confidence in the competence of accredited professionals; and possibly becoming agents for disclosure (perhaps through a public feedback system like TripAdvisor?).
>
> (Morrell, 2015, p. 7)

If the pillars of professionalism are ethics, knowledge and professional judgement, Chartered Architect status needs to represent a pinnacle in all three.

Back in 1964 Higgin made the astute observation that if the profession:

> fails in its social purpose, if it puts the interests of its practitioners ahead of its service to society, it will very quickly forgo the public's confidence in favour of a more relevant challenger, to become another Worshipful Company in our social museum, no longer having meaning for contemporary experience.
>
> (Higgin, 1964, p. 145)

The RIBA recently made a call for ideas about what it should do with its beloved but very formal premises in 66 Portland Place. How to make a twenty-first-century institution for the next generation is an exciting question. Without a root-and-branch strategy for promoting the knowledge of architects, 'the UK risks exporting some of its most valuable and pioneering knowledge offshore, and with it a versatile and highly sought after workforce' (Sheil, 2015, p. 113).

The development of the research culture of architects is too important to leave to chance. A process is needed to make it happen. Models of change deriving from management and leadership research are useful in considering how this might be done. Kotter, in his pragmatic staged model, lists eight stages in the process:

1. Establishing a sense of urgency;
2. Creating the guiding coalition;
3. Developing a vision and strategy;
4. Communicating the change vision;
5. Empowering broad-based action;
6. Generating short-term wins;
7. Consolidating gains and producing more change; and
8. Anchoring new approaches in the culture.

(Kotter, 1996, p. 20)

In December 2015 the RIBA Council unanimously voted to support the vision that: 'By 2020 the RIBA will be the leading architectural intelligence network, facilitating innovation, and improving practice effectiveness and outcomes through research and knowledge sharing'. A significant result of this motion is that knowledge is embedded within the new RIBA strategy at every level (RIBA, 2016a). A vision and a broad strategy are therefore now in place. In September 2017, under the auspices of the recently inaugurated president Ben Derbyshire, it voted for the creation of a new role, Vice President for Research. A key task will be 'communicating the change vision' and 'empowering broad based action' (Kotter, 1996, p. 20).

Conclusion

There is much to be done to foster research across the project team. By carefully choreographing the procurement of their buildings clients can unlock the innovation potential of their project teams with concomitant benefits for all. There are some remarkable practices that are taking their business development to new heights, often in order to achieve ethical and sustainable outcomes. Clients should not accept anything less.

The institutions, most notably the RIBA, have a major role in supporting and facilitating these cultural changes in the name of a future-proof profession and a better built environment. At the moment practitioners who want to get involved in research are floored at the first hurdle by the unfamiliar requirements of academic research. A pragmatic approach is needed, involving carrots of encouragement as well as sticks of rigour, to help them on the path towards externalizing their knowledge and utilizing its value.

References

ARUP, 2016. 'Building User Survey' (BUS). www.busmethodology.org.uk/

Braziotis, C., 2013. 'Team performance in collaborative and partnered supply chains'. *Team Performance Management: An International Journal*, 19, 7/8.

Brown, T., 2009. *Change by Design: How Design Thinking Transforms Organizations and Inspires Innovation*. HarperCollins, London.

Buntrock, D., 2014. *Japanese Architecture as a Collaborative Process: Opportunities in a Flexible Construction Culture*. Taylor & Francis, Oxford.

Clegg, P., 2012. 'A Practitioner's View of the "Regenerative Paradigm"'. *Building Research and Information*, 40, 3, pp. 365–368.

CreativeSpaceman, 2015. Creative Space Management. www.creativespaceman.com/the-team/

Davies, J. 2016. Email to author 26 October 2016.

Designing Buildings Wiki, 2017. 'PPC 2000'. www.designingbuildings.co.uk/wiki/PPC_2000 (accessed 3.1.17).

Duffy, F., 1995. *Strategic Study of the Profession, Phases 3 & 4: The Way Forward*. RIBA London.

Duffy, F., Worthington, J., 1977. 'Organizational Design'. *Journal of Architectural Research*, 6, 1, pp. 4–9.

Edwards, B., Naboni, E., 2013. *Green Buildings Pay*. Routledge, London.

Edwards, R., 2017. 'Pocket Living', presentation at the University of Reading School of Architecture, 8 February.

Edwards, R., 2016. 'West Green Place Community Centre'. Pocket Living. www.pocketliving.com/competitions/competition/id/west-green-place

Esty, D., Winston, A., 2009. *Green to Gold: How Smart Companies Use Environmental Strategy to Innovate, Create Value, and Build Competitive Advantage*. Wiley, London.

Fedoruk, L.E., Cole, R.J., Robinson, J.B., Cayuela, A., 2015. 'Learning from Failure: Understanding the Anticipated–Achieved Building Energy Performance Gap'. *Building Research and Information*. 43, 6, pp. 750–763.

Flanagan, R., 2017. 'Global Construction Practice'. Presented at Professional Practices in the Built Environment Conference, School of Architecture, University of Reading.

Hay, R., Samuel, F., Watson, K.J., Bradbury, S., 2017a. 'Post-occupancy Evaluation in Architecture: Experiences and Perspectives from the UK'. *Building Research and Information*, online, pp. 1–13. www.tandfonline.com/doi/full/10.1080/09613218.2017.1314692

Hay, R., Bradbury, S., Dixon, D., Martindale, K., Samuel, F., Tait, A., 2017b. *Building Knowledge: Pathways to POE*. RIBA/University of Reading.

Higgin, G., 1964. 'The Architect as Professional'. *RIBA Journal*, 71, 1, pp.139–145.

Hughes, W., Champion, R., Murdoch, J., 2015. *Construction Contracts*. Routledge, London; New York.

Kotter, J.P., 1996. *Leading Change*. Harvard Business School Press, Boston, MA.

Leaman, A., Bordass, B., 1999. 'Productivity in Buildings: The "Killer" Variables'. *Building Research and Information*, 27, 1, pp. 4–19.

Leski, K., 2015. *The Storm of Creativity*. MIT Press, Cambridge, MA.
MacLaren, A., Thompson, N., 2017. 'The Portfolio Professional = Education + Skills + Commercial Environment + Communications Network', in: Hay, R., Samuel, F. (eds), *Professional Practices in the Built Environment*. School of Architecture, University of Reading, pp. 80–92.
Menteth, W., 2015. 'Procurement', in: Dye, A., Samuel, F. (eds), *Demystifying Architectural Research*. RIBA Enterprises, Newcastle-upon-Tyne, pp. 139–144.
Morrell, P., 2015. *Collaboration for Change*. Edge, London.
Nowotny, H., 2015. *The Cunning of Uncertainty*. Polity, London.
Nowotny, H., Scott, P., Gibbons, M., 2001. *Rethinking Science: Knowledge and the Public in the Age of Uncertainty*. Wiley, London.
Project Compass, 2017. 'Project Compass'. http://projectcompass.co.uk/ (accessed 18.7.17).
RIBA, 2016a. *Advancing Architecture*. RIBA, London.
RIBA, 2016b. *POE Primer*, RIBA, London. www.architecture.com/knowledge-and-resources/resources-landing-page/post-occupancy-evaluation
Roszynski, K., Keeling, T., 2017. 'A collaborative approach to POE', in: Hay, R., Samuel, F. (eds) *Professional Practices in the Built Environment*. School of Architecture, University of Reading, pp. 102–109.
Saint, S., 2016. 'Build to Rent'. Vision 2016, London Olympia.
Samuel, F., Coucill, L., Tait, A., Dye, A., 2013. *RIBA Home Improvements: Report on Research in Housing Practice*. RIBA. www.architecture.com/knowledge-and-resources/resources-landing-page/home-improvements-housing-research-in-practice
Sheil, B., 2015. 'The After Life', in: Harriss, H., Froud, D. (eds), *Radical Pedagogies*. RIBA Publishing, Newcastle-upon-Tyne.
Tavistock Institute, 1966. *Interdependence and Uncertainty (Digest of a Report from the Tavistock Institute to the Building Industry Communication Research Project)*. Tavistock Institution, London.
TheFulcrum.eu, 2017. www.thefulcrum.eu/
UK Gov, 2015. 'Digital Built Britain'. www.gov.uk/government/news/launch-of-digital-built-britain
UK Gov, 2013, 'The G-Cloud Framework on the Digital Marketplace'. www.gov.uk/guidance/the-g-cloud-framework-on-the-digital-marketplace (accessed 7.18.17).
Wieczorek, I., 2017. 'Materialized Immaterialization', in: *Serie SOLID – Interior Matters – A+t Architecture Publishers Tienda Online*. A+t Architecture Publishers, Harvard GSD, MA, pp. 60–65.
Wright Associates, 2017. 'Research and Policy'. www.andrewwrightassociates.com/docs/content.php?id=4:0:0

Chapter 14

Risk and research strategy

Architects are continually worrying about when the next recession will come. This chapter is concerned with ways in which the profession can retrofit itself collectively to strategically manage the risk of continual economic, social, environmental and technical change (Hood et al., 2001), something that will require new professional mindsets. The chapter begins with a discussion of risk and moves on to the way it can be reduced through strategic thinking.

14.1 Risk

Architects may fetishize futuristic visions but 'The future' is 'conditional on how one assesses the present and how one adjusts mind and behaviour' (Nowotny, 2015, p. 36). Change has now become so rapid that the need to use cutting-edge knowledge to make projects as future-proof as possible has become intense. The seven societal challenges set out by the European Union (EU) are:

> Health, demographic change and wellbeing;
> Food security, sustainable agriculture and forestry, marine and maritime and inland water research and the bioeconomy;
> Secure, clean and efficient energy;
> Smart, green and integrated transport;
> Climate action, environment, resource efficiency and raw materials;
> Europe in a changing world – inclusive, innovative and reflective societies;
> Secure societies – protecting freedom and security of Europe and its citizens.
>
> (Synchrone, 2017)

Each of these risks has a built environment dimension which architects should be well placed to address. A visit to Philippines brings the urgency of the situation into clear relief (Figures 14.1 and 14.2). Turning a blind eye is not really an option any more.

'The practices of architects, like other urban design professionals, are implicated in the construction of risky objects and their mitigation by recourse to systems of managerial governance' (Imrie and Street, 2011, p. 21). Governments and funding agencies increasingly ask for promises of performance as organizations

Figure 14.1 **Homes in BASECO region, Manila, Philippines (2016). Photo © Rizalito M. Mercado.**

Figure 14.2 **Children foraging in flood waters, BASECO region, Manila in the Philippines (2016). Photo © Rizalito M. Mercado.**

want as much certainty as possible (Nowotny, 2015). This is why risk management has become a familiar administrative practice (ISO, 2009). Risk registers, as evidence to auditors, trustees and so on of due diligence on the part of an organization, are now playing a key role in the construction industry – as elsewhere (Buro Happold, 2012). Managers speculate on likely organizational hazards, assess the harm that could result, designate the likelihood of occurrence, suggest mitigating actions and then set out the residual risk. In my experience this can be quite a perfunctory process, but think what might happen if risk registers accommodated real knowledge about probabilities and impact, potentially fuelled by big data.

Different types of contract allocate risk in different ways (Hughes et al., 2015). The risk to future generations of inappropriate, cheaply constructed, ugly buildings and infrastructure is immense. As the authors of *Cradle to Cradle* make clear, waste equates to food (Braungart and McDonough, 2009). One way to unpack the real cost of projects over a long period is life-cycle analysis (LCA), in terms of both energy (ISO, 2006) and social value (UN Environment, 2017). In the built environment this is encapsulated in a systematic set of procedures for gathering and assessing the inputs and outputs of materials in terms of energy and the cost to society together with the environmental impacts that are directly attributable to the materal during the life cycle of a building (including disposal). Duncan Baker-Brown argues that 'while we wait for a truly circular economy to materialise, humankind needs to clean up the mess we have made over the last century through mining, making and consuming stuff without a thought for the end-of-life consequences on our environment' and that architects 'will play a major role in unpacking "traditional" design and procurement strategies that will ensure our future buildings and cities are "material banks for the future" and that they are "designed for re-manufacture'" (Baker-Brown, 2017, p. 63).

There is growing government recognition that 'smarter, more inclusive' cities can drive 'shared prosperity' and reduced risk (UK Gov, 2015a, p. 27). It is worth noting that the UK government has a strategic commitment to provide 'a platform through which a wide range of suppliers (including SMEs) and other stakeholders can be engaged in finding the best informed lifecycle solutions to infrastructure problems and in them be in a position to bid to supply solutions' (UK Gov, 2015b). It seems only to be a matter of time before such assessments extend beyond environmental impact into the social and cultural realm. With the growing tide of consumer protection law the possibilities of legal action enter into new territory. Speculations are, for example, already taking place at Yale Law School about the legal implications of discrimination caused by architects and urban planners through the design of space (Schindler, 2014). In a few years architects could be asked why they didn't design for climate change, given that temperature projections have been readily available for some time (UK Gov, 2009; Gupta et al., 2017). Those such as the Leeds-based practice, Bauman Lyons Architects, who make design for climate change a practice priority will be well prepared (Bauman Lyons Architects, 2015).

14.2 Strategy

To create a practice without a vision is like 'building on quicksand' (Preddy, 2011, p. 36). Simon Foxell's book *Starting a Practice* is a good place to begin (Foxell, 2015). Information on developing business strategy and new models of business is widely available (Osterwalder and Pigneur, 2010), but 60% of UK architectural practices have no business plan (Hurst, 2015), perhaps because this requires considerable leadership (Delong et al., 2007). However, firms that have enjoyed high levels of profitability over a long time, for example the architects Scott Brownrigg, have an extensive business planning process in place, with input from professional advisors. A vision forms the basis of strategy and, most importantly, the firm's attitude to fees. Interestingly Frank Gehry attributes his success in business to a set of rules that he made for himself when he was starting out:

> That I wouldn't borrow money. That everybody was going to get paid. And that I had to get enough peace to do the work the way that I wanted. Dumb simple, but it has led to what we are doing and it is a very comfortable kind of process. Architects are supposed to make 20 percent profit. We are lucky if in a year we make 7, 8 or 10 percent profit. But doing the work, having the kind of pleasure doing it that we do, that's very adequate.
>
> (Gehry, 2004, p. 28)

Everything flowed from his decision to be a solvent business.

Shouldn't we all be developers? is the title of a book by architect Roger Zogolovitch, which makes the point that architects really ought to take control of their situation, at least in the case of the residential market (Zogolovitch, 2015). Certainly it helps them specialize (Building Futures, 2011; Reinholdt, 2015b). Specializing means that investment and training can be focused and costs reduced (Green, 2011). Specialization facilitates economies of scale as well as the efficient and focused use of new technologies and skills, something that practices typically find difficult (Oliveira et al., 2016). Most building types lend themselves to systematized development, refinement and mass production (Woudhuysen and Abley, 2004). This is no less true of services and tools. Lisa Raynes's franchise organization Pride Road offers high quality of service to domestic clients. At the same time it helps women architects return to practice after taking time off to look after children, by supplying them with a ready-made platform from which to work (Raynes, 2016). At the opposite end of the scale, Gehry's spin-out company Gehry Technologies has been developed to promote, and leverage, income through its specialist software (Gehry, 2004). Innovations in the field must be protected by appropriate intellectual property safeguards – patents, copyright and trademarks – (UIA, 2014). This is an area where the profession needs help. Architecture practices frequently generate innovations – tools, components and processes – which, with some thought, could be used to help them earn money while asleep (Reinholdt, 2015a).

An interesting new development is the sale of products as services – we can see this with music platforms such as Spotify. It is notable that 'asset-based consultants' rarely do any consulting any more, but instead sell their clients the rights to use their apps and tools. In the field of law the US firm LegalZoom.com sells generic legal documents online (Susskind, 2016). An alternative example is www.acclimatise.uk.com, which, as a world leader in helping governments assess environmental impact, offers its documents online for a fee. Such thinking must underpin the website www.buy-architecture.com, which offers off-the-peg generic designs. Given sensitivity, rigour and parametric models, this could be the future. Interaction and service design have now become an important new field but information technology (IT) in architecture and the wider construction industry is being used only 'at a fraction of its potential' (Woudhuysen and Abley, 2004, p. 223).

Specialization also helps practices enter new markets. Carl Turner Architects, for example, has developed a specialism in 'meanwhile use' architecture (the temporary use of spaces listed for development) which has led to commissions for other types of community buildings. ZCD Architects were able to scale up from individual home design to larger housing developments based largely on the research activity of Dinah Bornat (now one of the Mayor of London's Design Advocates) in the field of community space for children. She writes:

> Our practice invested a considerable amount of time on the research, equivalent to 10% of annual turnover, which is comparable to other speculative work such as entering competitions. In the short term this has led to commissions in what is a highly competitive market. In the long term we hold onto evidence that is valuable to the industry.
>
> (Bornat, 2017, p. 144)

It is very difficult to get a commission in certain sectors if a practice has not had specific experience of that building type, but a research track record in that area can certainly help. Research activity can also open doors, offering practices a significant opportunity to grow their networks, influence and reputation. So passionate is the highly innovative London-based practice AStudio (an example is its Co-Innovate work with Brunel University, Co-Innovate, 2017) about the key role of research in their practice strategy that they have it on display all along a wall of their reception area (Figure 14.3). Once a research vision is in place, a good place to start thinking about research strategy is projected research income, including UK tax credits for research and development (R & D), scaling up after the first three years.

Most importantly architects need to have a very clear idea about the work they are ready and prepared to undertake and should think twice about taking on a client whose values do not align with practice strategy. The process of working with such clients can be overly resource hungry, wasteful and ultimately unrewarding (Bos-de-Vos et al., 2017). Architects in my experience feel a tremendous pressure to keep staff on their payroll, something that drives them to work with unsuitable clients particularly in times of recession, but this doesn't help anybody in the long run. If a practice can find clients whose work aligns with the strategic thrust of the practice, there will be benefits both to the project and to the overall learning of both parties.

Architects also have a cultural resistance to filling in their time sheets accurately, as they tend to do whatever it takes to get a design right (Bos-de Vos et al., 2015), but it is of key importance to know how a practice uses its time (Figure 14.4). David Maister divides tasks in professional service firms into three categories, 'Brains, Grey Hair and Procedure', each with a different cost. Whatever you call them, it is important to deploy the right people to the right task (Maister, 2003, p. 4) at the right time. Lack of strategy with regard to time impacts directly onto the earnings of architects.

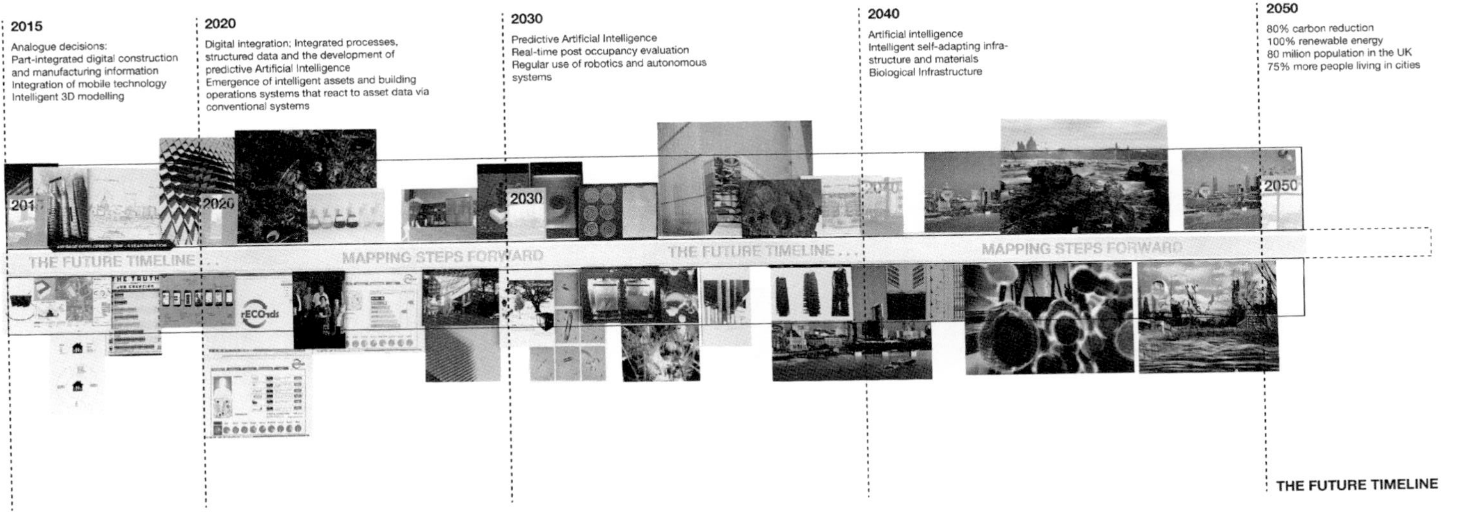

Figure 14.3
AStudio research strategy timeline to 2050. © Emma Flynn/AStudio.

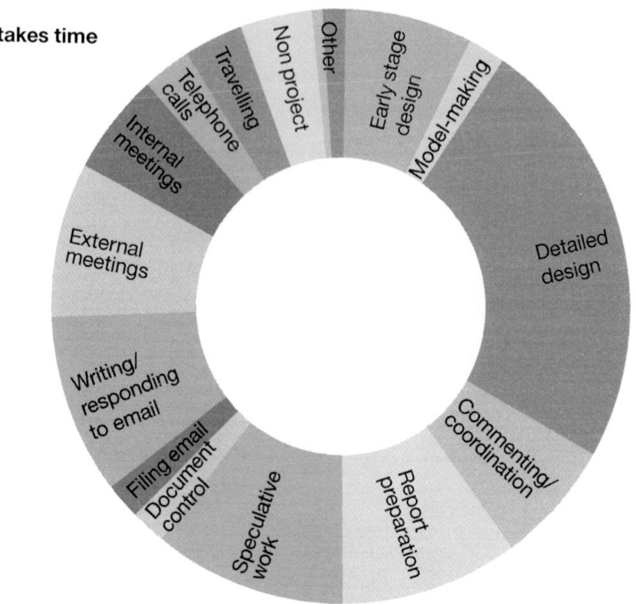

Figure 14.4 **Diagram showing how the practice Hawkins\Brown uses its time (2016). © Hawkins\Brown.**

Rothwell and Zegfeld have identified four challenges to small manufacturing firms which seem to have equal applicability to small practices working in the construction sector (Lu and Sexton, 2009). First, such firms suffer from a shortage of appropriate skilled staff. Second, very few resources are allocated to external relations, meaning that the flow of knowledge back and forth is limited. Third, they are often dominated by the owner or management team, who themselves may have poor strategic skills. The last factor of course is cash flow for ongoing investment, hence the need for strategic planning (Rothwell and Zegfeld, 1982). Practices need to set aside the necessary resources to improve their use of knowledge. That this is key to the development of organizational culture is evident from the global practice research case studies in the book *The Changing Shape of Practice* (Hensel and Nilsson, 2016).

14.3 Aligning knowledge to context

> Design is precious.
> Businesses listen.
> Understand your competitors.
>
> (Flanagan, 2017)

With technology moving at an extraordinary pace, the future-proofing of practice must become a professional priority. As I argued in Chapter 10, this is more to do with the development of generic research and business skills than soon-to-be-outdated knowledge, although subject-specific knowledge will be a key offering of specialist firms.

> Mass customisation replaces standardization as algorithms easily accommodate variations in form and choice. Parametric design tools like Grasshopper, Generative Components, Revit and Digital Project enable new user groups to interact with, navigate and modify the virtual designs, and to test and experience arrays of options at unprecedented low cost – recognizing laypeople as design-decision making agents rather than just consumers. Open source codes and scripts enable designers to share and compare information and collectively optimize production through modular components, accelerating the historical accumulation of shared knowledge. BIM and related collaboration tools and practices enable cross-disciplinary co-location of design information and integration of a range of platforms and timescales. Rapid prototyping and other 3D printing technologies enable instant production of physical artifact, both representational and functional, even on an architectural scale, to an ever-wider audience.
>
> (Ratti and Claudel, 2015, p. 125)

Increasingly there is a convergence between the digital and the biological 'where biological becomes informatics and data is made to work as if it was living' (Nowotny, 2015, p. 98). Major advances are being made in predicting the health of individuals based on their unique genomic make-up; soon personalized precision medicine will be designed for individuals based on probabilities. Helga Nowotny speculates about the possibility of biotechnology developing into a new art form and becoming domesticated in the same way that computers have been (Nowotny, 2015). Such developments make experiments in growing the fabric of buildings begin to look quite plausible (Armstrong, 2016).

In the UK, as in much of the world, there is a widely acknowledged housing crisis, which could be helped considerably by the advent of off-site construction. Such methods require considerable upfront investment to pay for the plant that will build the systems off site and the staff that can run the systems. 'To crack this market, offsite producers will need to innovate' and to bring about a 'cultural change'. Most importantly business leaders and investors will have to be confident that 'the future market is real' (Construction Industry Council, 2013, p. 3). Given advances in technology, the paucity of skilled construction workers and the lack of training for apprentices, all the signs suggest that more and more buildings need to be built in a modular way off site. Yet, as the *Off Site Housing Review* has shown (Construction Industry Council, 2013), the UK is woefully unprepared for such changes, particularly in comparison with other economies – three prefabricated housing factories were recently opened in one year alone in Melbourne, Australia. It is going to require new levels of collaboration to achieve the robot-controlled building sites that seem now inevitable. It is not really a question of when it will happen, but who will get there first – and there is little sign of its being the UK.

It is of course sensible to make sure that practice strategy aligns with government priorities, for example 'the UK government's Smart Cities Strategy to bring together expertise in design, planning, construction, operations, funding, technology and risk management', which it hopes will 'enable the UK to capitalise on the essential need to provide infrastructure and its services to our citizens and across the world' (UK Gov, 2015b, p. 13). This will operate through 'built asset data resources' as well as the 'wider market for data analytics and big data' (UK Gov, 2015b, p. 12). Architects are well placed to have an integrating design role in this agenda, the funding for which is set to grow.

Infrastructure continues to be a major issue for the UK as it upgrades its ageing facilities. Sadie Morgan of architectural practice DRMM leads on design for HS2, the UK's new high-speed rail link, due to cost over £100 billion over the next five years. However, the profession needs to do more to make sure that the importance of architecture is promoted within the Department of Trade and Industry (DTI), as not enough architects are involved in this area. A recent speech by the UK Minister for Transport on the need to improve the quality of transport architecture – 'the journey to beauty' – may be cause for hope (Hayes, 2017), but there is a skills shortage in the field of infrastructure architecture, meaning that expertise has to be pulled in from across the world. It all comes back to being strategic, developing focused knowledge and horizon-scanning for future opportunities.

Clients, like architects, are not a homogenous group. It doesn't help that 'the client' on a job taking place over a long period can frequently change, this churn making 'the client' a shifting target. One way to get under the skin of a client organization is to understand the metaphors that it uses to describe itself (Green, 1996). A client body that sees itself as a machine will need inputs of quantitative data to assist it in achieving its process-led targets. A client body that sees itself as a community may want participatory knowledge generated bottom up. A meeting of cultures is needed for projects to be successful (McDonnell and Lloyd, 2014). When acting as a client advisor I have been surprised to see how poor architects can be at pitching their work in a manner that aligns with client values. 'Illustrate, don't tell' is key to developing trust with clients (Maister, 2003, p. 206). A track record in building beautiful and well-loved buildings ought perhaps to speak for itself when pitching for work, but it can have little traction when the client team is trying to justify its decision to its board, funding body or fund managers. In an audit culture each of these bodies has to demonstrate its purpose through key performance indicators (KPIs), individuals being tied to SMART (specific, measurable, achievable, realistic, timebound) objectives, so it makes sense to try to deliver information easily regurgitated in this format as well as seductive imagery. Research can be extremely persuasive in this context, especially given the profession's reputation for business ditsiness.

Clients need to be involved in the design of their projects right at the start. Immersive tools are already becoming more common in architectural practice (an example is Cullinan Studio's Virtual Reality Lab), allowing clients to imagine their way into their projects at a much earlier stage. At the University of Reading smells and other sensory features are being integrated into the experience (Figure 14.5).

Figure 14.5 **A lecture at the University of Reading on using photogrammetry to capture existing buildings and create virtual models in immersive virtual reality. Photo Dragana Nikolic/ University of Reading.**

The next generation of clients brought up on SimCity and Second Life will be happy to design their own spaces, perhaps using a customizable kit of parts suggested to them on the internet, perhaps as a result of other lifestyle choices such as taste in music or films. Architects need to have a role in their development (or else who will think about the overall impact of such buildings on the wider environment?) but this will only happen if they can make a strong case for what they bring to the table.

'Although architects provide plans which eventually result in a building, what they offer is primarily a service, the quality of which is judged by clients on the basis of the overall experience, rather than the end product alone' (Winch and Schneider, 1993, p. 926). Working with an architect ought to be an instructive and enjoyable experience.

> I have developed behavior that endears me to the people who pay money to get me to do work. That's a kind of pandering to the audience. I try to make buildings that feel good, so that's pandering. There are architects' frames of mind and there are artists' frames of mind that are very critical of the things I do. For that reason – because I have a particular personality. I like people. For me, the building of a building, the process of working with people, is more exciting than the final building.
>
> (Gehry, 2004, p. 32)

Architects have much to learn from the large businesses that have entire teams working on 'customer experience' (Grönroos, 2000). Clients need to be able to comment on the service at critical junctures in a non-threatening way or they just 'slip away' (Preddy, 2011, p. 132). Service design, an extremely healthy area of the creative economy (Madano Partnership, 2012) and one that emerges out of 'customer experience', is a key, yet underrated, part of the profession. It is worth noting in this context that Stickdorn and Schneider, authors of *This is Service Design Thinking*, offer a 'post service period' for the readers of their book in the form of an online resource (Stickdorn and Schneider, 2014). Perhaps architects should offer something similar for their buildings.

While architects have long joked that they should be therapists and marriage guidance counsellors, there is actually a very serious part of the service which relates to helping others realize themselves (Brown, 2007), particularly in the sphere of domestic design. Working with an architect then can become a transformational experience as well as a way to get your organization or your home fixed (Burnside, 2015; Raynes, 2016). Very often the best architects are highly energizing and positive people. The employment of an architect, certainly at the domestic level, seems set to become a lifestyle choice like having a personal trainer – a learning experience that builds on the burgeoning language of coaching and self-development which self-consciously plays upon the aspirations of the client. Working with an architect needs to become a treat and make clients feel special. It is all wrong that people are prepared to spend more money on their hair, beard or nails than on an initial consultation with an architect when homes are generally our biggest asset.

Conclusion

There are high levels of risk inherent in the ways in which architectural practitioners as a whole are using, or rather not using, their knowledge. There is a strong risk of the profession's further marginalization if it is not able to marshal its knowledge to the benefit of its members and wider society. This is coupled with the risk of reduced fees and extreme dissatisfaction of the Generation Y architects, now mired in debt, who rightly expected and hoped for something better. In 1988 Robert Gutman wrote optimistically of the 'rising demand for architectural services' (Gutman, 1988, p. 3). While the profession has since then experienced a series of haemorrhaging recessions, I believe he is correct, but everything depends on how those 'architectural services' are framed in relation to the work of others. This requires strategy.

References

Armstrong, R., 2016. *Star Ark: A Living, Self-Sustaining Spaceship*. Springer, London.

Baker-Brown, D., 2017. 'A matter of living or dying'. *RIBA Journal*, 124, 4, pp.63–64.

Bauman Lyons Architects, 2015. 'Adapt and Save – Climate Adaptation Strategies', in: Dye, A., Samuel, F., *Demystifying Architectural Research*, RIBA Enterprises, Newcastle-upon-Tyne, pp.19–24.

Bornat, D., 2017. 'The benefits of research for a small practice', in: Hay, R., Samuel, F. (eds.), *Professional Practices in the Built Environment*. University of Reading, pp. 139–146.

Bos-de-Vos, M., Lieftink, B., Wamelink, H., Kraaijeveld, J., 2017. 'Challenges in the Business Models of Creative Professional Service Firms', in: *Professional Practices in the Built Environment*. School of Architecture, University of Reading.

Bos-de Vos, M., Volker, L., Wamelink, H., 2015. *Prioritizing Quality Over Profit: Value Tade-offs within Architect-Client Relations*. www.arcom.ac.uk/-docs/proceedings/cbb0136f8fd5aa19c739fcff89e952d2.pdf

Braungart, M., McDonough, W., 2009. *Cradle to Cradle. Remaking the Way We Make Things*. Vintage, London.

Brown, T., 2009. *Change by Design*. HarperCollins, London.

Building Futures, 2011. *The Future for Architects?* www.buildingfutures.org.uk/projects/building-futures/the-future-for-architects

Burnside, J., 2015. 'Co Design for New Lifestyles', in: Dye, A., Samuel, F. (eds.), *Demystifying Architectural Research*. RIBA Enterprises, Newcastle-upon-Tyne, pp. 55–60.

Buro Happold, 2012. 'Risk Register for Building Design and Construction'. www.designingbuildings.co.uk/wiki/Risk_register_for_building_design_and_construction

Co-Innovate, 2017. 'Co-Innovate Collaboration: AStudio'. https://co-innovate.brunel.ac.uk/success-stories/co-innovate-collaboration-astudio/

Construction Industry Council, 2013. *Off Site Housing Review*. offsite-housing-review-feb-2013-for-web.pdf

Delong, T.J., Gabarro, J.J., Lees, R., 2007. *When Professionals Have to Lead: A New Model for High Performance*. Harvard Business School Press, Boston, MA.

Flanagan, R., 2017. 'Global construction practice'. Presented at the Professional Practices in the Built Environment, School of Architecture, University of Reading.

Foxell, S., 2015. *Starting a Practice*. RIBA Enterprises, Newcastle-upon-Tyne.

Gehry, F.O., 2004. 'Reflections on Design and Architectural Practice', in: Collopy, F. (ed.), *Managing as Design*. Stanford Business Books, Stanford University Press, Stanford, CA, pp. 19–36.

Green, S.D., 2011. *Making Sense of Construction Improvement: A Critical Review*, Wiley Blackwell, Chichester; Ames, Iowa.

Green, S.D., 1996. 'A Metaphorical Analysis of Client Organizations and the Briefing Process'. *Construction Management and Economics*, 14, 2, pp.155–164.

Grönroos, C., 2000. *Service Management and Marketing: A Customer Relationship Management Approach*. Wiley, Chichester.

Gupta, R., Barnfield, L., Gregg, M., 2017. 'Overheating in Care Settings: Magnitude, Causes, Preparedness and Remedies'. *Building Research and Information*, 45, 1–2, pp. 83–101.

Gutman, R., 1988. *Architectural Practice: A Critical View*. Princeton Architectural Press, New York.

Hayes, J., 2017. 'The Journey to Beauty'. www.gov.uk/government/speeches/the-journey-to-beauty

Hensel, M., Nilsson, F., 2016. *The Changing Shape of Practice*. Routledge, London.

Hood, C., Rothstein, H., Baldwin, R., 2001. *The Government of Risk.* Oxford University Press, Oxford.

Hughes, W., Champion, R., Murdoch, J., 2015. *Construction Contracts.* Routledge, London; New York.

Hurst, W., 2015. '60% of Architects Have No Business Plan'. *Building.* www.building.co.uk/60-of-architects-have-no-business-plan/5036636.article

Imrie, R., Street, E., 2011. *Architectural Design and Regulation.* Wiley Blackwell, Oxford.

ISO, 2009. *Risk Management,* ISO 31000. www.iso.org/iso-31000-risk-management.html

ISO, 2006. 'ISO 14040 Environmental Management – Life Cycle Assessment – Principles and Framework'. www.iso.org/standard/37456.html

Lu, S., Sexton, M., 2009. *Innovation in Small Professional Practices in the Built Environment.* Wiley Blackwell, Oxford.

Madano Partnership, 2012. *Scoping Study on Service Design.* London. www.ahrc.ac.uk/documents/project-reports-and-reviews/scoping-study-on-service-design/

Maister, D.H., 2003. *Managing the Professional Service Firm.* Simon & Schuster UK, London.

McDonnell, J., Lloyd, P., 2014. 'Beyond Specification: A Study of Architect and Client Interaction'. *Design Studies,* 35, 4, pp 327–352.

Nowotny, H., 2015. *The Cunning of Uncertainty.* Polity, London.

Oliveira, S., Marco, E., Gething, B., Organ, S., 2016. 'Outwith Domain…Within Terrain Effects of Early Design Energy Modelling on Architect's Design Practice', in: *Building Our Future.* Presented at the International Conference on Integrated Design (ID@50), University of Bath, UK. http://eprints.uwe.ac.uk/28805

Osterwalder, A., Pigneur, Y., 2010. *Business Model Generation: A Handbook for Visionaries, Game Changers, and Challengers.* John Wiley & Sons, Hoboken, NJ.

Preddy, S., 2011. *How to Run a Successful Design Business.* Routledge, Oxford.

Ratti, C., Claudel, M. (eds.), 2015. *Open Source Architecture.* Thames and Hudson, London.

Raynes, L., 2016. 'Pride Road'. www.prideroad.co.uk/

Reinholdt, E.W., 2015a. *Architect and Entrepreneur: A How To Guide, Innovating Practice, Tactics Models and Case Studies in Passive Income.* CreateSpace Independent Publishing Platform.

Reinholdt, E.W., 2015b. *Architect and Entrepreneur: A Field Guide to Building, Branding, and Marketing,* CreateSpace Independent Publishing Platform.

Rothwell, R., Zegfeld, W., 1982. *Innovation and the Small and Medium Sized Firm.* Printer, London.

Schindler, S., 2014. 'Architectural Exclusion: Discrimination and Segregation through Physical Design of the Built Environment'. *The Yale Law Journal,* 124, 6, pp.1836–2201. www.yalelawjournal.org/article/architectural-exclusion

Stickdorn, M., Schneider, J., 2014. *This is Service Design Thinking: Basics – Tools – Cases.* BIS, Amsterdam.

Susskind, D., 2016. 'The Way We'll Work Tomorrow'. *RIBA Journal*, 123, pp. 63–64.

Synchrone, 2017. 'Horizon 2020: The 7 Societal Challenges'. www.ncpwallonie.be/en/project-horizon2020-challenges (accessed 11.4.16).

UIA, 2014. 'UIA on Recommended International Standards of Professionalism in Architectural Practice'. www.uia-architectes.org/sites/default/files/UIAAccordEN.pdf

UK Gov, 2015a. *National Security Strategy and Strategic Defence and Security Review*. First Annual Report. www.gov.uk/government/publications/national-security-strategy-and-strategic-defence-and-security-review-2015

UK Gov, 2015b. *Digital Built Britain Level 3 Building Information Modelling*. www.gov.uk/government/news/launch-of-digital-built-britain

UK Gov, 2009. 'Climate Change Adaptation'. www.gov.uk/government/policies/climate-change-adaptation

UN Environment, 2017. 'Life Cycle Initiative'. www.lifecycleinitiative.org/starting-life-cycle-thinking/life-cycle-approaches/social-lca/

Winch, G., Schneider, E., 1993. 'Managing the Knowledge-Based Organization: The Case of Architectural Practice'. *Journal of Management Studies*, 30, 6, pp.923–937. doi:10.1111/j.1467–6486.1993.tb00472.x

Woudhuysen, J., Abley, I., 2004. *Why is Construction so Backward?* Wiley Academy, Chichester.

Zogolovitch, R., 2015. *Shouldn't We All Be Developers*. Solidspace, London.

Chapter 15

Managing knowledge in practice

Both surveyors and architects have so far failed to take advantage of the data about building capacity and building use which is piled high in every one of their offices.

(Duffy, 1998)

This book is an argument for respecting the knowledge of architects, but architects have to respect their own knowledge before expecting others to do the same. In Chapter 9 I posited that 'knowledge architects' are key to the future of the profession and that they play a vital role in parcelling up the knowledge of architects for use by others. It is, however, equally important for practices to assess the knowledge they already have in their organization in order to help the development of organizational learning and innovation and, not least, to improve their own commercial advantage. Architects need to 'anticipate the new tasks that will have to be done, to identify those that require their unique talents, and to develop the skills that will therefore be required in years to come', among them 'knowledge engineering' and 'process analysis' (Susskind, 2016, p. 64). All this needs to be seen against a backdrop of growth in the knowledge economy (DTI, 1998, p. 1; Seidel et al., 2012), with knowledge management 'begging for a bigger role' (Kransdorff, 2009).

15.1 Collecting and sharing knowledge in practice

In order to maximize value, practices need to be highly strategic about the way in which they develop and choreograph the knowledges that flow through their walls (Hansen et al., 1999; Kamara et al., 2002; Lu and Sexton, 2009). Practice organograms such as the one produced by AHMM (Figure 15.1) may take a long time to put together but they are very important in showing how knowledge is passed from one area of the business to another. Practices need to develop 'cost-effective methodologies and tools for the live capture of project knowledge' (Kamara et al., 2002, p. 66). Each project produces a wealth of knowledge including:

A product (or service) delivered for an internal or external customer.
Project knowledge related to the product, its production and use.
Technical knowledge concerning the product, its parts and technologies.

Procedural knowledge concerning producing and using of the product and acting in a project.
Organisational knowledge concerning communication and collaboration.
(Kasvi et al., 2003, p. 571)

The content and quality of this knowledge varies, as does the ability of the organization to utilize it properly. Hansen has identified two strategies for managing knowledge: the first 'codified strategy', the use of information technology (IT) and databases for the collection of data under agreed headings, and the second 'personalisation strategy', which relies on people to spread the word (Hansen et al., 1999, p. 107). While most architectural practices have adopted the latter, the need for the former is becoming more pressing as there is an ever-larger amount of data to manage. The power of knowledge is evident to those who have experienced the layers of vetting and encryption necessary to work for governments and security organizations. That architects can be trusted to generate and handle information in an ethical and secure manner also seems set to become extremely important (BSI, 2015).

In Chapter 3 it became apparent that there are gaping holes in the professional knowledge of architects and that very often these represent gaps in the market. An example is 'knowledge about the aesthetic appreciation of the

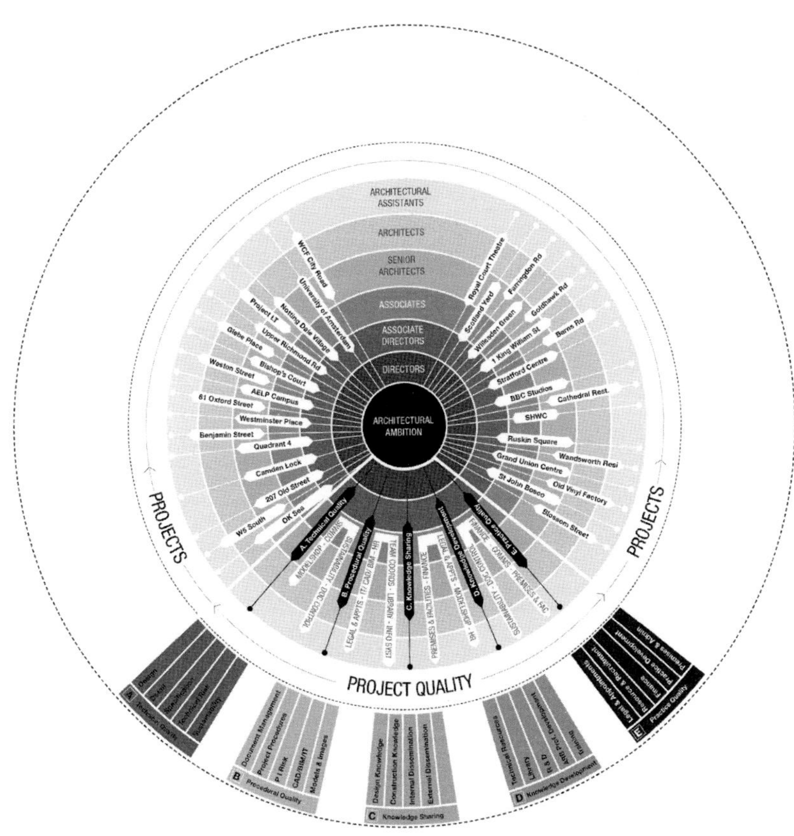

Figure 15.1
AHMM Practice Organogram (2017).
© AHMM.

public, which remains an uncomfortable void in the articulated knowledge base of architects, but something that other fields of design and marketers have been quick to exploit' (Norman, 2005, p. 10). If architecture is to impact positively on people, it must have resonance with their sense of taste. Although evidence suggests a strong divergence between the aesthetic sensibilities of architects and the public (Devlin and Nasser, 1998; Brown and Gifford, 2001; Fawcett et al., 2008), the disabled (Quayson, 2007) and even children (Horton et al., 2015), this is an area that is rarely addressed head on (Darke, 1984). These issues impact on shopping. The relationship between architecture and the retail sector is largely unexplored and represents a significant gap in knowledge (Watson et al., 2016). If the way in which commodities are lit influences attitudes to buying, then what might the impact of the environment be on buying behaviour (Gilboa and Rafaeli, 2003; Ballantine et al., 2010) or on the fast growing food and beverage industry (Heide et al., 2007; Ryu and Han, 2010)? This is just a single example.

'We innovate because we know that innovation is as much about finding simpler ways of doing things better as it is about finding new things to do' (AHMM, 2017). With innovation, commonly separated into 'product innovation' and 'process innovation', it doesn't really matter if the idea is actually that new; what matters is that it is new within its particular context (Lu and Sexton, 2009). There are therefore opportunities in taking architectural ways of working into terrains that may be well trodden by others but where architects can offer a fresh perspective. Collopy and Bolland's use of design studio in management has already been discussed in Chapter 11; another example might be the use of design studio as a form of leisure or therapy. Such areas, of which there are many more, may provide architects with important new work opportunities.

Archives and practice intranets are important resources for organizational learning, but only if structures are put in place to ensure that they are used. Knowledge management strategies work best when aligned with the overall strategy of the practice (Egbu, 2004) and when they have buy-in from its members. The Royal Institute of British Architect's (RIBA) *Handbook of Practice Management*, now in its ninth edition, is unusual in including a very helpful section on knowledge management based on the author's experiences of practice management at Hawkins\Brown Architects (Ostime, 2013). Unfortunately practice intranets are bespoke, meaning that they don't lend themselves to information-sharing. The London office of AHMM is leading on the development of an intelligent office intranet with funding from Innovate UK. Considerable competitive advantage can be derived from the ordering of practice knowledge.

At the same time it is important that knowledge is shared between practices, something that can bring benefits to all without endangering intellectual property (Nicholson, 1992). DesigningBuildings Wiki is an example of useful co-created resource knowledge sharing, while platforms such as CarbonBuzz allow practices to collate data anonymously with benefits to all. Effective knowledge sharing requires rigour and uniformity in the way in which it is gathered. For this to take place more leadership is needed.

'Managing knowledge is a value-creating process in most organisations and is particularly important in knowledge intensive firms' (Robertson et al., 2001, p. 334).

Large practices have problems maintaining a sense of practice culture and continuity, while small practices are vulnerable to knowledge being spread unevenly across the organization. Both kinds of practice often seem to suffer a crisis of confidence on the retirement or departure of the founding partners, partly because so much of the practice knowledge was bound up in that person or people. The way in which a practice manages its knowledge is tied to its culture and identity.

Historians too have an important role to play in framing architectural knowledge into a form in which it can be saved and shared. A recent symposium by the Architectural Historians of Great Britain on 'The Official Architect' revealed how little is known about the recent history of architectural practice and, further, how many practice archives are being lost – a problem that perhaps paradoxically is becoming more acute with digitization. Loss of 'organizational memory' is a major problem across many business sectors (Kransdorff, 2009).

A particular problem is 'the female brain drain' that occurs as women leave the profession. This generally occurs when they start having children as a result of the difficulties of juggling practice and childcare, and is 'financially damaging both to practices and to the individual' (de Graft-Johnson et al., 2007, p. 179). The waste involved in training a professional only to lose them due to inadequate office support systems is immense. In the USA JustDesign are asking architects to sign up to a charter which guarantees fair treatment of staff (JustDesign, 2017). Not only do such systems help people; they also enhance practice brand and can even foster innovation:

> companies must develop and deploy two kinds of diversity: inherent – meaning more women and people of color make up the workforce – and acquired, meaning leaders behave inclusively to foster the speak-up culture that unlocks a broad spectrum of perspectives and toolkits. Companies replete with both inherent and acquired diversity, we find, out-innovate and outperform the competition. Employees who work for companies like these are 45% more likely to report that their company improved market share in the last 12 months. And they're 70% more likely to report that their company captured a new market in that time frame. That's a remarkable testament to the impact of diversity – not just on innovation, but on market growth.
>
> (Hewlett, 2013)

A diverse workforce maintains a diversity of knowledge and will appeal to a diverse range of clients. New sorts of practice will attract new sorts of client. Architects need to think seriously about the new types of service that might appeal to new and increasingly powerful markets and adjust their services accordingly.

Innovation can be 'market based', prompted by external drivers, or 'resource based', instigated by the practice itself in an attempt to influence the market (Lu and Sexton, 2009, p. 9). The two types need to exist in balance (Sexton and Barrett, 2003). Incentivizing innovation should play an important part in practice strategy, whatever its size. Many global multidisciplinary practices have a well developed research structure, Arup, for example, has its own 'University', delivering educational programmes for its staff and others, and an increasing number of smaller practices are finding ways to prioritize staff time for research and development. A well known and influential strategy for mobilizing staff entrepreneurialism is the Google 80/20 policy, which allows employees to pursue personal projects and is potentially of great benefit to the business. Bauman Lyons Architects currently work in this way. However, it has become apparent that, though a useful tactic, Googletime is not a 'silver bullet' for innovation (Townsend, 2013). Effective innovation requires a concerted effort on many fronts.

The way that innovation happens in large firms tends to be 'mechanistic', while that in small firms tends to be more 'organic', making them agile and resilient (Lu and Sexton, 2009, p. 4). This is reflected in the way in which practices draw on their knowledge networks. An example is Steven Smith of Urban Narratives, who went from being a Director at DEGW, a very large practice, into a micro practice. He considers himself still to be working in a large interdisciplinary community, as he has a mature network of collaborators that he draws on around the globe to make a particular project happen (Smith, 2016). Large practices sometimes draw in smaller ones temporarily to help them out in specific niche areas or to cluster capital when going for bids. In the field of law, experts gather on virtual networks such as 10 EQS and Axiom Law (Susskind, 2016). This surely must be the model for micro practices going forward when connectivity is key.

Lu and Sexton's in-depth study of a small architectural practice shows the importance of building on existing knowledge. Sharing knowledge across the team in this way facilitates organizational learning (Lu and Sexton, 2009). When new members arrive in a practice it is important to exploit the knowledge that they bring with them. The education described in Chapter 10 supports the development of highly skilled problem-solvers, yet many young architects going into practice are quick to lose ambition as they are put to mundane tasks for which they are radically overqualified, because of the 'twisted priorities' of their bosses (Woudhuysen and Abley, 2004, p. 222). This comes back to the importance of strategy discussed in Chapter 14.

15.2 Collecting and sharing knowledge across the construction team

It is time for architects to acknowledge that they work in a knowledge-based service sector. They create boundary objects – models, drawings, reports, events, experiences – that facilitate organizational learning and the transfer of knowledge from one place to another, from the client to the building contractor, from citizens to planners, from communities to policy and so on. They also create experiences and transformations.

At present discussions of knowledge sharing across the construction team eventually revert to Building Information Modelling. 'We simply cannot afford to fall back in the BIM arms race' (UK Gov, 2015, p. 6). As part of the 2011 Government Construction Strategy (now fully embraced by the *Industrial Strategy for Construction, Construction 2025*), the UK has taken a world lead in the adoption of digital technologies thanks to the delivery of the Level 2 BIM programme (UK Gov, 2015). Matt Thompson gives an account of the large

Danish practice Arkitema coming to the UK on a fact-finding mission (Thompson, 2016). This is interesting on two counts: first that the UK is seen as having something to offer in this area and second that Arkitema is investing in its knowledge-gathering. Non-UK practices are right to be interested in what is happening over here, but BIM (discussed more extensively in Chapter 2) is just one of a plethora of tools on offer for the sharing of knowledge and is currently being used at just a fragment of its creative potential.

The building industry is working together to develop standardized terminology that can feed into collaborative working tools such as BIM. COBie (Construction Operations Building Information Exchange) initially developed by NASA; Industry Foundation Class – Uniclass 2015, which classifies objects; and the developing ISO 11000 are all examples of evolving classifications, while at the other end of the classification spectrum are the 'controlled vocabularies' and 'name authorities' used by the Getty Research Institute, and many librarians and archivists, to collate aspects of historical architectural practice, but there is no meeting between these two cultures. As yet there is no controlled vocabulary for contemporary research-based architectural practice, making it difficult to catalogue, to archive and to find or indeed share through search engines. Filling this void will also be important for the integration of construction with the wider creative economy.

As integrated project delivery seems to be the direction of travel, practices also need to develop the ability to communicate knowledge in a way that facilitates the process of production (Sinclair, 2017). This is most pressing in the field of design for manufacture (Sinclair, 2016). In the future there is likely to be greater used of components in building; with standardization of procedure requiring performance data to be more readily available through product libraries (UK Gov, 2015). Artificial intelligence is rapidly becoming far more common and plays an important role in the experimental work of practices such as Zaha Hadid Architects (Figure 15.2). When off-site production takes off, taking a large part of the construction of buildings

(a)

Figure 15.2a **AiBuild Interior Finishes research showing a 2.3m high wall finish printed in twenty-four hours. Photo © Zaha Hadid Architects.**

Figure 15.2b **AiBuild puddle chair. Photo © Zaha Hadid Architects.**

Figure 15.2c **AiBuild's formwork technique for casting concrete. Photo © AiBuild Ltd.**

Figure 15.2d **Thallus designed by ZHCODE and fabricated by AiBuild large-scale 3D printing technology with Philips Lighting. Photo © Zaha Hadid Architects.**

into factories, standardization will come to the fore (a corollary of which will of course be practice specialization). Collective Custom Build systems, such as the Lightboxhouse system designed by Ash Sakula (Ash Sakula, 2017), seem set to make inroads into the market as they offer choice, speed and the chance to acquire an architect-designed home while reducing risk (Figure 15.3). The idea of house as product goes right back to Le Corbusier and even beyond, but is only now becoming a reality. Given the investment it takes to set up such systems, it seems very unlikely that all projects will be undertaken in this way, particularly those involving retrofit, but automation is an important force and architects have to ensure that they are ready for it. Bauman Lyons is trying to take control of the 'reluctant supply chain'

Figure 15.3 **Ash Sakula Lightbox custom build housing system. Photo © Ash Sakula.**

through the development of demonstrator projects intended to wake up industry to the potential of these processes from the very bottom up (Bauman, 2017).

Conclusion

The need 'to energize data that exist within practice through new, more flexible institutions and new, more inventive modes of research' (Duffy, 2008, p. 655) grows ever more necessary. Focused strategic thinking and horizon-scanning is needed to decide which kinds of information will be needed in the coming years. The knowledge of each individual practice and of architects as a group and the wider industry needs to be categorized, collated, evaluated and disseminated in an intelligible form useful for sharing with others. It is, however, hard to imagine how this can be done without post-occupancy evaluation (POE) becoming an industry norm.

References

AHMM, 2017. 'About Us'. www.ahmm.co.uk/About-Us/

Ash Sakula, 2017. 'Lightboxhouse'. www.lightboxhouse.co.uk

Ballantine, P.W., Jack, R., Parsons, A.G., 2010. 'Atmospheric Cues and Their Effect on the Hedonic Retail Experience'. *International Journal of Retail and Distribution Management*, 38, 8, pp. 641–653.

Bauman, I., 2017. 'The Reluctant Supply Chain', in: Hay, R., Samuel, F. (eds), *Professional Practices in the Built Environment*. University of Reading, pp. 18–24.

Brown, G., Gifford, R., 2001. 'Architects Predict Lay Evaluations of Large Contemporary Buildings: Whose Conceptual Properties?' *Journal of Environmental Psychology*, 21, 1, pp. 93–99.

BSI, 2015. *PAS 1192–5 Specification for Security-minded Building Information Modelling, Digital Built Environments and Smart Asset Management.* British Standards Institute/Centre for the Protection of National Infrastructure, London.

Darke, J., 1984. 'Architects and User Requirements in Public-sector Housing: 1. Architects' Assumptions about the Users'. *Environment and Planning B*, 11, 4, pp. 398–404.

De Graft-Johnson, A., Manley, S., Greed, C., 2007. 'The Gender Gap in Architectural Practice: Can We Afford It?', in: *People and Culture in Construction.* Spon Research, London, pp. 159–183.

Devlin, K., Nasser, J.L., 1998. 'The Beauty and the Beast: Some Preliminary Comparisons of "High" versus "Popular" Residential Architecture and Public versus Architect Judgements of Same'. *Journal of Environmental Psychology*, 9, 4, pp. 333–344.

DTI, 1998. *Our Competitive Future: Building the Knowledge-driven Economy.* HMSO, London.

Duffy, F., 2008. 'Forum Linking Theory Back to Practice'. *Building Research and Information*, 36, 6, pp. 655–658.

Duffy, F., 1998. *Architectural Knowledge: The Idea of a Profession.* Spon, London.

Egbu, C.O., 2004. 'Managing Knowledge and Intellectual Capital for Improved Organizational Innovations in the Construction Industry: An Examination of Critical Success Factors'. *Engineering, Construction and Architectural Management*, 11, 5, pp. 301–315.

Fawcett, W., Ellingham, L., Platt, C., 2008. 'Reconciling the Architectural Preferences of Architects and the Public: The Ordered Preference Model'. *Environment and Behaviour*, 50, 5, pp. 599–618.

Gilboa, S., Rafaeli, A., 2003. 'Store Environment, Emotions and Approach Behavior: Applying Environmental Aesthetics to Retailing'. *International Review of Retail, Distribution and Consumer Research*, 13, 2, pp. 195–211.

Hansen, M.T., Nohria, N., Tierney, T., 1999. 'What's Your Strategy for Managing Knowledge?' *Harvard Business Review*, 77, 2, pp. 106–116.

Heide, M., Lærdal, K., Grønhaug, K., 2007. 'The Design and Management of Ambience – Implications for Hotel Architecture and Service'. *Tourism Management*, 28, 5, pp. 1315–1325.

Hewlett, S.A., 2013. 'How Women Drive Innovation and Growth'. *Harvard Business Review*, August 23. https://hbr.org/2013/08/how-women-drive-innovation-and

Horton, J., Hadfield-Hill, S., Krafti, P., 2015. 'Children Living with "Sustainable" Urban Architecture'. *Environment and Planning A*, 47, 4, pp. 903–921.

JustDesign, 2017. 'Help Us Identify Firms with Best Architectural Labor Practices'. http://justdesign.us/ (accessed 4.5.17).

Kamara, J.M., Augenbroe, G., Anumba, C.J., Carillo, P.M., 2002. 'Knowledge Management in the Architecture, Engineering and Construction Industry'. *Construction Innovation*, 2, 1, pp. 53–67.

Kasvi, J.J.J., Vartiainen, M., Hailikari, M., 2003. 'Managing Knowledge and Knowledge Competences in Projects and Project Organisations'. *International Journal of Project Management*, 21, 8, pp. 571–582.

Kransdorff, A., 2009. *Knowledge Management: Begging for a Bigger Role*. Business Expert Press, New York.

Lu, S., Sexton, M., 2009. *Innovation in Small Professional Practices in the Built Environment*. Wiley Blackwell, Oxford.

Nicholson, R., 1992. 'Architects Who Open the Books'. *Architects' Journal*, 19 and 25 August, p. 11.

Norman, D.A., 2005. *Emotional Design: Why We Love (or Hate) Everyday Things*. Basic Books, New York.

Ostime, N., 2013. *Handbook of Practice Management (9th edition)*. RIBA Publishing, London.

Quayson, A., 2007. *Aesthetic Nervousness: Disability and the Crisis of Representation*. Columbia University Press, New York.

Robertson, M., Sørensen, C., Swann, J., 2001. 'Survival of the Leanest: Intensive Knowledge Work and Groupware Adaptation'. *Information Technology and People*, 14, 4, pp. 334–352.

Ryu, K., Han, H., 2010. 'Influence of Physical Environment on Disconfirmation, Customer Satisfaction, and Customer Loyalty for First-time and Repeat Customers in Upscale Restaurants', in: International CHRIE Conference Refereed Track. University of Massachusetts, Amherst.

Seidel, A.D., Kim, J.T., Tanaka, I.B.R., 2012. 'Architects, Urban Design, Health and the Built Environment'. *Journal of Architectural and Planning Research*, 29, 3, pp. 241–268.

Sexton, M., Barrett, P., 2003. 'Appropriate Innovation in Small Construction Firms'. *Construction Management and Economics*, 21, 6, pp. 623–633.

Sinclair, D., 2017. 'Redefining Construction', in: Duncan, J. (ed.), *Retropioneers*. RIBA Enterprises, Newcastle-upon-Tyne, pp. 51–58.

Sinclair, D., 2016. 'RIBA Plan of Work 2013: Designing for Manufacture and Assembly'. www.offsiteschool.com/documents/dfma-web-pdf3.compressed.pdf

Smith, S., 2016. http://urbannarrative.com/Steven-Smith

Susskind, D., 2016. 'The Way We'll Work Tomorrow'. *RIBA Journal*, 123, 7, pp. 63–64.

Thompson, M., 2016. 'Where is BIM Taking Us?' *RIBA Journal*, 123, 7, pp. 61–63.

Townsend, C., 2013. 'Innovate or Die: Why Google's 80/20 Rule is a Red Herring'. *WIRED*. www.wired.com/insights/2013/08/innovate-or-die-why-googles-8020-rule-is-a-red-herring/ (accessed 1.12.16).

UK Gov, 2015. 'Digital Built Britain'. www.gov.uk/government/news/launch-of-digital-built-britain

Watson, K.J., Evans, J., Karvonen, A., Whitley, T., 2016. 'Re-conceiving Building Design Quality: A Review of Building Users in Their Social Context'. *Indoor Built Environments*, 25, 3, pp. 509–523.

Woudhuysen, J., Abley, I., 2004. *Why is Construction so Backward?* Wiley Academy, Chichester.